THE BIRTH
OF THE
ENGLISH MAJOR

THE BIRTH OF THE ENGLISH MAJOR

An Origin Story

Dayton Haskin

Louisiana State University Press
Baton Rouge

Published by Louisiana State University Press
lsupress.org

LSU Press Paperback Original

DESIGNER: Michelle A. Neustrom
TYPEFACE: Fournier MT Pro

The manufacturer's authorized representative in the EU for product safety is Mare Nostrum Group B.V., Doelen 72, 4831 GR Breda, The Netherlands.
Email: gpsr@mare-nostrum.co.uk.

COVER ILLUSTRATION: Unsplash/Susan Wilkinson

LIBRARY OF CONGRESS CATALOGING-IN-PUBLICATION DATA

Names: Haskin, Dayton, author.
Title: The birth of the English major : an origin story / Dayton Haskin.
Description: Baton Rouge : Louisiana State University Press, 2026. | Includes bibliographical references and index.
Identifiers: LCCN 2026028834 (print) | LCCN 2026028835 (ebook) | ISBN 978-0-8071-8724-1 (paperback) | ISBN 978-0-8071-8829-3 (epub) | ISBN 978-0-8071-8830-9 (pdf)
Subjects: LCSH: English literature—Study and teaching (Higher)—United States—History
Classification: LCC PR51.U5 H37 2026 (print) | LCC PR51.U5 (ebook)
LC record available at https://lccn.loc.gov/2026028834
LC ebook record available at https://lccn.loc.gov/2026028835

For Mary Anne and David

Aesthetic teaching is the highest of all teaching because it deals with life in its highest complexity. But if it ceases to be purely aesthetic—if it lapses anywhere from the picture to the diagram—it becomes the most offensive of all teaching.

—GEORGE ELIOT, Letter to Frederic Harrison

Literature classrooms are in the business of creating literary value, not merely receiving or reproducing it.

—RACHEL SAGNER BUURMA and LAURA HEFFERNAN, *The Teaching Archive*

"English literature" has always been something more than an object of study. . . . It has also been implicated in its audiences' libidinal dramas and in their understandings of their families and their erotic histories—hence English studies' eccentric relation to the norms of publicness and impersonality that seem to govern other knowledge-producing occupations.

—DEIDRE SHAUNA LYNCH, *Loving Literature*

CONTENTS

PROLOGUE 1

INTRODUCTION 8

PART I: English Back in the Day

1. What Was Going to College Like? 19
2. Elocution and Composition 31
3. Commencement Orations 43

PART II: What Would "English" Be?

4. Philology as a Turning Point 53
5. A Love for English Words 62
6. Professors of English in the Scientific Schools 71
7. An Ardent Desire to Learn: A College for Black People 83
8. Competing with the Boys: A College for Young Women 89
9. Acting English Plays: A College for the Sons of Immigrants 96

PART III: Literature in English as a Field for Study

10. Entrance Examinations 105
11. Taking Notes 117
12. The Study of Masterpieces 134

PART IV: What Constitutes an English Major?

13. The Idea of a Major 153

14. English as a Special Subject at Cornell 161

15. A Concentration in English Studies at Harvard and the "Harvard Annex" 175

16. The English Major at Wellesley College 193

Coda: A Library 210

ACKNOWLEDGMENTS 223

NOTES 227

BIBLIOGRAPHY 239

INDEX 251

THE BIRTH
OF THE
ENGLISH MAJOR

Prologue

WHEN OXFORD UNIVERSITY floated the idea of instituting a degree in English literature in the late nineteenth century, the proposal met with vociferous resistance from august members of the faculty. The university went ahead and opened a School of English in 1894, nonetheless. But the antipathy against literary study continued to reverberate in a withering and memorable phrase that the Professor of Modern History, E. A. Freeman, had infused into the acrimonious debate. Freeman dismissed the prospect of teaching English literature as a lame attempt to dignify "mere chatter about Shelley." These words long outlived all the ones he had poured into his scholarly writings. (Cambridge did not institute a set of qualifying examinations, called a *tripos,* for a bachelor's degree in English until 1917.) Well into the twentieth century, disdainful skeptics found the phrase "mere chatter about Shelley" useful for characterizing what goes on in college English departments.

In our time antagonism toward literary study is more likely to come from politicians and influencers than from history professors. Fourteen years before the Trump administration began cutting federal funding to universities, President Barack Obama, who had majored in political science and studied English literature at Columbia, was urging in his State of the Union address that college students pursue STEM subjects. He spoke repeatedly about the importance of scientific and technological education to the nation's economic well-being, and he called for recruiting one hundred thousand new STEM teachers. Attempts to gauge the value of a college education wholly in economic terms had by this time won the day.

After the Great Recession of 2008, reports on the English major began charting a steep downturn in its popularity. According to statistics from the National Center of Education, the number of English majors declined by more than 25 percent over a fifteen-year period. The decline has touched even liberal arts colleges known for their distinguished English departments. To take one example, at Swarthmore College in the 1990s, nearly 17 percent of the graduating class had majored in English. By 2021 the figure had dropped by more than 10 percent. The relatively low status currently accorded the study of English in American colleges is not unprecedented. In fact, the meager place English occupied in the early nineteenth-century curriculum hovers over the story that this book means to tell.

Even before AI became readily available to college students and their professors, obituaries announcing "The End of the English Major" (as a February 2023 *New Yorker* essay proclaimed) were proliferating. Autopsy reports offered this diagnosis as the principal grounds for what many people believed was already a fait accompli: a loss of consumer confidence in the humanities and the likelihood that following a STEM major will lead to financial security. Various detractors, not least those who credit the notion that English departments are in the business of indoctrinating students with a liberal bias, have been happy to celebrate the death of the English major.

While the emergence of AI has required large adjustments in the ways in which English is taught and studied, the accumulated mass of obituaries for the subject may be premature. English is the most widely useful common language that the world has ever seen, and it continues to mutate across the globe. The study of English has a yet-to-be-determined future. This book investigates how college English studies were born and how they developed in the face of long-standing resistance. It brings its narrative down to the time when it became possible for undergraduates to choose a principal focus for their academic experience and English emerged as an especially popular choice.

The broad narrative of what's routinely called "the rise of English" has been known for decades. It was disseminated by scholars who framed it for their fellow English professors. It explained how their discipline took shape within graduate programs at elite universities. The narrative offered a sociological perspective, highlighting the centrality of research, the emergence of professional organizations and journals, and the training of specialists. By contrast, this book focuses on undergraduate education. As an origin story rooted in archival research, it excavates the process by which teachers and students made literature in English a worthy object for college study. It explores decidedly different ways in which the subject might have been defined and practiced, and it assumes that while the birth of English studies can never be replicated, the subject can be reinvented.

The first of the book's four parts concerns the merely marginal place colleges allotted vernacular literature "Back in the Day"; that is, in the decades leading up to the Civil War. Parts II and III—"What Would 'English' Be?" and "Literature in English as a Field for Study"—move through the 1860s and 1870s, when colleges began opening the curriculum to new subjects. Part IV—"What Constitutes an English Major?—traces the practice of "majoring'" back to its origin in graduate study at Johns Hopkins University. It then illustrates how three exemplary institutions created distinctly different English majors. The concluding coda, called "A Library," draws on a story by Nathaniel Hawthorne to explore how the creation of new methods for classifying books cemented the idea that writings from the United States and from England constitute two separate literatures.

The book bears the subtitle "*An* Origin Story" because the resources for recounting how English rose are variegated and the story is inexhaustible. My version grows out of years visiting the archives at institutions of higher education in England and in the United States. Comparing what I found in institutional records at more than thirty colleges and universities enabled me to construct a basic story. But unique documents created by individual students and their professors inspired my writing. They also made it possible to point up distinct differences in the ways individual institutions went about defining their conception of what English studies were to consist in.

Because what we think of as college English owes far more to exploring literary works in the classroom than it does to professional literary criticism, this book directs attention to a variety of unpublished notes generated by the first generation of "English" students and their teachers. Generally speaking, professors' notes and papers manifest admirable industry and earnestness. They give evidence of a determination to make the study of English engaging, productive, and nourishing. Some reveal a quirkiness on the part of maverick instructors whose impatience with the way that things were routinely done inspired risky experimentation and led to lasting innovations. Notes that students took in their English courses show that, by the last two decades of the nineteenth century, decisive changes had taken place since the days when colleges expected the professors of rhetoric and oratory to train students for public speaking. If in retrospect the changes look to have been inevitable, nonetheless, as with other life-altering processes, many features of their emergence were contingent. The process through which the changes occurred, and the general excitement that they generated among those who were fostering them and those who first benefited from them, will never be repeated.

Each chapter in the book might be read independently of the others. Read in sequence, however, the chapters offer a roughly chronological narrative that moves back and forth in time. Typically, a chapter takes up some practice or feature (for instance, reading literary masterpieces, or taking notes during lectures) that helped to birth English as a subject. Many chapters exhibit how something exceptional played out in one or another college. In some cases, a chapter features an institution because it offers unusually colorful or amusing evidence to explore. In other chapters I have singled out a college in which administrators promoted an environment where sudden advances were likely to take place; in still others, I have attended to an English department that experimented with something unlike anything I had found elsewhere. This range makes it possible to tell a common story while simultaneously highlighting some distinctive ways that various colleges were composing their own versions of it.

As all this implies, the book has no simple provenance. It has grown out of an interest that began when I was in college. As a sophomore, I wrote a term paper for an education course that traced the changes in my college's curriculum through two decades after its founding. While the paper itself faded from my memory, I can see in retrospect that this modest project spawned an enduring interest in how curricula are constructed. It also sparked my curiosity about the rationales on which they purport to rest. Many years later, that early experience served me when I was working on a book about how John Donne was lodged in nineteenth-century literary culture. Noticing that T. S. Eliot had remarked that he first read the metaphysical poets as a freshman, I went into the Harvard archives to see what could be learned about Eliot's English course. What I found there changed the principal focus of my research from literary criticism to education.

The extraordinary treasure trove of materials available in the archives prompted me to start learning about the curriculum that Eliot had encountered. Two fascinating books built on archival records at Harvard showed me how nineteenth-century teaching could be reconstructed. Bruce Kimball's *The Inception of Modern Professional Education* reveals how C. C. Langdell introduced the case method into law school classrooms. Caroline Winterer's *The Culture of Classicism* unveils how the teaching of Latin and Greek developed. These models inspired me to imagine that something similar might be done with English studies. But I had my book to finish, and I was not yet thinking that I might be the one to write about how the study of vernacular literature entered the curriculum. I did, however, devote the book's climactic chapters to revealing how Harvard became the first institution to turn John Donne's writings into an academic subject.

My research then took two further turns. I began visiting other archives to augment what I was finding at Harvard and to learn more about how other writers were taught. I also began introducing students to the idea that our study of literature could be enriched by realizing that it has a history. To disabuse advanced students from thinking that reading the latest scholarship on, say, *Othello* constituted doing research, I began creating assignments that asked them to find something original and surprising to write about. I encouraged them, for instance, to look into the introductions and notes in early textbook editions of a play, where they could discover curiously different ways in which teachers and students had once been thinking about it. I offered a graduate course called "The Invention of the Renaissance in the Nineteenth Century," brought the students to Harvard's hospitable archives, and helped each one to create a research project focused on an author of their choice. I was fortunate to be teaching in a college where English was for many years the most popular major. It proved easy to find undergraduate research assistants who were eager to learn how to share my archival work. I remain grateful to many students for what their projects taught me. But it took a long time for me to begin confronting the kinds of questions that I might have been raising all along. It was after I encountered James Turner's *Religion Enters the Academy*, a book that demonstrates how philological perspectives generated the scholarly study of religion, that I began to raise the questions that inspired me to write this book.

—When did colleges and universities first start teaching English literature?
—What were the circumstances that led to the creation of English courses?

—How were the boundaries of the subject defined? Who defined them?
—By what methods was literature written in the students' own language to be taught?
—How did someone who had never taken a course in the subject manage to teach it?
—How did the introduction of courses on literature affect the teaching of writing?

The Birth of the English Major has grown out of what I have found by pursuing questions like these. Like everyone who writes history, I have benefited from a large mass of published work by other scholars. Many published sources that underlie the book are referred to in the notes, which I have nonetheless tried to keep to a minimum. Here, I wish to single out a book that richly articulates a theoretical rationale for the archival work on which my book is based: Rachel Sagner Buurma and Laura Heffernan's *The Teaching Archive: A New History for Literary Study.* The excitement that I first felt in Harvard's archives endured. I felt it again every time I went into a different college's archives. And I have often felt it anew. Writing this book has occasioned recalling the experience of reading books I have loved and remembering students whose own experiments doing archival work expanded and deepened their knowledge and mine.

A FEW WORDS OF clarification are in order. Some terms appearing in these pages were employed, especially before c. 1870, in senses different from what we are accustomed to.

(1) Class. Until the emergence of a curriculum that allowed for a wide choice among electives, a *class* generally referred to the group of students who entered the college together and were slated to graduate in the same year, e.g., the class of 1846. The word was not used to refer to what is now known as a *class period.* Typically, students attended *recitations* and sometimes *lectures.*

(2) Course. My practice in this book is to capitalize this word when it refers to a complete degree program: the Classical Course, which led to the BA degree; the Scientific Course, leading to a BS degree; the English Course, which might lead to a BS or BPhil degree; the Ladies Course, which led to a certifi-

cate. Until the last two decades of the nineteenth century, typically students did not take *courses* in our sense; they studied *subjects*. Harvard eventually required that every year students pass four yearlong *courses* in our sense of the word. In the early 1880s it began to offer what were called *half-courses*. These met for only one of the two terms or met twice a week during one term.

(3) **Department.** This word was used differently in different institutions at different times. It sometimes referred to a subject matter, such as the classics or chemistry. Sometimes it named what we would now consider a separate *school* within the institution. In the 1850s, Yale had three "Departments" that prepared students for a profession: Law, Medicine, and Theology. Yale students seeking a Bachelor of Arts degree studied in the Academical Department, the equivalent of what we call the undergraduate college. By the 1870s, as separable disciplines were organized into discrete groups, many colleges began employing the word *department* to refer to the faculty who taught that discipline; for instance, the chemistry department.

(4) **English.** Colleges traditionally gave names to many subjects and to departments on the basis of languages: Latin, Greek, French, German. English departments arrived belatedly. Well into the 1880s, the scope and contents and methods of college English were still being defined. In places where I mean to signal the merely inchoate nature of this new subject, I generally place "English" in quotation marks.

UNLESS OTHERWISE NOTED, italicized words that you see within quotations were italicized in the original. Double quotation marks surround material quoted from somewhere else or call attention either to a characteristic or to an unusual way a word or phrase was being used.

Introduction

Reading is going toward something that is about to be,
and no one yet knows what it will be.

—ITALO CALVINO, *If on a Winter's Night a Traveler*

ASSIGNMENTS LIKE CRAFTING an essay about *Pride and Prejudice* or writing a take-home exam on Shakespeare's tragedies have long been known to college students, but they have not existed from time out of mind. They have a history. They emerged as part of an unprecedented development that took place in the United States during the last decades of the nineteenth century. That's when college English departments first emerged. Questions about why and how this happened have as many answers as there were colleges and universities that went about creating courses in which students read literature in English. The courses sprung up like azaleas here, daffodils there, and tulips a bit later somewhere else, spotting the nation's landscape in different shapes and colors. By the early 1870s some institutions had created what was designated a Department of English. Others took their time. Every institution devised its own ways of deciding what its version of "English" was going to look like.

Whoever the first teachers of literature in English were, they had never taken a course on it themselves. By choosing this poem and that book or even a Shakespeare play for sustained attention, instructors wrought a startling innovation. It was not obvious just which works were to be taught or how teaching them was to be accomplished. There was no established canon to be studied everywhere. Some colleges started students out with Anglo-Saxon, others with Chaucer or Shakespeare. Still others reversed the process, beginning with recent literature. The contents and methods in the first English courses varied from one college to the next, and within each college these changed from year to year. Whatever students were assigned to read became the de facto measuring sticks that they would bring to the next works they read. As they processed what they were reading, students themselves contributed to defining what college English was to be.

FOR SEVERAL DECADES after the American Revolution, only a tiny portion of the population—fewer than 2 percent of young white males aged fifteen to twenty—attended college. High schools began appearing in the 1820s, but high-school education became widely available only after midcentury in the North and even later in the South. Random adolescents here and there might be reading a novel by Walter Scott or a play by Shakespeare. But formal study of vernacular literature was unimaginable, even for college students. Those who went to college were young, and the level of instruction on offer was pretty much equivalent to what we experience in early high school. To gain admission, they needed to learn languages they would never speak. Once they matriculated, they would be required to study Latin, Greek, and mathematics to make their way toward a Bachelor of Arts degree. Many were expecting to become ministers or to go into the family business. Some planned to be teachers. Some would enter public life. Colleges put every student into competition with all the other members of his entering class. They aimed to produce—by teaching basic math, by imparting a knowledge of material coded in secret languages, and by requiring practice in public speaking—a nonhereditary meritocracy from which the country's leaders would emerge.

During the first two decades of the nineteenth century, college attendance was at low ebb. Alternatives to college were springing up: institutions that offered training in law, medicine, and theology. Churches found that pastors who had attended divinity school were better prepared than college graduates to do the practical work required of them. After 1820, many new denominational colleges were founded, especially in the West, where it was necessary to accommodate applicants who had little knowledge of the classical languages. Few offered a full four-year program, and they had a more diffuse curriculum than the classical colleges. Many of their students had barely entered their teens. New options appeared in New York State, where West Point taught engineering and a school opened in Rensselaer that would develop into a polytechnic institute. Amherst College, founded in 1821 in the spirit of the Great Awakening, began offering a practical alternative to its Classical Course. Students recognized its inferiority, however, and few opted to follow it. Thomas Jefferson's University of Virginia opened in 1825 and provided a secular model for organizing a curriculum that was meant to be more practical. The opening of Mount Holyoke in 1830 and of Oberlin College in 1834 meant that young women might also pursue higher education. Expensive female colleges in the South catered, as the University of Virginia did, to wealthy families. Southern colleges stuck with the classical curriculum. The University of North Carolina was an exception: it allowed fourth-year students to move into the study of engineering or agriculture. Still, through the antebellum period generally and throughout the country, the Classical Course held its own against a welter of attempts to debunk its prestige. It was the only path to the Bachelor of Arts degree.[1]

Since the seventeenth century there had been grumbling about the central place that Latin and Greek occupied in higher education. "Can there be any thing more ridiculous," John Locke had asked, "than that a father should waste his own Money, and his Son's time, in setting him to learn the *Roman Language*, when at the same Time he designs him for a Trade?"[2] Locke insisted that only "Custom," not real necessity, dictated that ambitious young men had to study Latin; students were seeking the prestige attached to a knowledge of the classical languages merely as a symbol of status. In nineteenth-century America, where a knowledge of Latin was available to persons of the middle class as well as to the wealthy, Yale's president and fellows acknowledged the critique as early as 1828. They launched an in-depth inquiry "into the expediency of . . . altering the regular course of instruction" by "substituting other studies" for "the study of the *dead languages*."[3] But the faculty concluded that the traditional study of Latin and Greek must remain the foundation of a liberal education, and other institutions continued to follow Yale's lead. Cogent critiques of the established system, and reasonable proposals for a better way forward, mostly met with silence.

A decade and a half after the influential Yale report appeared, the *Nassau Monthly*, a small fledgling journal located in Princeton, New Jersey, published a telling call for "Popular Collegiate Education." It articulated the grounds on which the study of English literature should replace the classics. Without directly mentioning the local college by name, an anonymous writer offered a bold vision of how that institution might transform American higher education. "The whole classical course," he observed, takes "about six years." Most of that "is spent with Greek, Latin, and Mathematics." Yet "nine-tenths of the graduates will in a few years have forgotten almost all they ever learned."[4] No student who studies Greek and Latin, the writer observed, ever learns to think in those languages. Prolonged familiarity with the syntax and inflections found in the long sentences characteristic of classical writing teaches students to write stilted English prose. But Shakespeare and Milton are as beautiful, profound, and sublime as Homer. Their writings, "in the very language we drink in with our mother's milk," could provide the same "mental discipline" that classicists claim for the established curriculum: "Why not study them?"[5] Still, the full classical curriculum remained in place.

The perennial questions about the utility of Latin and Greek began percolating again during the Civil War. The Morrill Land-Grant Act of 1862 meant to answer them by funding new state-sponsored public institutions that would teach agriculture and the mechanic arts. The wartime deaths of such an extraordinarily large number of persons, many of whom had been college students, brought a new edge to the questioning and penetrated into the traditional colleges. What good had it done them to have studied Latin and Greek for years on end?

After the war, rumblings about traditional forms of education multiplied. The demand for scientific and technical education increased. Some colleges were now offering, in addition to the Bachelor of Arts degree, a second-class program. In the 1840s, Harvard and Yale had shown the way by creating separate "Scientific Schools." In 1851 Harvard's Lawrence School began to grant a Bachelor of Science degree. The University of Michigan followed in 1855. By the early 1870s Michigan was offering a Bachelor of Letters degree as well. When Lafayette College opened its Pardee Scientific Course in 1866, it acknowledged that, increasingly, "great universities and colleges" were offering programs like theirs in "parallel" to the Classical Course.[6] As alternative Courses multiplied, a much larger number of students began attending college. Opportunities for Black people, immigrants, and women opened up. Families accustomed to imagining that their sons would attend traditional liberal arts colleges began to suspect that a classical curriculum might turn out to be irrelevant. Early in 1869 Charles W. Eliot, then a young man teaching analytical chemistry at the newly opened Massachusetts Institute of Technology, published an essay aimed to dispel this fear by turning attention to emerging opportunities for young men. Titled "The New Education," Eliot's essay appeared in the country's leading magazine, the *Atlantic Monthly.* It helped to set the institution we now know as MIT on its way to international notoriety. It also launched Eliot's career as an educational reformer.

In the opening paragraph of "The New Education," the author speaks in the voice of a parent contemplating a college education for his child: "What can I do with my boy? I can afford . . . to give him the best training to be had." Then, as if to recall that the purpose of college had long since been to train ministers and teachers, the father goes on to articulate a dilemma troubling the affluent: "I should be proud to have him turn out a preacher or a learned man; but I don't think he has the making of that in him. I want to give him a practical education; one that will prepare him, better than I was prepared, to follow my business or any other active calling. The classical schools and the colleges do not offer what I want. . . . Here is a real need and a very serious problem."

Eliot's own voice has begun to rise out of the imaginary father's. Having hit his stride, he goes on to open a wide vista with large implications for the future of higher education in the U.S.: "The difficulty presses more heavily upon the thoughtful American than upon the European. He is absolutely free to choose a way of life for himself and his children; no government leading-strings or social prescriptions guide or limit him in his choice. But freedom is responsibility."[7]

Eliot's essay provides a wide swath of information and informed opinion. It describes the present state and future promise of a practical education designed to prepare young men to contribute to scientific progress. It reports on how technological education is currently carried out in Germany, France, and England. Then it examines in detail the leading scientific schools in the U.S., including the Sheffield School at Yale and the Lawrence School at Harvard, where Eliot had begun his teaching career. The essay climaxes with an answer to the bewildered father's dilemma: it offers an elegant celebration of a new kind of education at the Massachusetts Institute of Technology.

Within months of the publication of "The New Education" Eliot resigned his position and returned to Harvard. Largely on the basis of the vision articulated in the essay, and not without controversy among its overseers, Harvard had hired him to be its president. However eager the majority of the overseers may have been for the college to be headed by an innovator, Eliot soon found that he would have to think in practical terms about his claim that there is a profound difference between a newly created polytechnic school and a traditional college with an entrenched faculty. His new position required him to navigate the difference between what he had claimed were two incompatible "tempers." His essay had defined the *literary spirit* as appropriate for students attending college where "the desire for the broadest culture, for the best formation and information of the mind, the enthusiastic study of subjects for the love of them without any ulterior objects, the love of learning and research for their own sake, should be the dominant ideas." By contrast, *the practical spirit* was said to befit the "temper or leading motive" of the polytechnic or scientific school, where "a mental training inferior to none in breadth and vigor, a thirst for knowledge, a genuine enthusiasm in scientific research, and a true love of nature" are pursued as training for a specialized scientific or technological profession. Before Eliot had served even six months as Harvard's president, an item in the popular press would cast "the literary" and "the practical" as warring factions and declare the latter winner of a decisive victory.[8]

On December 18, 1869, what sounded like a definitive answer to Eliot's question "What can I do with my boy?" made its way through the mails to households all around the country. *Frank Leslie's Illustrated Newspaper*, a weekly that had gained a circulation in the tens of thousands thanks to its coverage of the war, ran a piece on a new institute recently opened in Boston. It was going to change higher education forever. A handsome sketch of the Massachusetts Institute of Technology's new building caught readers' eyes. The edifice was manifestly an achievement of architects and engineers of the caliber that the Institute meant to train. It was situated in the Back Bay, a new area of the city created by filling in a tidal bay to accommodate the construction of luxury housing. The property abutted the first public botanical garden in the United States. The accompanying prose called attention to the beauty of the structure and designated the building a monument to a hard-won victory over the deadening effects of a classical education. In keeping with this message, it discreetly omitted mention of the building's classical façade and instead celebrated the Institute's large significance as the model for the education of the future:

> In the fairest portion of Boston, just adjoining the pleasaunce of the Public Garden, with its flowers and fountains, and in the neighborhood of the palaces of that region, there stands a handsome and massive building of brick and brown-stone . . . sheltering the operations of an institution which is destined to assume a part in the education of a people never played before. This building is the tomb of dead languages. The day on which its first stone was laid sealed the fate, it is to be hoped, of that system by which our youth waste the best portion of student-life in burrowing into the grammars and dictionaries of races less enlightened than their own, of a literature whose beauties their immature minds cannot perceive—literature already sufficiently displayed by translation, and whose general pursuit is of no further earthly use to any one alive.[9]

This prophetic voice intimated that it spoke for power and wealth. Condescending towards ancient civilizations, southern European "races less enlightened," it put the traditional colleges on notice that their curriculum belonged in a mausoleum and that they should not expect to keep conducting business as usual. The gleeful display of hostility to the classical languages evinced what Charles Eliot had called the "freedom" available in the U.S. to radically remake educational structures. In the next three decades, that freedom would also make it possible for colleges to create departments of English in which students could study vernacular literature.

When Eliot assumed the presidency of Harvard in 1869, both the Massachusetts Institute of Technology and Yale's Sheffield Scientific School were beginning to experiment with making English a full-fledged academic subject. It was assumed that reading and writing in their native language would better prepare students to lead productive lives than studying Latin and Greek. Through the last four decades of the century, many new colleges opened, and many traditional colleges created alternative degree programs. Some traditional colleges metamorphosed into modern universities. To make room for previously marginal subjects to develop into disciplines, most administrators reduced the scope afforded to the classical languages. Gradually, traditional colleges began creating English departments that took their place alongside burgeoning departments of chemistry, mental philosophy (psychology), political economy (economics), history, and even fine arts. Increasingly, ambitious adolescents in the U.S. had reason to feel that the study of vernacular literature would betoken their entrance into modernity.

Given the freedom that institutions of higher learning enjoyed, and the American propensity to glorify individualism, each college, in creating an English department and developing its curriculum, had nonetheless to work with limited resources. But by the 1890s courses on English literature were available nearly everywhere, and they were multiplying and filling up. This development was celebrated in a journal published in Chicago, where a new private university was just opening. In 1894 *The Dial,* as a feature of its attempt to revive the Transcendentalist journal once edited by Ralph Waldo Emerson and Margaret Fuller, began publishing detailed accounts of how the study of English was being organized in colleges nationwide. Semimonthly installments, each from a different institution, reported at length on what various English departments were doing and how literature was coming to be studied. Enthusiastic "professorial testimonies" came from traditional Eastern colleges, from state-supported institutions of the Midwest, and from newly created private universities endowed by private philanthropy. When an associate editor of the journal gathered the series into a collection titled *English in American Universities,* the published volume made it plain that, in what he referred to as the country's "leading institutions," "English" was no longer the name for a nontraditional second-class degree program. The subject was flourishing from New Haven to Ann Arbor and onward to Palo Alto and Berkeley. The study of literature, the editor concluded, had garnered "its full share of attention" and had become "recognized as a true university subject with its own methods and aims."[10]

PART I

ENGLISH BACK IN THE DAY

I

What Was Going to College Like?

> We have known young men graduate with considerable honour, who knew absolutely nothing of History and of Shakspeare [*sic*] and Milton. . . . And yet these were young men who had passed through a regular academic and collegiate course, and were supposed by their friends to have a finished education which fitted them for any employment within the grasp of the human intellect.
>
> —*Nassau Monthly* (1844)

EARLY IN 1888, readers of the *Book Buyer,* a monthly literary review based in New York, encountered a notice about an examination recently given at Harvard. It may have raised some eyebrows. It probably warmed a few hearts. The briefest of notes, it nonetheless intimated that a metamorphosis in how English literature could feature in a college student's life was in the offing. Arlo Bates, the review's regular correspondent on the literary scene in greater Boston, reported he had become "much interested in an examination paper in the mid-year examination of English 14." Confident that most readers had never come up against anything like it and would be as surprised as he was, he quoted a sample question:

> Discuss the following passage: "In the works of Middleton 'we are far away from the rising freshness of Greene, and Peele, and Marlowe; we have left behind the upland valleys of Ben Jonson; we have passed in a sort of St. Gotthard tunnel beneath the alpine heights of Shakespeare; and now we are on the other side of the Alps, with beautiful, corrupt Italy before us.'"

"I should have liked to see the faces of the students when they read the paper," Bates remarked. "They are said to have done unexpectedly well, . . . but the digs who had been cramming dates and the like must have been somewhat disconcerted at being required to use their reason instead of their memory." Bates pointed up the contrast between what could now be found in contemporary departments of English and "the list of questions with which our student days were familiar."[1]

English 14 was a newly created course on Elizabethan and Jacobean dramatists, excluding Shakespeare. The focus on a genre and on a particular historical period was unprecedented at Harvard, though not elsewhere. The sample question and its "we" suggest camaraderie among the students and with their instructor. It invites the examinees to think of the first half of their course as having been a journey and encourages them to recognize themselves as characters in a travel narrative. Even as the prompt expects students to display knowledge of Thomas Middleton's plays and to evince understanding of their place in an unfolding story, it welcomes originality. Whether the examiner, Bates's friend Barrett Wendell, had found the quotation somewhere or (more likely) had fabricated it for the purpose, the writing prompt encourages the students to think of the instructor as a kind of tour guide and then to use their imaginations. By quoting a single question from the exam, Bates provided a glimpse of a new dispensation in the history of studying English literature.

We can know a great deal about the workings of Harvard's English 14, far more than we do about hundreds of other late nineteenth-century courses that entailed the study of English literature. The Harvard archives preserve about a dozen notebooks in which students transcribed what they heard during lectures in English 14. Extraordinarily, while Wendell was first giving the course, he himself kept an elaborate notebook which he eventually donated to the archives. On the right-hand pages, he wrote out his lectures. On the left, he recorded reflections and an occasional anecdote that might prove useful the next time he gave the course. He also folded in copies of the midyear and final examinations, and listed how many students had received an A (4), B (10), C (12), D (10), or E (2) as their final grade.[2] (Many Harvard students considered belonging to the right club and participating in extracurricular activities more important than grades. Not a few regarded C as a perfectly acceptable mark.

Some actually sought, if indirectly, to acquire a C. It demonstrated that they were not "digs" or "grinds.")

THE DISCONTINUITY BETWEEN emerging practices in late nineteenth-century English courses and what readers of the *Book Buyer* might be expected to remember from "our student days" raises questions about what the study of literature had been like through the preceding decades. Bates had graduated from Bowdoin in 1876 and likely had in mind an audience that had attended college before students had much space to elect their courses and when there were no literature courses centered on a genre or a literary period, on versification, or on a single author not named Shakespeare. What had colleges been like for earlier generations of students? What sort of acquaintance with English literature had colleges afforded students through the first six or seven decades of the century?

In the first half of the century, when high schools did not yet dot the landscape, applicants to college prepared to pass an entrance examination on Latin, Greek, and the lower mathematics either by attending an academy or by receiving instruction from a private tutor. Some college students were as young as twelve when they matriculated, and colleges took an in loco parentis approach in dealing with them. Gradually, it was required that students be at least fourteen.

Many colleges simply served local populations. West of New England, most institutions were allied with one or the other Protestant denomination, and sectarian squabbles set them in competition with each other. A majority would fail before century's end. Small colleges had only three or four faculty members, all of them male, and enrolled fewer than a hundred (male) students. Few instructors proved as competent as the faculty in a good preparatory academy.[3] By 1869, when Charles Eliot became president of Harvard, among liberal arts colleges, Amherst was considered large with 251 students. Harvard and Yale were the largest colleges. Harvard's catalogs show that for the 1869–70 academic year the college had 24 faculty members and 563 undergraduates. Yale's catalog for that year lists twenty-some faculty in the Department of Philosophy and the Arts (the college) and 519 undergraduates preparing for the BA degree. In addition, both colleges also employed contingent faculty and tutors. Yale's Sheffield Scientific School numbered 140 students. Yale's other Departments—theology, law, and medicine—had still fewer students. (Nowhere did admission to studies leading to a profession require one's having first earned an undergraduate degree.) When Bates was at Bowdoin in the early seventies, the "Academical Faculty" of the college numbered fifteen, and he was one of about 220 undergraduates. Here, we might note that by that time women made up about a quarter of the collegiate population in the U.S.; their numbers would grow to 37 percent by 1900.[4] In later chapters we will take up women's increasing attendance in college.

BEFORE MIDCENTURY, the technology available for classroom activities had been sparse. The invention of a blackboard facilitated instructing students in groups. Each student had a slate for writing and could compare his computations while doing a math problem, say, with the solution that the master wrote on the board. Paper was made from linen and old cotton rags and was expensive. Students wrote with quill pens, and their masters spent a good deal of time mending their quills with a penknife, one by one.

Custom—what Francis Bacon once called "the principal magistrate of man's life"—ruled in the daily schedule. In many colleges, the school day was punctuated by a series of recitations. Typically, Monday through Friday, three recitation periods structured the students' time. (On Saturdays students had only two recitations.) One recitation took place in the early morning, the second in the middle of the day, the third in the late afternoon. Between the first recitation and the second, and again between the second and the third, students had time for what was called "polling," to ready themselves for the next period when they would be quizzed on some limited amount of work. There were other names for studying as well: "cramming" and "digging" and "grinding." A recitation period lasted for an hour. Many instructors did not think of their classroom as a site where teaching and learning took place; it was the place where the instructor checked up on how well students had learned the assigned work. It served as a sort of theater, where one by one students were summoned to perform. Nearly everyone dreaded being called on to provide the solution to a math problem. For their Latin recitations, students needed to reproduce information crammed into their short-term memory or to declaim, say, a passage from Virgil learned by rote. They generally encountered Latin and Greek texts not as literature but in short excerpts that served as specimens for exercises in grammar and for practice in elocution.[5] While one student performed, everyone else sat by with little to do except worry about being called on. Short of witnessing an electrifying humiliation of an insufficiently prepared classmate, they found the whole procedure boring.

On several counts, literature in English was assumed to be unworthy of collegiate study. The general populace regarded knowledge of English simply as a birthright. They held it up as the standard to which immigrants needed to conform in order to become "American." Adults learning English—however sophisticated their mastery of their native language—found it difficult to be taken seriously by native English speakers. Most educators who insisted on the study of the classical languages shared the prejudice against nonnative speakers and refused to countenance the possibility that, like other languages, English was worthy of advanced study. Few were ready to acknowledge that speaking one's mother tongue was an accomplishment; though, when we give it some thought, we understand that learning their native language is actually the major intellectual achievement of the vast majority of members of the human race.

The human capacity to use language is inborn. But every language anyone acquires—including the first—is comprised of grammatical knowledge unique in its distinctive properties of syntax, semantics, lexical facts, etc., the basics of which need to be learned in order to participate in a community that is bound together by sharing it.[6] This is what makes acquiring one's native language a substantial accomplishment. It is also what makes studying the English language and its literature a rich opportunity for those who have long-standing experience in using it. Assuming that the country's dominant language is simply a birthright, rather than acknowledging that acquiring one's native language is an achievement, retarded the long process through which English came belatedly to be regarded as a respectable college study.

Literature in English provided diversion and entertainment for native speakers quite apart from any schoolroom. By the 1840s some families were spending Sunday afternoons in the parlor reading the latest installment of a Dickens novel in a periodical. Many people knew phrases out of Shakespeare and something of his great characters. College students were free to read whatever literature they wished on their own. But before the Civil War, and in many places thereafter, English literature was scarcely to be found in the curriculum. In accord with literary theories dating from the age of Queen Anne, students learned to treat poems not as wholes but as containers for isolated nuggets, touchstones said to illustrate the poet's brilliance. Professors of rhetoric and oratory sometimes exposed students to famous passages drawn from orations by Daniel Webster and Edward Everett, or from a play by Shakespeare. The practice of considering a literary work in its entirety lay undeveloped until much later in the century.[7] Excerpts in the vernacular served to illustrate a rhetorical device or to provide inspiration for a writing assignment. When, in the 1840s and 1850s, some colleges began offering alternative degree programs in which French and German stood in as alternatives to Greek and Latin, even in these living languages, students encountered their literatures piecemeal, as storehouses of grammar, syntax, and vocabulary, or as isolated instances of aesthetic beauty.

Meanwhile, the general populace had scant knowledge of what was done in college or any reason to care. In the 1840s, two young men at Williams College, "yet in their 'teens,"[8] composed sketches of college life, remarking that people tended to think either that college students live in a "heathen paradise," where they experience "one continuous round of gaiety and dissipation," or that they dwell in "a sort of monastery, where Science and Religion, clothed in the sternest garbs, govern like tyrants."[9] To counter these delusions, the Williams students compiled from a private journal, purportedly kept by one of their fellows through all four years, choice excerpts meant to exhibit college life. The journalist praises, for instance, "the affable and familiar manner"[10] in which faculty members treat him. He gets back an essay he's written and begins to suspect that the instructor's ambiguous comments are subtly critical. When his geometry course ends, he joins his classmates in a mock funeral service for Euclid. Suddenly, in sophomore year, he begins to recognize how little he knows.

What's telling about the place of English literature in college shows up in a pair of entries that virtually bookend all the others. The first records the student's excitement at having joined a literary society shortly after matriculating. College literary societies had begun springing up in the late eighteenth century. They were independent institutions run by students. They offered respite from the grind of thrice-daily recitations, a place in which to cultivate friendships and to hone skills in debating. Many had much more ample libraries than the colleges. (College students rarely had need to consult library books for their studies. Their daily recitations required them simply to memorize material out of textbooks.)

Most colleges had two competing literary societies, and nearly every student joined one or the other. The Dialectic Society at the University of North Carolina was founded in 1795 to promote "useful" knowledge. A rival Philanthropic Society soon split off, and the groups competed with one another for recruits. According to legend, the rivalry descended into dueling, and the administration intervened to establish rules for membership based on the geographical locales from which the students came. Literary societies were different from fraternities, which, when they emerged somewhat later, were exclusive. Fraternities admitted prosperous candidates. Others were not invited. Frat brothers often scorned religiously inclined students—"theologs"—as being no fun at all.[11] Literary societies had more ambitious intellectual aims. Members thrashed out their views on current events or something controversial such as the institution of slavery. They wrote and sometimes performed their own poetry, essays, and music. They held debates and sponsored addresses by public figures. (The most well known was Ralph Waldo Emerson's "American Scholar" address delivered to Harvard's Phi Beta Kappa society.) Since they maintained their own libraries, their members could take their fill of literature in English. At North Carolina, each society eventually donated more than ten thousand books to establish the university's first library.

The Williams students, urging that literary societies are where the "majority of men make most progress in literary pursuits,"[12] quote from the journal a passage in which the newly enrolled student tells about an early visit to his society's well-furnished library. It inspires in him a desire to read widely. He resolves on a program of extracurricular reading. It will focus on history, biography, and, climactically, English literature: "Shakspeare [*sic*], Milton, Addison, Pope, Young, Swift, Goldsmith, Burke, and Cowper. I think this course, well pursued, will employ me," he writes, "through college, and make me at graduation a man of great general information."[13]

Many passages later, as the student's years in college are coming to an end, a climactic excerpt lays bare an attempt to come to terms with how much he has missed out on: "How little do I know? How little have I read? How feeble the execution of the scheme of reading which I find entered on my journal during the buoyancy of Freshman year! . . . Would that I could enter college again with my present experience!"[14]

The majority of students, if they were to read English literature seriously, needed the kind of structure that the college would provide, but there was no available curricular space for this. Nearly everywhere students followed a uniform curriculum. They studied the same subjects, and they were graded on all their recitations and examinations in relation to their peers. In most cases, at commencement each graduate left college knowing the exact number of his rank in class. Here and there, a college allowed students some modest choice of coursework in senior year, but not English literature. If a student showed literary propensities, his Latin and Greek courses were thought to provide a suitable outlet. Slowly, however, educators began to acknowledge it a failing that most graduates left college with almost no knowledge of literature in their native tongue.

By midcentury a few classical colleges began offering a short set of lectures on English literature. Far from overcoming the piecemeal handling of literary works characteristic of rhetoric courses, these lectures exacerbated the problem. Typically, students heard a lecture one day a week for a term or two. Sometimes the professor of rhetoric delivered it. More often it was an inexperienced tutor. Most lecturers simply provided information available in a handbook. In Canada's colleges, students were obliged to become acquainted with the contents of William Spalding's *History of English Literature* (1862). It was written in an oral style that enabled instructors to read from it aloud. Students took notes, and there may have been no need to purchase the book. In a later edition, Spalding included sample exam questions in an appendix keyed to the text, presumably for the students, but perhaps for inexperienced instructors. It showed that a question as apparently daunting as "Sketch the changes which English literature underwent from Elizabeth to Anne" could be answered on the basis of having memorized the contents of as few as three of Spalding's paragraphs.[15]

Students who heard lectures in U.S. colleges frequently met with Thomas Budd Shaw's popular *Outlines of English Literature* (1849). Like Spalding's *History*, this inexpensive textbook acquainted them with the names of authors and literary works, and with dates. Handbooks disseminated second-hand information, much of it erroneous. They dealt with the merely external features of literature, not with literature itself. They fostered the illusion in the teachers as well as the students that they knew something about English literature. Once students rehearsed the information they had memorized, they could forget it.

WHEN IT CAME TO lectures on literature, Harvard stood as the exception that proved the rule. There, decades of serious instruction on modern foreign literatures provided the soil from which Wendell's drama course would eventually crop up. The college made an early commitment to introducing students to several vernacular literatures. Already in the 1820s and 1830s it had secured the services of George Ticknor, whose four years of literary study in European universities had furnished him with an unparalleled authority to lecture on Spanish and other European literatures. Many people from outside the college attended his lectures. The tradition continued into the second half of the century as Henry Wadsworth Longfellow and James Russell Lowell succeeded him. They lectured on the literatures of the Romance languages, Longfellow notably on *The Divine Comedy*. They freely made reference to English authors as well, especially Shakespeare and Milton. But they no more taught English literature as a subject in its own right than did Harvard's Boylston Professor of Rhetoric and Oratory, Edward Tyrrel Channing. In 1856, Channing's *Lectures Read to Seniors in Harvard College* were posthumously put into print. They take up one rhetorical subject after another, presented with grace and learning. Not a single lecture, however, provides a sustained treatment of any English author or work of literature.

The standard rhetoric textbook at Harvard was known casually as "Whately's Rhetoric." Richard Whately, an English rhetorician, had composed it with British readers in mind. The two-hundred-some pages of his *Elements of Rhetoric* offer no specimens from English classics. Instead, readers find occasional allusions to short passages in Shakespeare's plays, a line from *Twelfth Night* here, a passing reference to "Caesar and Lear" there, all delivered with the confidence that the readers are familiar with the plays. This feature of the textbook makes it surprising that several other colleges, perhaps simply because they were following Harvard's lead, employed Whately's *Rhetoric*. Channing's confidence that Harvard students could navigate its allusions to classic English literature was unusual. Students elsewhere were out of their depths with it.

Through the middle decades of the century, college students across the country varied considerably in the range of their reading experiences. At Bowdoin, where Longfellow and Nathaniel Hawthorne had studied as classmates in the 1820s, the newly appointed professor of rhetoric, Samuel Newman, wrote his own rhetoric textbook. *A Practical System of Rhetoric* often quoted whole passages from Milton. That Shakespeare appeared less often is consonant with the fact that Milton had been much better known in the colonies and had inspired the founding fathers' views on freedom of the press and on the rights of private conscience. The kind of accommodation that *A Practical System* offered students can be seen in Newman's explanation of an allusion made to Shakespeare in a recent and highly regarded essay on Milton written for the *Edinburgh Review:*

> This allusion is to the Othello of Shakspeare [*sic*]; and such is the rank and antiquity of his writings, that allusions to passages found in them, are regarded much in the same manner as classical allusions. We have in fact our English classical writers, who have outlived their century, and who, from their preëminence, may be supposed to be familiarly known by every English scholar. To such writers it is lawful to make allusions as those whose works should be known; and such allusions, when happily introduced, will please us in the same manner and degree, as those made to the ancient classics.[16]

Newman's *Rhetoric* went through over sixty editions and was still the textbook at Bowdoin in the 1870s, when Bates took sophomore rhetoric. It enjoyed wide popularity beyond the college and affords an impression of what students knew and did not know about English literature through the middle decades of the century: in short, they knew next to nothing. In 1870, when Yale's Sheffield Scientific School hired Thomas Lounsbury as the university's first professor of English, the criticism that had been lodged in Princeton's *Nassau Monthly* three decades earlier was still pertinent. "Assuredly," Lounsbury wryly remarked, "it is no wild statement to make that in many of our colleges a man might go through a four years course, and never hear once from the lips of his teachers the names of Shakespeare or Milton; and there are still very few of our schools in which he would ever be reduced to the necessity of reading a single line of their works."[17]

Sprinkling a few famous passages of English literature into a rhetoric course did not make English a college subject like Latin or Greek or French. Except for rare exceptions like the courses George Ticknor taught at Harvard, courses named for foreign languages were directed above all to the languages themselves. Instructors brought from the literatures of the classical languages exemplary passages that would illustrate features of the grammar and syntax and vocabulary. Native speakers of English had encountered the comparable features of their vernacular from their youth. They had acquired a relatively large vocabulary. Even if they could not articulate many basic rules of grammar, they knew them implicitly. Professors of rhetoric were not going to waste time reviewing what students should have encountered in school.

In the decades when students learned about English literature from the likes of Shaw's *Outlines,* lecturers were teaching it as a minor subfield of history. Instructors could examine students on what they knew *about* literature. The names and dates of authors, the titles of literary works, and other facts could serve as the answers to objective questions in an examination. Such a procedure would hardly make "English" the name of a respectable subject. As we will have occasion to see in subsequent chapters, another expedient embraced by those who sought to teach English to college students was to focus on earlier stages of the language. Many colleges came to require their students to study Anglo-Saxon, and some had students begin with the Middle English that could be illustrated from passages in Chaucer. This seemed to make English sufficiently difficult to justify a place for it in a college curriculum. Eventually, however, the state of the language at the time of Shakespeare would become a kind of compromise. It proved different enough from contemporary usage to offer difficulty. It was the medium for literary works that might be thought prestigious enough to rival those of Homer and Virgil. Yet it was familiar enough to enable a degree of imaginative engagement for most students that only the most accomplished of Latin scholars ever achieved in reading the *Aeneid.*

WHEN ARLO BATES QUOTED an examination question from a course on the dramas written by Shakespeare's contemporaries, he made a perfect choice for illustrating the discontinuity that would surprise and fascinate readers who had gone to college a generation or two earlier. The question required of students a degree of familiarity with the names, relative dates, and particular works of several authors. It allowed for but did not precisely require students to draw upon what they may have heard in lectures. It asked them to make distinctions among a body of materials, to consider how several plays fit within an unfolding narrative, and to demonstrate a relatively sophisticated understanding of the history of the genre. It encouraged them to use their imaginations and allowed for original insights. It abandoned the crude idea that without actually reading literary works oneself and then entering into dialogue with other readers one could have a knowledge of literature. The chapters to follow are meant to illustrate something of the slow, circuitous process by which literature in English was turned into a respectable college subject and to show how that subject came to flourish.

2

Elocution and Composition

In books, we see the result of thought and of fancy. In the living speaker, we see the thought itself, as it rises in the speaker's own mind. And his countenance often indicates a *perception* before it gets upon his tongue. I have been charmed by observing this operation of minds which are truly great and vigorous; so that I sometimes am as much moved, as in reading a part of Milton and Shakespeare, by a striking and able argument, although on the driest subject.

—DANIEL WEBSTER, writing a letter while listening to Henry Clay speaking in the House of Representatives, 17 January 1825

DURING THE FIRST HALF of the nineteenth century, colleges regarded the production of effective orators as their crowning achievement. Professors of rhetoric and oratory bore the chief responsibility for seeing that students learned to speak well and to write English effectively. In some colleges, instruction in writing was largely confined to matters of grammar, penmanship, and spelling. In most colleges, instructors directed students' attention chiefly to speaking, and they interacted with them by hearing their recitations and declamations. One by one, students were required to recite from memory some celebrated passage in English. This practice left no room for the student to express a living thought of his own. Perhaps the best that might be said for it is that, by listening to one another's performances, students gained familiarity with a snippet of accomplished vernacular writing and noticed that individual oral interpretations of the same phenomenon can vary widely. With the benefit of an effective instructor, over time they would also learn something about different rhetorical styles.

Shakespeare, widely regarded as shared cultural property, offered countless possibilities for classroom elocutionary practice and declamations. Noah Webster, who favored American orators, included only a small sampling of speeches by Shakespearean characters in his popular *Grammatical Institutes.*[1] But other authors of elocutionary handbooks represented the Bard's art as transcending genre and insisted that the educational value of his writing lay in his mastery of spoken English. Increase Cooke, compiler of *The American Orator; or, elegant extracts in poetry and prose* and its *Sequel* (1813), claimed Shakespeare for American oratory. Speeches from *Julius Caesar* and *Hamlet* became standard fare in teaching elocution.

Extracts from American works enjoyed equal popularity. William B. Fowle's *The New Speaker, or Exercises in Rhetoric* (1829) included nine selections from Daniel Webster and eight from Edward Everett.[2] Everett's 1824 Phi Beta Kappa lecture at Harvard, attended by an overflowing audience, proved to be a seminal moment in American cultural history. His inspired handling of his subject, "Circumstances Favorable to the Progress of Literature in the United States of America," loomed behind, cast a shadow over, and sometimes directly infused the activities that many a professor of rhetoric had in mind for his students. Consideration of this speech can give us a feel for how teachers of rhetoric and oratory made use of vernacular oratorical literature.

A pair of published passages, one describing the circumstances and effects of Everett's speech, the other drawn from the address itself, illustrate two different, sometimes overlapping, rhetorical styles: the *epideictic* style that awards praise or assigns blame and the *deliberative* style that enters into a controversy and develops a logical argument on one side rather than the other.

First, an example of the epideictic style, from a contemporary's account of the hour-long speech that Everett delivered from memory:

> Mr. Everett came forward in the full glow of manly beauty . . . , without any manuscript or brief in his hand commenced in clear, untremulous and silvery tones his oration upon the Circumstances Favorable to the Progress of Literature in America. He sketched with inimitable grace and graphicness the fields open for the ambitious—broad as our prairies, grand as our lakes and cataracts, stirring as our colonial history and revolutionary struggles, of which he gave some brilliant pictures. The sympa-

> thies of the vast audience kindled as the form of the orator expanded and his face glowed with the increasing interest of his theme. As he approached his grand climax, the whole audience were of one countenance, thrilled with one emotion. It was a grand musical instrument, every string responding to the skillful touch of the orator.[3]

The style sounds rhetorical, using the term loosely. It picks up on imagery actually employed by Everett: *fields, prairies, lakes, cataracts.* It delivers expansive sentences housing diction that redoubles Everett's spatial and temporal themes: *open, broad, vast, expanded, whole.* It conveys that Everett looked both to the country's past (*revolutionary struggles*) and to the future that it holds out for *the ambitious.* It inflates its praise with a generous infusion of adjectives: *inimitable, brilliant, grand, skillful.* It moves that praise along by deploying active verbs and verbal and deverbal adjectives: *sketched, stirring, kindled, glowed, approached, thrilled, responding.* As it reports on the climax of Everett's speech, it offers its own climactic metaphor, the responsive stringed *instrument.* It supplies an example of the kind of writing that professors of rhetoric and oratory encouraged.

By contrast, Everett's own style is deliberative. It looks not to something that has already happened but to the future. It takes up a controversial subject: whether conditions in the new republic are favorable for creating a distinctive national literature. It attempts to make a logical case and to persuade each member of the audience, Phi Beta Kappa graduates of varying ages, that they have something to contribute to the matter at hand. The argument waxes triumphal, though it modulates this tone with a cautionary note: "Should our happy Union continue, this great continent, in no remote futurity, will be filled up with the mightiest kindred people known in history; our language will acquire an extension which no other ever possessed; and the empire of the mind, with nothing to resist its sway, will attain an expansion, of which, as yet, we can but partly conceive. The vision is too magnificent to be fully borne."[4]

Everett's recurring contrast of American educational institutions with European ones incorporates the ancient tropes called *translatio imperii* and *translatio studii*, referring to the movement of empire and culture westward from Greece to Rome. It anticipates what will be called the country's "manifest destiny." Everett urges that American institutions are free from governmental control, and he proposes that people, because they all employ one language, need not squabble with one another. He observes that the language is a native tongue, not the Latin that Milton, though he could compose beautiful musical strains like those heard in his vernacular "Il Penseroso," had to employ when he wrote his defenses of the English people. Beyond these advantages, Everett calls attention to the sheer size of the continent, the "teeming growth" of "our" population: the promise of westward expansion that had once transferred the center of learning from Greece to Rome and onward to England would one day belong to the continental United States.

Everett's oration inspired—and sometimes intimidated—a generation or more of college faculty and their charges. Students who had never heard of Everett learned about him in college, as he himself made his way up a ladder that included stints as minister to Great Britain, Harvard's president, governor of and then senator from Massachusetts, till he became secretary of state under President Fillmore. Professors of rhetoric would sometimes encourage or even require students to write themes describing how Everett's prediction of an accomplished national literature could be brought to fulfillment.

Everett's orations, like those of Daniel Webster, helped to enhance the prestige of instruction in vocal culture. They provided both models for public speaking and actual sources of passages for declamation, and they constituted a significant component of such literature in English as featured in the early nineteenth-century rhetoric curriculum. Speeches that Shakespeare had written for players to perform proved useful for elocutionary practice as well. Standard rhetorical textbooks printed Hamlet's advice to the players and Portia's speech encouraging Shylock to show mercy. A competent educator would insist that to declaim a passage successfully a student would need some relevant knowledge of the dramatic moment to which it belonged, and he would devise ways to broaden his students' knowledge of the salient features of the play. If he was assigning for memory "The quality of mercy . . ." from *The Merchant of Venice,* students would have to develop an awareness of what Shylock's situation was, what effects were created by Portia's appearance in disguise, and above all what was at stake at the tense moment when the speech was delivered. The best teachers of elocution begot in their students a desire to make the acquaintance of the entire work from which a passage had been excerpted. Not surprisingly, given the classical curriculum in every college, Marc

Antony's oration over the dead body of Julius Caesar proved another favorite passage:

> Friends, Romans, countrymen, lend me your ears.
> I come to bury Caesar, not to praise him.
> The evil that men do lives after them.

One astute handbook, *The Philosophy of the Human Voice; Embracing its Physiological History*, by James Rush, showed how paying close attention to diction can yield information that bears, sometimes subtly, sometimes conspicuously, on developing a right tone. Directing attention to two other lines spoken by Antony—"Pardon me thou bleeding piece of earth / That I am meek and gentle with these butchers"—Rush observed, "The syllable 'Par' . . . has a natural quantity, which, without impropriety, may be doubled or more in expressive utterance; and the same may be said of 'bleed. . . .' The circumstances of the scene . . . inform us that Mark Antony's sentiments, as first expressed in the passage, are those of love, grief and contrition; his feeling of revenge does not appear until the second line."[5] When the study of whole plays began decades later, *Julius Caesar*, long a favorite for elocutionary exercises, stood among the most frequently assigned for reading.

Besides Shakespeare, Milton offered apt materials for elocutionary exercises. Teachers included his writing for a reason not immediately relevant to the purpose: Milton's republican politics and literary achievements had led to the claim that he "is more emphatically American than any author who has lived in the United States."[6] The vigorous republican rhetoric that animates Milton's antimonarchical prose got students sharpening their tongues on poetic speeches that thunder with rebelliousness, such as Satan's bold declaration:

> Farewell happy fields
> Where joy forever dwells: hail horrors, hail
> Infernal world, and thou profoundest Hell
> Receive thy new possessor: one who brings
> A mind not to be changed by place or time.
> The mind is its own place, and in itself
> Can make a Heav'n of Hell, a Hell of Heav'n.[7]

Milton's blank verse speeches were meant to illustrate deliberative rhetoric. Excerpts of this sort likely inspired at least a few students to begin reading the poem for themselves. Whether and how they managed to fit much outside reading (as we would call it) into their routine seems difficult to imagine. Except at Harvard, where Edward Tyrrel Channing served as the Boylston Professor of Rhetoric and Oratory from 1819 until 1850.

When Harvard's Boylston Professorship was created at the start of the century, the college had fewer than 150 students. The university's overseers spelled out in considerable detail the responsibilities to be borne by the holder of the chair. He was to listen to freshmen recite bits of classical literature translated into English; to hear declamations by members of all four classes every week of the year; to assign compositions to sophomores and fortnightly themes to juniors and seniors; to train juniors to speak at public exhibitions; and to lecture to juniors and seniors twice weekly. When Channing took up these duties in 1819, he soon realized that the overseers and administrators were content to overlook how irrelevant these stipulations were becoming and how burdensome they were for the professor. Channing was convinced that students learn more from reading and writing than from providing oral interpretations of others' speeches. He sensed, too, that those most responsible for the curriculum had little idea that the old-fashioned practices meant to prepare students to live in an oral culture were outdated. (The authorities responsible for evaluating the Bolyston Professor's work were unwilling to spend time themselves reading the writing that Harvard students were producing. They considered attending an occasional exhibition in which students gave declamations sufficient for the purpose.) Channing foresaw that the future lay not with public speaking but in reading and writing. He regarded the development of clear, cogent writing as the very heart of his work.[8]

Channing taught composition, elocution, and forensics (the commonly used term for *argumentative writing*). He set a high standard and in time exerted widespread influence. A competent classical scholar, he had read widely in English literature: Shakespeare and Spenser and Milton, Burke, Dr. Johnson, Goldsmith, Fielding, Richardson, and especially Walter Scott. He knew the writings of his contemporaries as well: Irving, Cooper, and Bryant. He admired Longfellow's poetry before it became prominent. He held contemporary British writers in relatively low regard, but admired Dickens for his humor and pathos. He had no brief to teach vernacular literature in his courses, but apart from the curriculum he freely met with students to talk about literary works in English. He urged reading an author right through without allowing footnotes supplied by an editor to summon attention away from the text, even when one is reading unfamiliar language like Chaucer's.[9] As an undergraduate, Henry David Thoreau especially valued this experience and read widely in English poetry.

For all the written polish of his lectures on rhetoric, Channing was not himself an inspiring speaker. In 1829 Harvard hired a British physician, Jonathan Barber, to supplement Channing's work. Barber taught elocution, in particular the art of gesturing with one's hands called "Chironomia." He claimed to have mastered the best schemes for cultivating this practice. He favored a physiological approach and emphasized the mechanical components of gesturing. He constructed out of bamboo poles a contraption into which a student would enter. As the budding orator declaimed some select passage, he was to gesture by touching certain gaps between poles as if they were variously located on the circumference of a sphere, each point being connected with a distinctive gesture to be employed as a physical extension of a particular interior emotion. Meanwhile Barber composed a volume titled *A Practical Treatise on Gesture,* which explained and illustrated his teaching practices.[10] Several pages show how he taught students to gesture when declaiming Brutus's speech on the death of Caesar. This oration, spoken from a decidedly republican vantage point, was thought to be more pleasing to an American audience than Antony's better-known "Friends, Romans, countrymen." Barber's book printed Brutus's "Romans, countrymen, and lovers! Hear me for my cause" as prose, leaving spaces above all its thirty-some lines of type for a vast array of symbols (numbers, lines of varying lengths, uppercase and lowercase letters), each placed over a syllable, word, or phrase to indicate some specific hand gesture to be made in the direction of a particular point on the imaginary sphere. Barber then followed the annotated excerpt with a seven-page "Glossary explanatory of the symbolical Letters in Brutus' speech." All this elaborate gesturing seems to have been too much for the freshmen, and the administration reassigned Barber to teach the juniors and seniors. While some students felt gratitude for what they learned from him, others made fun of being required to enter his "cage." One night a few students got hold of the contraption and took it outside and set it up on a barber pole for all to see. Their instructor was not amused. He left Harvard shortly thereafter and published his treatise with a local publisher, almost as if to say, "Look what you're missing!" Channing went back to his usual work, which included assigning all the sophomores, juniors, and seniors a theme to write every fortnight. He also returned for a time to a component of obligatory responsibilities he deemed useless, hearing memorized declamations.

To prepare students for the literary future that Everett had sketched out in his Phi Beta Kappa speech, Channing moved away from teaching writing in traditional ways. As Everett had opened a vista onto the possibilities for an independent body of American writing, Channing promoted a kind of writing for the future. He did away with imitation, especially with following classical models. He gradually found ways to have others hear the required declamations. Meanwhile, throughout his thirty-two years as Boylston Professor, he quietly turned what "rhetoric" had entailed at Harvard into instruction in composition.[11] He assigned topics on which he wanted to see students write: *dueling,* for instance; *President Jackson; writing to make a living; Shakespeare.* He kept a record of all the topics he assigned, lest he give the same one out more than once in four years.[12]

While mid-nineteenth-century college students produced untold thousands of pieces of writing, today the archives of their colleges retain only the tiniest fraction of them. Most colleges had no interest in preserving academic writing. Harvard and Yale and a few other institutions are remarkable exceptions. They have troves of curricular materials largely because, by the end of the century, they were self-consciously aware that their educational reforms had been of historic importance. In the 1890s Harvard established a special department in its library to archive materials, and the university made its interest in preserving documents known to its alumni. The majority of nineteenth-century essays now found there were accessioned decades after they had been written.

After, say, the death in 1921 of an alumnus from the class of 1867, his grandchildren, finding in an attic old papers he had saved from college, might have enough of a sense of history to inquire whether his college had an interest in preserving them. These extant writings enable us to develop a richer picture of college students' ideas and experience than can be discerned from perusing documents like catalogs and presidents' annual reports. But unlike official annual records, the preservation of writing by students was contingent upon a variety of factors, most of them unknown, and the impressions that we form on the basis of them do not generate a representative picture. That ought not to dissuade us from examining what is there.

From the hundreds of themes from the first half of the century now held in Harvard's archives, it is possible to read many on literary topics. John William Bacon wrote, for instance, in April 1843 on "Which class of literary publications offers to writers the best pecuniary return?" and on "What dangers to literature are apprehended from the present low prices of books in this country?"[13] Henry Burroughs produced an essay headed "Of our unwillingness to be told how a novel will turn out, yet we confidently anticipate the results and are displeased if our conjecture was wrong."[14] Every week Channing read, with an enthusiasm rare among instructors, hundreds of pages of writing by students. He seldom wrote even a summary comment on a composition. Instead, he responded to each student's work in conversation. On every other Friday, he spent the whole afternoon talking with students about their writing, either one-to-one or with small groups.

IN 1851, WHEN FRANCIS CHILD succeeded Channing as Harvard's Boylston Professor, things moved even more decidedly in the direction of literary education. Only five years earlier, as valedictorian at Harvard's commencement, "Stubby" Child (as he was known on account of his short stature) had given the class oration to great applause. He then had the opportunity to study in Germany, first at Göttingen, where Everett and his teacher George Ticknor had studied. (Göttingen later granted Child a degree on the basis of the scholarly publications he had produced.) At the Friedrich Wilhelm University in Berlin, he heard the Grimm brothers lecture on language. Returning to Harvard, where he would teach for half a century, he seems to have put no more stock in the efficacy of declamations than his predecessor had, although he continued to oversee them.

Child's judgment that prose composition was of greater importance than public speaking owed a good deal to technological improvements, ones that facilitated a transition from what might loosely be called an oral system of education to a written one. Together, the introduction of blackboards, the replacement of quills by steel pens, and particularly the machine production of cheaper paper from ground wood pulp and of books on rotary presses made this change possible. These developments rendered drill-based recitations obsolete and turned rhetoric into a writing-based discipline. They confirmed Child's sense, inherited from Channing, that the future would belong to writers. Instead of training students to write scripts for orations to be delivered to a live audience, Child expected them to address cogently argued themes to intelligent readers. He set essay topics that involved the use of deliberative rhetoric, on the model of debating: students were required to argue on one side or the other on a controversial topic.

Most topics on which the students were assigned to write engaged moral or political issues. Some were cultural or literary. The archives hold a collection of essays by Francis Henry Brown (class of '57), for instance, that includes the following topics:

> "Whether the original and untrained impulses of human nature incline more to good or to evil."
>
> "Whether Despotic or Free Governments are more likely to pursue an aggressive policy toward other States."
>
> "Whether a Representative in Congress is bound to submit his own opinions to the opinions and wishes of his constituents."[15]

Child set some timely topics and some that had long been of enduring interest. Essays composed by George A. Fiske (class of '61) include "What just grounds of complaint have the Southern States against the Northern States?"; "The position [occupied] by Humboldt among the scientific men of the present century"; and "The opposite reflections suggested by the contemplation of the grander and the minuter objects of Creation." Child sometimes assigned students to write an abstract of one or two Shakespeare plays. Fiske wrote on *As You Like It.*[16] Francis Brown composed an essay on "Whether Shakespeare intended to represent Hamlet as insane." (This assignment did not presuppose that Child had taught *Hamlet.*) Brown's six-page handwritten essay shows that he knew how to bring textual evidence to bear in developing an argument. He quotes many passages to argue that Shakespeare designed the play to show that Hamlet knew just what he was doing as he carried out his plan to avenge his father.

From 1846 when Child began as a tutor to 1896 when he died, the number of undergraduates at Harvard increased from 279 to 1771. Increasing enrollment meant that, week after week, year after year, Child was marking hundreds of essays. Only when A. S. Hill succeeded him as the Boylston Professor in the late 1870s did Harvard fully adopt the expedients of teaching writing in large lecture classes and of hiring several tutors to help mark the essays. Child's long experience convinced him that while college students should be required to write frequently, courses on composition per se did not belong in the college curriculum. His view—which manifestly did not prevail—was that whenever instructors in any department gave writing assignments, their students should be able to expect an expert in the relevant field to oversee and evaluate their compositions.

Elsewhere, teaching "composition," as we have learned to call it, proved to be an intractable problem.[17] The ratio of one or two instructors to hundreds of students rendered utterly impossible the old college ideal summed up in a widely quoted anecdote ascribed to President Garfield. Having studied at Williams College, Garfield endorsed the way its president, Mark Hopkins, used to carry out his teaching duties, casually sitting on one end of a log with the student on the other. As the number of college students increased, one-on-one interactions with the professor faded from view. The bugbear of required composition courses discouraged faculty and students alike. Timothy Bancroft, overworked as a professor of rhetoric at Brown, left a shocking example of faculty burnout. He kept suffering nervous breakdowns and, despairing, went out for a walk one December day and disappeared. Two months later his body was found in a frozen pond, where he had drowned.[18]

AS THE COLLEGE POPULATION continued to grow through the last decades of the century, college administrators, even as they hired numerous assistants to provide guidance in the science labs, failed to acknowledge the importance of giving students individual commentary on their writing. Two notably successful teachers of rhetoric and composition eloquently called out the abuses that were routinely heaped upon composition teachers and their students. John Franklin Genung, hired by Amherst College in 1882, urged that responding to each student's paper is itself "laboratory work" and protested against "the makeshift way in which time was grudged out to [writing] in the curriculum" once a week, "at some irregular hour supposedly unavailable for anything else."[19] In the early 1890s, Fred Scott, who oversaw writing courses in the much larger University of Michigan, reported that he was marking over three thousand essays a year. He had surveyed the general situation in colleges across the country and observed that required freshman writing courses were being packed with large numbers of "heterogeneous" students, most of whom write "crudely, some execrably, and only a few as well as could be wished." He pointed out that no provisions were being made to instruct students in accord with their differing needs. Looking back with admiration at how Harvard's Ned Channing attempted to respond to every essay his students wrote, Scott urged colleges to remedy the deplorable conditions in which academic writing was taking place by increasing the teaching force to provide individual students with the guidance they need.[20]

We can appreciate just how distinctive Channing's and Child's teaching of composition was, and how profoundly they entangled much of it with literary considerations, by contrasting it with the sort of themes students at Amherst were writing before Genung arrived. The Amherst archives house a smaller but nonetheless telling collection of essays composed during the middle decades of the century. These materials, to be considered in the chapter that follows, show that the college continued to train students to become influential public speakers, men of "character" who could carry forward a crusade for religious and moral reform.

3

Commencement Orations

QVI NOVIT NEQVE ID QVOD SENTIT EXPRIMIT PERINDE EST AC SI NESCIRET
[Whoever knows something but does not express what
he feels might as well not know it.]

—Nineteenth-century Latin inscription over a
classroom door at Amherst College

AMHERST COLLEGE HAS long been admired for its strong tradition of cultivating excellent writing. The tradition began late in the nineteenth century with John Franklin Genung, whose teaching career as the professor of rhetoric made him known as "The Quintilian of Amherst." Genung shared the priorities set at Harvard by Ned Channing and Stubby Child, and he saw to it that effective writing displaced eloquent speaking as the principal concern of rhetoric. Looking back as the century neared its end, he acknowledged, however, that for decades the college had provided "incompetent and inexperienced teachers" to oversee what the students wrote.[1]

Through the middle decades of the century, when eloquence dominated the goals of Amherst's professor of rhetoric and oratory, students had been writing. What was their writing like? The faculty hoped that their graduates would prove to be men of good character, and they encouraged student writers to imagine themselves speaking, if not in the pulpit, then out on something like the Lyceum circuit, where they would provide adult education. To this end, four years of daily recitations were sometimes supplemented by disputations, an inheritance from the medieval university, so that students could gain experience in debating. But instructors did not require students to bolster their arguments by using the library, which had but scant holdings. They encouraged broadly generalizing speeches on topics that might promote moral reform and good citizenship. Students composed their orations on the model of what they heard in chapel, where each day a member of the faculty took a turn in the pulpit. Titles affixed to many student essays suggest a predilection for literature and a belief in its moral force: "Literature essential to a nation's strength." "Influence of poetry on character." "Christian Poetry Superior to that of Mythologies."

Soon after the founding of the college in 1821, Commencement Day became the dramatic climax of an Amherst education. The ceremonies gathered the students, their friends, their families, returning alumni, and various dignitaries to join the faculty and the overseers. Delayed until August when the local populace had finished the hard work of summer and were ready for a holiday, commencement also attracted the townsfolk and people from neighboring villages. Hucksters and vendors, auctioneers and self-appointed orators crowded into Amherst's streets. (Perhaps in her girlhood Emily Dickinson ventured out to join them.) Many people came to hear the speeches, especially when the principal address was to be delivered by a well-known figure such as Ralph Waldo Emerson or Henry Ward Beecher. Each year several graduates received the honor of addressing the assembly as well.[2]

Surviving programs from the commencement exercises provide a glimpse of the kinds of writing that the most accomplished Amherst students were doing. In the 1830s and 1840s, when graduates doled out praise or blame (the bread and butter of epideictic oratory), attendees heard various kinds of compositions. Speeches ranged widely and included topics like scientific skepticism, civilizing the Indians, and the responsibilities of eminent writers.

By the 1850s, the number of student orations had multiplied. Attendees at commencement ceremonies could be seen coming and going in the course of a long day. In 1853, nineteen students were honored with the opportunity to orate before the crowd, and many chose to speak on literary topics. The first oration was in Latin, the rest in English, beginning with one titled "American Literature." Other topics included "Earnest Feeling as related to Eloquence," "Our Literature in its Influence on our Political Institutions," and "The English, the Future Universal Language."[3] After every few presentations, music punctuated the verbiage. The climactic presentation was called *The English Oration*. To give it was the highest honor an Amherst student could receive.

After the honoree had delivered it, the ceremony kept going on and on. The proud parents and dutiful siblings who sat through this exhausting ritual helped to inaugurate a tradition that has continued unabated in many colleges into our own time.

For all the achievements celebrated at commencement, three features of the atmosphere at Amherst College in the mid-nineteenth century help to account for Genung's implication that the college had been inattentive to the students' writing: the absence at various times of an effective professor of rhetoric and oratory, the intense orientation towards a particular sort of Congregational theology, and a competitive ethos that left behind the weaker students. These deficiencies did not altogether preclude successful writing. A surviving collection of compositions in the college archives reveals that most were composed as oratorical scripts. Many were actually delivered. Taken together, although the extant materials suggest the collectors' predilection for literary subjects (and for Milton, a hero in Amherst's oratorical tradition), they display notably different rhetorical practices from the ones found in the sorts of essays that Harvard students were writing.

Amherst's pedagogical practices, like those of many other colleges, fostered a competitive ethos. On winter days in the 1840s students got up in the dark and, before going to breakfast, made their way through snow to an unheated chapel for prayers. Then, by the light of oil lamps, they attended a Greek recitation.[4] During their recitation periods they worried about what the instructor thought of their performance. Typically, the instructor marked something down after each student recited. Students did not learn what it was or how it affected their standing. Instead, after four years, the evaluative marks made by all their instructors were massed together to generate a rank in class. As the college did not reveal to the students where they stood until graduation, the faculty observed a good deal of fawning behavior in the meantime.[5] The teachers must have repressed recognizing how much resentment lay behind it and how much insincerity this practice begot in their charges.

Many Amherst students experienced pressures that touched their consciences. The college was dedicated to making converts to a particular type of Protestantism that had become widespread in the seventeenth century. During England's civil wars, men and women who had developed an assurance that Jesus Christ was their personal savior had been required, in order to join a local congregation, to produce a narrative that described their conversion to Christ. They laced their narratives with Bible verses that demonstrated familiarity with what they claimed was the sole source of religious authority, and they illustrated the process of their conversions through scriptural precedents. (Bunyan's *Grace Abounding to the Grace of Sinners* became the most famous of these accounts.) While Amherst College was guided by persons whose Christianity operated in this tradition, applicants to the college were not required to have had a conversion experience before entering. In fact, to accomplish the college's goal of multiplying the number of those who could be considered genuine Christians, it needed students who had not yet been converted. Revivals (called "Quickenings") began in the 1840s and intensified thereafter. In 1855 the college distributed a closely printed single page headed the "Religious Condition of Colleges." It reported on the state of piety and number of conversions at some fourteen colleges from Maine to Ohio, judging for instance that of the 150 students at Bowdoin only 52 are "pious" and of the 340 students at Harvard only 33 are "professing Christians."[6] Amherst could now claim for itself that 156 of its 234 students were "professing Christians," and that more than a hundred were "preparing for the gospel ministry." One of these latter, William Otis Carr, described the conversion of a classmate who long had "gloried in his wicked ways and seemed the first in any forbidden scheme." When this student got religion, "his first act was to banish from his room the servants of sin." He poured out the contents of his brandy bottle. He burnt his cards and the cane he had used to "row the Freshmen."[7] Nonetheless, many students made their way through college simply conforming outwardly to the requirement to attend daily chapel and Sunday services.

As for the instruction that students received from Amherst's professors of rhetoric, it was fitful. The best of these professors was William Chauncey Fowler, a graduate of Yale and a genuinely learned man. He came to Amherst in 1838 from Middlebury College, where he had been professor of chemistry and natural history. Amherst students applauded his teaching, sometimes sarcastically. One day the applause went on for so long that Fowler interrupted it to say that the students should applaud for as long as they liked and then, when they stopped, they should never applaud him again.[8] But not long afterwards, students were complaining that this instructor had too high an opinion of himself, and they petitioned for his removal. In 1843 he resigned, and the position of professor of rhetoric and oratory remained vacant. In subsequent years, as Genung observed, actual instruction in rhetoric and composition was rarely on offer.[9] Nonetheless, among a dozen or more surviving scripts from the 1850s and 1860s that were to be delivered as orations, there is evidence that contradicts the charge that the college neglected rhetoric and composition. Some scripts suggest that an ideal Amherst graduate was a man who displayed literary interests, nearly all that a model alumnus would pursue a career as a preacher or teacher—or both.

One script titled "Milton" has almost nothing to say about poetry and little about religion. It shows that, although students did not study Milton's poetry, they had learned to boast that its surpassing achievement was beyond question. Their assumed familiarity with great literature enabled them authoritatively to promote the sort of civic and political orientation that the college favored. As was common in the U.S. at the time, the oration emphasizes Milton's republicanism. It praises the example of his independent mind, his strong Protestant principles, and the forcefulness of his controversial prose. It rehearses well-known features of Milton's youth: his studious nature, the long years spent at university in Cambridge, his subsequent years of private study, his education rounded out by an extended sojourn on the continent, etc. The would-be orator presents Milton as a model for young American scholars since, after long years of preparation, he took on himself the twin vocations of instructing youth and of writing to expose political threats to godly citizens. Emphasizing that the Stuart enemies against whom Milton wrote were tyrants who trembled at his words, the young orator intimates the importance of curtailing Catholic immigration, lest the United States of America repeat England's descent into being governed by "papal counsels [*sic*]."[10] (Probably, the student meant "councils.")

THE CAREER OF ANOTHER student illustrates the sort of life that midcentury Amherst faculty regarded as a genuine credit to the college. A script composed by Henry Sabin (class of '52) and titled "Literature essential to a nation's strength" offers a cogent glimpse of the literary ideal that he had learned to cultivate. Written nearly three decades after Edward Everett had given the widely celebrated Phi Beta Kappa speech that enumerated circumstances favorable to the creation of a distinctively American literature, it proposes related criteria. "There are three ingredients peculiarly essential to a national strength," Sabin writes: physical force, attachment to laws and institutions, and a national literature. Sabin proposes that the American present is "open . . . [to] a new and ever living fountain of national strength in a pure and high toned literature" and urges that "the ready pen of a single writer can move a thousand earnest thinking hearts."[11]

Whatever he was thinking when he wrote this, Sabin did not become that writer. Nor did he become a preacher. Yet what he wrote largely predicted his future as an educator and as a consummate apostle of Amherst's emphasis on building character. After his graduation, Sabin toiled in remote areas of the country, training rural teachers and earning a reputation as "the Horace Mann of the West." He abandoned whatever hope he himself may have had for contributing to America's "pure and high toned literature." He devoted himself to bringing the light of public education to the disadvantaged children of farmers and the gospel of patriotism, hard work, and capitalist success to their parents and neighbors. He became at last a widely sought-after public speaker.

Sabin eventually settled in rural Iowa, where schoolchildren had no idea of modern progress and virtually no expectation that they might ever move away. Iowa was dotted by more than a thousand tiny ungraded schools, in which children of different ages were instructed by young women, often teenagers themselves. Sabin rose to the role of the state's superintendent of public instruction. He saw to the consolidation of schools and began to set standards for the education of teachers. Increasingly, he found himself exercising the role of a public orator for which his education had prepared him. Each year when his town's school year ended, he gave a commencement address, attended by the admiring townsfolk. He unfailingly emphasized a theme that epitomized what an Amherst education had meant to teach him: character is the key to every child's future. He urged that if education's "whole tendency is not to lead the soul up and back to Him who gave it, it is defective in its nature, and wholly unsuited to our wants."[12] So popular were Sabin's speeches that neighboring towns also secured his services for their own commencement exercises.

Every summer Sabin went from town to town, addressing teachers and members of the public, seeking to create "an aristocracy of character" to leaven the Christian nation. By this phrase, he meant leaders with good old

Protestant, Anglo-Saxon values. He insisted that the children of German immigrants be taught only in English. He organized two- and four-week institutes for training teachers, modeling them on religious revivals like the Quickenings he had known in college. Prayers and hymn-singing punctuated each day's activities, and some edifying entertainment occupied the participants in the evening. Sabin urged educators to shift their emphasis from intellectual to moral training, inculcating industry and obedience. Ordinary people did not need science, he insisted. Expert knowledge, problem-solving, and the creation of a strong national literature was to be left to their betters.

While Sabin's career represents a fulfillment of the goals of a midcentury Amherst education, the career of another Amherst graduate, the polymath Francis March, made an original and influential contribution to American letters by developing scholarly methods and practices far more sophisticated than Sabin ever imagined. Part II will provide a context for the intervention in the 1850s by which March managed to introduce the study of English literature into the curriculum at Lafayette College.

PART II

WHAT WOULD "ENGLISH" BE?

4

Philology as a Turning Point

It used to be chic, dashing, and much ampler in girth. Philology reigned as king of the sciences, the pride of the first great modern universities. . . . It meant far more than the study of old texts. *Philology* referred to *all* studies of language, of specific languages, and (to be sure) of texts. Its explorations ranged from the religion of ancient Israel through the lays of medieval troubadours to the tongues of American Indians—and to rampant theorizing about the origin of language itself.

—JAMES TURNER, *Philology: The Forgotten Origins of the Modern Humanities*

EVERY AMERICAN COLLEGE found its own way to open the doors to the study of English literature. As a college subject, English came in by stops and starts, at moments defined more by contingent adaptations than by any overriding inevitability. No single account of how and why an English major developed could satisfy the desire of someone who, having enjoyed studying literature, feels curious about how their own college's story compares to those from other colleges. Later chapters in this book will draw upon plentiful, teemingly various, and inevitably partial evidence, here from one college, there from several, to probe features in the collegiate landscape that fostered the flowering of literary studies or revealed that it had already taken place. Each chapter offers a snapshot from a larger and far more variegated story than can be coherently told.

The first two chapters here in part II situate the story in relation to its German background. The "rise of English" as a discipline in American higher education took place not in relation to England, where English literature had been written.[1] The innovators in the U.S. who devised the earliest courses on

English literature looked instead to Germany. There, in the first modern universities, *Philologie* named the study of language and of texts. Its practices inspired American scholars to experiment with teaching English literature in ways that would parallel and even surpass those in which the classical languages and literatures were taught. Chief among the innovators was Francis March, who in the 1850s introduced the philological study of English literature into the curriculum at Lafayette College. March recognized that his students' knowledge of the vernacular equipped them to read literature composed in their native language in more sophisticated ways than they could read Latin and Greek. The next chapter will take up the exemplary manner in which, drawing on philological methods and perspectives, March demonstrated that English could be profitably taught and studied. By the 1870s, as later chapters will show, many institutions regarded study in Germany as an integral component of a candidate's readiness to teach the new subject.

WHAT WAS PHILOLOGY? I raise the question in the past tense because philology has been a shape-shifting sort of beast. By the 1890s in the United States some teachers of literature were distinguishing what they were doing from "mere philology," which they sought to consign to a separate field called linguistics. Through much of the twentieth century academics often used the term pejoratively, as if its essence had been perfectly summed up in George Eliot's portrait of Mr. Casaubon drearily searching for the key to all mythologies. But in the mid-nineteenth century philology named a hallowed set of practices found in German universities, and ambitious scholars were flocking there to learn them. The German philosopher Friedrich Nietzsche once praised it as "a goldsmith's art" and described its best workings as follows:

> In the midst of an age of "work," that is to say: of hurry, of indecent and perspiring hastiness, which wants everything to "get done" at once, including every new or old book—this art does not so easily get anything done, it teaches us to read well, that is to say, to read slowly, deeply, looking back and forward, with reservations, with doors left open, with delicate eyes and fingers.[2]

The German university was—unlike the French *lycée*, the German *gymnasium*, and colleges in the U.S.—a professional school. It provided specialized academic training and offered no program comparable to the U.S. bachelor's degree in arts or science. Tellingly, it was a realm of free inquiry (*Lehrfreiheit*). Its professors were specialists who, although they were obliged to give lectures, were not what we think of as teachers. Each student was responsible for training himself.

The heart and soul of the German university was its library. Its large holdings made it possible for each member of the institution to pursue his own specialized knowledge in whatever subjects he desired. Among the array of fields for study, philology fully enjoyed the status of a science. Its prestige rivaled the cachet of Newtonian natural science. Derived from the Greek words for "love" and "word," *philos* and *logos*, the word *philology* came to refer to the study of language itself, and to almost everything connected with language, including the radically different civilizations in which different languages flourished. It served as a byword for what we now call the humanities. The separable disciplines increasingly found in American universities by the turn of the twentieth century—history, archeology, literary studies, art history, and Latin and Greek (once the classical languages were reduced to just one discipline among a growing number)—all descended from philology as it had been practiced in Germany.[3]

Comparative philology differed markedly from traditional classical philology, which dated to the Renaissance. The older philology was directed to the study of the classical and biblical languages in their cultural surroundings. It sought to establish texts and to secure factual information. Comparative philology, a more empirical and speculative practice, explored many more languages and cultures. Keen to discover features of human experience that had long since vanished, its practitioners probed ancient languages (Sanskrit, Hebrew, Greek), more recent ones (Latin, Anglo-Saxon, Old High German), and ones as newly discovered as those of the Indigenous peoples of the western hemisphere. The most accomplished of these philologists sought to uncover the laws that govern particular languages, to trace language families, and to learn as much as possible about the origins of language itself.

Struck by the discovery of the spectacular resemblance that Greek and

Latin bear to Sanskrit, comparative philologists boldly posited a fissure in European history. They developed an integrated approach for reconstructing and exploring traces of long-lost human achievements. They found them lodged in the history, poetry, and physical and textual artifacts of the ancient world. Like geologists uncovering fossils in various layers of rock, they traced the long history of words back through earlier stages of language. They divined the possibility that the languages and culture of Europe derived from a part of the world considered remote, where the inhabitants once shared a common language, referred to now as *Proto-Indo-European*. Speakers of this language came to be called *Aryans*. By the middle of the century these new terms would sometimes become entangled with theories about race and racial hierarchies.[4]

Of course, not all philological scholars were productively adventurous, and some failed to turn up anything intellectually satisfying. Less than imaginative drudges also made their way into the universities, and hangers-on sought to align themselves with the august aura that philology cast. Looking back on philological practices through several decades, Nietzsche, who had been named a professor of classical philology at age twenty-four, could be fiercely critical of abuses and acknowledged he had been guilty of them himself. In *We Philologists,* he insisted that many plodders misspent their energies boring people with matters of small import. Windbags, he called them, and splitters of hairs.

Oxford and Cambridge were indifferent to philology, but some young men from Britain who had received a lengthy classical education went to Germany to learn philological methods first-hand. There they discovered freedom to practice a "New Humanism" quite apart from governmental or ecclesiastical control. Startlingly unfamiliar means for editing and interpreting classical texts bred in them fresh interests. They began to compare the cultures of the classical West with those of the ancient Near East. They encountered an enthusiasm for Hellenic culture. They learned to admire the ancient Greeks' fostering of human capacities for civic benefit, and they were fascinated with their love of beauty. Some traveled on to Greece, to visit the sites about which they had often read. Young Americans who studied in Germany had similar experiences. Harvard took the lead in encouraging its graduates to study in Germany, and many who did went on to assume leading roles in education, scholarship, and public service. In this chapter we will consider the careers of four men, all of whom studied at the university in Göttingen and brought back to the U.S. influential philological and pedagogical practices.

AT GÖTTINGEN, recognized in the early decades of the nineteenth century as the premier university for philology, George Bancroft (Harvard class of '17) and his elder companion Joseph Green Cogswell (class of '06) pursued a wide range of humanistic studies. Bancroft, in addition to the classical languages, studied French, Italian, and German literature; Platonic philosophy; and biblical interpretation. Once he took his degree, he toured Europe and sought out Goethe, Schleiermacher, Hegel, Wilhelm von Humboldt, Lord Byron, and other well-known artists and intellectuals. As for Cogswell, he paid at least as much attention to the methods instructors were employing as he did to the subjects on which they were lecturing. After returning to Massachusetts and teaching for several years at Harvard, together with Bancroft he founded an innovative school on German principles, where physical education was made integral to the daily schedule and corporal punishment abolished. Both men became distinguished librarians. Bancroft built a large collection of primary documents on the basis of which he wrote a multivolume history of the United States. It earned him the title "father of American History."

Not least because Harvard graduates had brought back from Germany a Hellenism adapted to revitalizing classical studies, at midcentury Boston was known as the Athens of America. Two of Cogswell's other companions in Göttingen, George Ticknor and Edward Everett, went on to especially influential careers. Harvard's administrators, seeking to build up the faculty and spotting unusual intellectual promise in the pair, hired them and immediately—before either was required to do any teaching—allowed them to go off to Europe (at their families' expense) to pursue language studies. Both men ended up staying for four years. As noted in the earlier chapter, "Elocution and Composition," Everett would eventually become president of Harvard, a senator from Massachusetts, and U.S. secretary of state. (He is also remembered for having given the two-hour oration at Gettysburg that was followed by President Lincoln's two-minute address.) Before all that, as a professor at Harvard, Everett brought an unprecedented enthusiasm for German methods and culture to the teaching of the classics. He created a Greek Reader filled with extracts from ancient texts that provided a literary focus to the study of the classical languages. Ralph Waldo Emerson was his appreciative student.

Ticknor's youthful experiences in learning modern European languages meant that his orientation differed from his friend's. He came from a prosperous Boston family and had studied at his father's alma mater, Dartmouth College. He found the instruction in the classics there much inferior to what he had received from his father and from tutors who had taught him French and Spanish. By his late teens he was already adept at reading German, and he was taking a passionate interest in Goethe's *Sorrows of Young Werther.* Before heading to Europe, having learned of the philological interests that Thomas Jefferson was cultivating in his retirement,[5] he traveled to Virginia to consult him. Jefferson was sufficiently impressed with Ticknor to entrust him with the task of buying European books for his library. Along with Everett, Ticknor made his way to Göttingen. He was astonished to find there that both rich and poor students were equals and that success in studies depended entirely on one's own aptitude and effort. He sometimes studied as much as fourteen hours a day. He read all the Goethe he could find, making a habit of comparing various passages both within a given work and across the entire corpus. That passages in *Werther* and *Faust* paralleled ones in Goethe's autobiography fascinated him. But Goethe's morals shocked him, and he felt disappointed that most German intellectuals were atheists.[6] Amidst this cognitive dissonance, he remained firmly committed to a New England Unitarianism that (for all of its liberalism) was fiercely intolerant of immorality. Through his whole career Ticknor's concern with the ethical component of literary works remained as strong as his interest in their historical and aesthetic value. After his two years at Göttingen—Harvard having hired him to fill a new professorship of French and Spanish—he made his way to Paris and then to Spain. In that Catholic country, to his surprise, the religious and patriotic fanaticism of decent ordinary people impressed him favorably. Here, drawing on the Romantic principle of *Volksgeist* to which he had been introduced in Germany, he developed an unparalleled knowledge of Spanish literature.

Back home, Ticknor adapted what he had learned to fit the U.S. college landscape. Harvard entrusted him with the task of creating the first program in the United States concerned with the Romance languages. In 1823, he published his *Syllabus for a Course of Lectures on the History and Criticism of Spanish Literature.* This laid the foundation for the work that he would go on to do over the next quarter-century. A novel document, extraordinary in its ambition, the *Syllabus* approached each individual work of literature with a concern to fix its date and to describe the circumstances in which its author had been writing. It modeled a brief characterization and assessment of each work and provided bibliographical references. Altogether, the treatment of hundreds of works helped to establish a proto-canon of Spanish literature. Even more influentially, it showed how literature could be put at the service of defining a national character. Ticknor's continuing work in this vein culminated in one of the most highly regarded scholarly publications of the era. By 1849 when he published it, he had amassed the country's most extensive library of Spanish and Portuguese materials.

Ticknor's three-volume *History of Spanish Literature* demonstrated that philological methods, far from being directed simply to the study of ancient texts, could prove effective for studying modern literature as well. It proposed to tease out of a nation's writing essential characteristics that, though subject to new inflections, remained basically unchanged over time. This claim owed a good deal to the New England Unitarian and Federalist moral perspective that Ticknor had acquired in his youth. He nominated intolerance in religion and strong loyalty to a leader as the distinguishing badges of Spanish culture. He proposed that from early on these two features of the country's writing made it fresh and original and helped to differentiate what was truly Spanish from "Mohammedanism." But in time, he concluded, these quintessentially Spanish attributes had degenerated into bigotry and despotism, with the result that, broadly speaking, the whole history could be summed up in a narrative about a rise and fall.[7] For readers interested in the subject of his friend Everett's Phi Beta Kappa lecture—how a distinctively American literature might take its place among European literatures—Ticknor's magnum opus must have seemed a cautionary tale. It also reinforced the idea that his own country's future depended upon the people's demonstration of their good character.

PHILOLOGY—thorough in its examinations of any subject, broad in its temporal and geographical scope, and often bold in its speculations—contributed to the emergence of English as a college subject through three principal phases. Everett's and Ticknor's careers illustrate the first two. Philological methods inspired Everett to bring a fresh new literary approach to the classical languages into Harvard's classrooms. The admiration his German colleagues had exhibited for Greek civic culture enhanced his motivation to commit himself to the public sphere, where—as an orator, administrator, and politician—he sought to make distinguished contributions to his nation. Ticknor took philological concerns and methods in a new direction when he adapted them to the study of distinctly modern materials. His disposition to regard literature as a window onto a nation's essential character owed a good deal to the ways in which German philology had drawn on ancient literatures to characterize various cultures. The lives of both men confirmed the traditional idea that developing a knowledge of what has been coded in foreign tongues ought to constitute an essential component of a college education. But neither foresaw the next stage of the process by which philological methods and perspectives contributed to making English a full-fledged college subject.

It was Francis March who wrought the breakthrough. He developed a mastery of philological methods that informed both his scholarship and his teaching. His book of 1864, *Method of Philological Study of the English Language*, ensured and burnished his international reputation as a philologist. Reprinted numerous times, this book also opened an unprecedented vista for instructors in other colleges. It treated English literature as a body of material worthy to be compared with the literatures of Greece and Rome. English literature, composed mostly in another nation and much of it surviving in seventeenth-century dress, was just foreign enough to serve something like the traditional purposes for studying Latin and Greek. March taught his students that they could read literature in English with the same care they had directed to classical literatures. His book showed other teachers that they could count on their students' knowledge of the vernacular to enable them to study the writings of Shakespeare more readily, even more deeply and extensively, than they could those of Homer and Virgil. It unveiled reading practices that proceed slowly and thoughtfully with small units of text, and it invited readers to examine in detail a few carefully chosen passages from, say, *Julius Caesar* or *Paradise Lost*. It demonstrated how to notice in a rich nugget a telling glimpse of a larger whole. By putting students in touch with the real thing, these practices diminished the likelihood that students would think that they were to learn *about* literature, as if it were a minor tributary feeding names and dates into the great River of History. Instead, their approach involved treating vernacular literature as worthy material for a goldsmith's art. For the teacher and students alike, philological perspectives certified the value of their native language and of a literary heritage to which it gave access.

5

A Love for English Words

Our students are made to write their own lectures.

—FRANCIS MARCH, "The Growth of Lafayette: A Post-Prandial Address" (1888)

WRITING IN THEIR old age to John Adams, Thomas Jefferson told of a difficulty he was anticipating as he drew up plans for his new university in Virginia. He acknowledged that those charged with launching the curriculum would need to be persuaded about offering one subject in particular: Anglo-Saxon. Concerned that students should become familiar with modern (i.e., postclassical) languages, Jefferson placed Anglo-Saxon in their company. He regarded it as the earliest form in which we have knowledge of English. This genealogical concept helps to make sense of a widespread pedagogical practice that later emerged in many colleges: Old English (as it is now more often designated) came to serve as the gate through which students needed to pass before beginning the study of English literature. That Anglo-Saxon was sufficiently difficult to be taught and that it could be examined on the model of Latin and Greek helped to promote the idea that English could be considered a respectable object of study.

Jefferson had first become interested in the language as a law student. He owned more than a dozen volumes of Anglo-Saxon grammars and texts. Although he had definite ideas about how the language should be studied, he underestimated what it would take to learn it. He informed Adams that "as an inducement to introduce Anglo-Saxon into our plan," he would assure the faculty that students could learn it with only a "*few weeks* of attention."[1] The concession here manifests a naïve understanding of the difficulties instructors and students would encounter. Few scholars in the United States had sufficient mastery of the language to teach it effectively. The situation would change, however, within a single generation.

Lafayette College, a small institution in the town of Easton, in Pennsylvania's Lehigh Valley, showed a surprising way forward. In 1858 the college's new president, G. Wilson McPhail, gave his inaugural address at the close of his first year in office. As he approached its climax, he called attention to Jefferson's idea that Anglo-Saxon should be part of a college education.[2] He then began to describe in striking detail the workings of a curricular innovation at Lafayette that was making the study of Anglo-Saxon foundational. It integrated the study of English not with modern languages but with the traditional study of Latin and Greek.

Before assuming his new position, McPhail had trained for the ministry at Yale and was running a law academy in Fredericksburg, Virginia. His accomplishments had caught the attention of the Presbyterian church in Easton, and it persuaded him to become its pastor. Some months previously, he had successfully recommended the young polymath Francis March, who was working on his teaching staff, for a position at Lafayette. "He knows more than all of us," McPhail assured the administration.[3] When the college subsequently offered the new pastor the opportunity to become its president, McPhail set to work with March, whose knowledge of constitutional law and several languages would enable them to undertake a radical transformation of the traditional curriculum. After a year of watching March's work up close, McPhail delivered his inaugural address, which culminated in a detailed description of the college's new literary curriculum.

In his address, without embarrassing his colleague by name, McPhail gave a wide currency to the innovations that March had set in motion. He called attention to the college's unusual decision to create a professorship of English and tied it to the importance of treating language scientifically. He reported that the philological approach now taken at Lafayette regarded words as "durable objects" to be studied as plants and minerals are studied. Much as "the geologist creates [a] history from the successive strata of rocks," the philologist traces the layered change in the history of a word, discreetly and imaginatively glimpsing its pre-history in oral culture before it was ever written down. Philology, McPhail urged, "exhibits language as a daguerreotype of the mind."

It shows us "the laws that govern . . . thinking." When the address was published, Lafayette's curricular innovations provoked wide interest, even in parts of Europe.[4]

FRANCIS ANDREW MARCH, who was to serve as Lafayette's "Professor of the English Language" for more than half a century, was born in Worcester County, Massachusetts, in 1825. When he was fifteen, his father's business failed and a kindly judge provided $200 for him to attend Amherst College. (The tuition was $33.00 per year, the total annual cost estimated at $78.00.) As it happened, the early 1840s began as the best of times for March to be studying there. Then things took a turn for the worse.

During March's undergraduate years Amherst College started heading for trouble. Enrollment was consistently diminishing, from 142 students when he was a freshman to 121 when he was a senior. By 1845 the college desperately needed an infusion of funds, and the professors agreed to take reductions in their modest salaries. The literary societies were in financial trouble as well; fraternities were eclipsing them. March nonetheless developed interests during college that would last a lifetime.

March became fascinated with the English language through the work of the lexicographer Noah Webster, who stimulated his interest in English and turned his attention to Anglo-Saxon. He acquired an intimate knowledge of Webster's *American Dictionary of the English Language.* He also took an interest in Webster's *American Spelling Book* and in his famous essay on the reform of English spelling. These writings inspired him to join a crusade that he would seek to carry forward through much of his career. Webster was chiefly responsible for a number of American alterations, such as dropping the superfluous "u" in words such as *favour* and *honour* and the "k" from words like *publick* and *musick.* Many other reform attempts, such as advocating the substitution of *masheen* for *machine,* would prove as unsuccessful for March as they had been for the master. Here, in a passage showing how German ideals had been appropriated, is a sample of the kind of radical reform for which March would be aiming (some difficult-to-reproduce marks placed over or through several vowels are omitted):

> Widhin dhi last fifti yirz a complit revolushun haz tekn ples in dhi aidialz and purpusez ov dhi scolarli clas. Dhi haiest wurdz ov dhi old scolarz wer "cultyur" and "buiti." . . . Dhi haiest wurdz ov dhi niu scolarz ar "progres" and "pauer."[5]

Clearly, not everything that March touched proved equally compelling. But his youthful fascination with Webster's work went far beyond matters of spelling.

During his first two years at Amherst March studied with Webster's son-in-law, William Chauncey Fowler, whose teaching career we glimpsed in the chapter on "Commencement Orations." Fowler modeled intelligent interest in Webster's work. As a professor of rhetoric he greatly improved the quality of instruction in vocal culture. He also encouraged students to read widely. March studied rhetoric, elocution, and the philosophy of English grammar with him and heard him lecture on English literature. Meanwhile Fowler was editing a new edition of *Webster's Dictionary* adapted to the needs of college students. During March's sophomore year, Fowler had the class making their way through the elementary rhetoric textbook that Bowdoin's Samuel Newman had composed for relatively unsophisticated students. As juniors, they were to advance to Whately's *Elements of Rhetoric*. But a series of events interrupted the study of rhetoric altogether. Amherst had no professor of rhetoric and oratory during March's junior year. When news reached Amherst that Noah Webster, one of the founders of the college and March's chief inspiration, had died, Fowler resigned to care for his father-in-law's grieving daughter. He managed nonetheless to get his adapted *Dictionary* into print and went on to produce an accomplished series of grammars for use in colleges and schools. March remained a grateful and admiring disciple, and in 1861 Lafayette College awarded an honorary degree to his former teacher, an honor as well to the tradition of Webster's work. Every year at commencement the college awarded a Fowler Prize to the student who had demonstrated "the greatest proficiency in English Philology."

IT WAS ONLY AFTER graduation that, although he did not study in Germany, March thoroughly familiarized himself with the science of comparative philology that had taken deep root there and which in time provided the context for inducting the study of English literature into a Bachelor of Arts curriculum. Long before other colleges came to expect their faculty members to produce original scholarship, the Lafayette administration ensured that March would have independent time to pursue scholarly research. The first hire that McPhail made was for a newly created position—a professor of rhetoric, who would oversee the students' compositions, freeing March to concentrate on philological work.

By the early eighteen-seventies March had gained an international reputation. He had achieved such a mastery of philological methods that his new book, *Comparative Grammar of the Anglo-Saxon Language, in Which its Forms Are Illustrated, by those of the Sanskrit, Greek, Latin, Gothic, Old Saxon, Old Friesic, Old Norse, and Old High German,* provided results that astonished professional philologists on both sides of the Atlantic. A reviewer in London's *Athenaeum* acknowledged that no other scholar in the English-speaking world could have produced it.[6] Princeton, Oxford, and Cambridge all awarded March honorary degrees. Offers of a position at Princeton and at other institutions, where he would be expected to lecture, never persuaded him to leave Lafayette. The framework that the college continued to provide for his teaching proved ideal, and his pedagogy raised the study of the English language to unprecedented prominence in American higher education.

Because McPhail and March wrote extensively about the Lafayette curriculum, we can reconstruct in unusual detail what a student's academic experience might have been in the years when March's book on Anglo-Saxon grammar was in preparation. The number of students dwindled during the Civil War, and the college almost failed. But the integrated curriculum that had been put in place in 1859 provided stability. Students now had to be at least fifteen to matriculate. While previously about half Lafayette's students had been preparing for the ministry, now young men seeking to become miners, engineers, and chemists were enrolling. By 1867–68 the number of students had climbed to 128, and the college added a Scientific Course in parallel to the Classical. While teaching in the Classical Course, March employed comparative philology to teach English literature in conjunction with Greek and Latin. While teaching in the Scientific Course, he adapted the procedure so that the students studied Anglo-Saxon in conjunction with French and German.

March once reckoned that over four years a student would attend a total of 2,070 recitations and lectures.[7] The academic year was divided into three terms. In all but two of the twelve terms, students in the Classical Course studied either Greek or Latin and usually both. Through all four years they wrote themes. As at Amherst and elsewhere, commencement ceremonies at Lafayette included student orations. What made Lafayette unusual was that its curriculum offered students opportunities to acquaint themselves, though only for a single term each, with a wide array of subjects, from surveying, political economy, and architecture to botany and constitutional law. Many courses, including the study of Hebrew, were elective. Typically, at the end of the first and second terms students had a straightforward examination on the material they had studied in each of their subjects. At the end of the academic year, external examiners gave them more probing examinations.

Entering students generally had a long wait before they could study with March. He did little teaching during the first term. Students, in their first two years, concentrated on language study with the classics professor, who prepared them for the synthetic work they would be doing with March as juniors. They studied languages and wrote themes for the professor of rhetoric and worked on vocal culture ("declamations") with him. Freshmen studied biblical literature in English translation. Sophomores spent a term with March in "the study of words." Then, beginning in the second term of junior year, intensive studies with March dominated the program through the rest of the year. Students pursued three interrelated subjects with him: Anglo-Saxon, Fowler's English grammar, and either *Paradise Lost* or *Julius Caesar.* Finally, in senior year they delved into English literature and began to practice comparative philology.

March aimed to teach the Anglo-Saxon language as Harvard's Bancroft and Everett had taught Greek and Latin; that is, philologically, "with a careful scrutiny of every word." He worked closely with students outside regular class time and expected them to do a great deal of preparation. He had them looking up etymologies, preparing questions on the history of key words, and exploring kindred words in other languages. Then they moved on to the consideration of syntax, and built up to larger questions about the civilization in which the language had been spoken and eventually written down.[8] March taught Fowler's English grammar comparatively, juxtaposing features of English grammar with those of the other languages his students were learning, Latin and Greek in the Classical Course, French and German in the Scientific. Teaching juniors three hours a day enabled him to blend his instruction of the three related languages they were studying comparatively. It allowed the class to explore literary texts for more than an hour at a time, sliding back and forth between abstract matters of grammar and concrete grammatical and lexical features in a passage from Milton or Shakespeare. March explained the process he and the students shared: "The text is minutely analyzed, the idioms explored, and synonyms weighed; the mythology, biography, history, metaphysics, theology, geography, are all looked up; and whatever else is necessary that every allusion may be comprehended."[9]

March wrote in detail about how he taught English literature, and we know more about how he was conducting a class in the 1860s than we do about any other contemporary English teacher's practice. He encouraged students to inquire for themselves by remarking that "there never was a pair of eyes made not worth looking through." He insisted that students "should look up information everywhere" and write about what they had found. Nuancing Bacon's famous remark in "Of Studies," he urged, "The habit of investigating and writing out results makes the full man and the exact man at once; it divests composition of ninety-nine parts of its horrors, and it quickens thought ninety-nine times as much as beating the brain for original brilliancies."[10] By the time a junior began reading Milton's epic, he had a host of ideas about what he might look for and no grounds for worrying what in the world he was going to write about.

Once March sensed that his students were sufficiently habituated to reading slowly, he pressed forward to encourage scrupulous attention both to the circumstances in which each author had been writing and to the wide varieties of style to be found among classic writers. Beyond this, he got his students to probe their reading from multiple perspectives. He had them look into the historical circumstances and natural environment in which a work had been composed. He encouraged them to consider the individual psychology of an author. He taught them to discern evidence of influence from previous writers. He asked them to compare the ways in which writers in other languages had treated a similar subject. He expected them to name what was distinctive, even unique, in each author's style.

In the classroom March encouraged conversation about whatever the students brought to the day's discussion. He expected students to ask questions of one another. In addition to daily reports, he assigned a weekly essay, often connected with the study of a particular author more generally. He eschewed the kind of essay that he and his classmates at Amherst had pretentiously composed. Your writing, he insisted, is "to be a simple recording of thought, and not one of the grand rhetorical performances" written "for great occasions." One hour each week was reserved for some students to read their essays to the group and discuss them with one another. Each week, too, some time was set aside for "declamations," attempts to read aloud passages on which students had written, to bring out "precise shades of meaning." After a few weeks, discussion would turn to the work as an aesthetic whole, and the class sought to place it in the broad history of literature.[11]

March held dear his opportunities to interact with students. By making space for them to express themselves, he got them reading widely and writing often. "We used to wish that Prof. March talked more," one former student recalled. "He seemed to think that we ought to do a good deal of the talking."[12] His former students couldn't remember his ever having given a formal lecture. He regarded that sort of teaching as an attempt to vaccinate "pupils against any sincere sense of love of learning, imparting only a chicken-pox form of the thing." Yet he took care to introduce "professorial palaver" in the classroom and encouraged his fellow faculty members to do likewise, the idea being that, whatever field students were to work in, they should strive to master the language spoken by experts. "Our students," he insisted, "are made to write their own lectures."[13]

The centrality of classic texts from Chaucer through Bunyan in Lafayette's undergraduate curriculum remained in place into the 1890s. Meanwhile, however, March encouraged students to read and to write about contemporary literature, British and American, adapting the methods they had learned as they began reading Spenser and Shakespeare to reading Browning and Emerson. In the 1880s the college began awarding a Francis A. March Prize to the student who had written the best essay on a particular author. While occasionally an eighteenth-century author (say, Samuel Johnson) was set for the competition, more recent writers—Poe and Bryant, Harriet Beecher Stowe and James Russell Lowell, Elizabeth Barrett and Robert Browning—were frequently featured.

WHEN FRANCIS MARCH had begun teaching at Lafayette in the late 1850s, he was seeking to integrate the study of both Anglo-Saxon and English literature with the work his pupils were doing in their studies of the classical languages. His adaptation of German philological methods soon led to success, and word of it spread widely. Teachers elsewhere took notice of the idea that Shakespeare and Milton could be studied as Homer and Cicero were, and many were attracted to the idea that Anglo-Saxon would provide the basis for this study. By the 1870s professors in several institutions, Francis Child at Harvard, for instance, had picked up on the idea that Anglo-Saxon could be made the gateway to studying English literature. Hiram Corson of Cornell insisted that students could not appreciate the glories of Elizabethan literature unless they approached it with a knowledge of the language and its literature from the time of Alfred the Great onward. A decade later the research faculty at the newly founded Johns Hopkins University, led by March's former student James Wilson Bright, established the study of Old and Middle English language and literature as the central focus of the English department. Across the country thousands of college students began studying Anglo-Saxon, regarded as the earliest form of English and the source from which the whole English literary tradition descended. Not surprisingly, however, a significant majority of those who were required to study the language felt that the long labors involved in acquiring it were not amply rewarded with enhanced pleasure in reading literature. At Columbia, seniors rebelled by shouting, slamming doors, and throwing firecrackers into the stove that heated the classroom.[14] Gradually, most colleges abolished the requirement, and courses on Anglo-Saxon became elective.

For his part, March continued to teach his integrated curriculum until he retired in the first decade of the twentieth century. He published an introductory Anglo-Saxon textbook for use in high schools and academies both in the U.S. and in England.[15] Some colleges sought to adopt the curriculum that he had created at Lafayette. Without the man himself to win students over to the study of Anglo-Saxon and to teach them how and why to read slowly, it was a difficult sell. Lafayette remained virtually unique in the ways that it integrated the study of English with the study of the classical languages.

6

Professors of English in the Scientific Schools

Drive your cart and your plow over the bones of the dead.

—WILLIAM BLAKE, *The Marriage of Heaven and Hell*

WHEN CHARLES W. ELIOT published "The New Education" in 1869, he began by contrasting the relative lack of institutions that were providing practical education in the United States with what he had found in Europe. He observed that Germany had established the first *Realschule* (practical school) more than a century earlier and that from the time of Napoleon government schools in France had been training young men in mining, agriculture, and commerce. The better to publicize what the Massachusetts Institute of Technology aimed to offer its students, he emphasized the freedom available in the U.S. to create alternatives to colleges that offered a classical education. As we noted in the Introduction, ceasing to require a knowledge of the classical languages was a foundational step in exercising that freedom. MIT, as it would come to be known, endorsed the superior practicality of instruction in the vernacular by hiring a professor of English. A year later Yale's Sheffield School hired one as well. But the two institutions defined "English" in radically different ways. The difference belongs to a moment when it was clear that English was likely to become an academic subject but not yet clear what its material and methods were going to be.

DURING THE DECADE BEFORE the onset of the Civil War, William Barton Rogers had gathered a group of entrepreneurs, businessmen, scientists, and scholars to lay plans for a new institute of technology in Boston. At the time, they had no thought of hiring a professor of English. They aimed to outdo the country's various scientific schools, none of which measured up to the standards they meant to set. Their goals prominently included demonstrating that scientific and technological studies could provide a more effective liberal education than classical colleges were offering. Still, they acknowledged that, in addition to training in a specialized scientific or technical field, students would need exposure to broadly humanistic subjects.

Through its earliest years people referred to the Massachusetts Institute of Technology not as "MIT," but as "Boston Tech." This sobriquet sorts oddly with the large pretensions declared for it when *Frank Leslie's Illustrated Newspaper* proposed that it was "destined to assume a part in the education of a people never played before."[1] Its students would not be found wasting their time "burrowing into the grammars and dictionaries" that were the daily companions of college students at Harvard and Yale. Their native language would be sufficient.

Although Boston Tech already had a plan for teaching English, *Leslie's* gleeful celebration of the burial of Greek and Latin said nothing of about it. The declaration that the Institute was "the tomb of dead languages" in fact owed a good deal to the man who was to become its first professor of English, William P. Atkinson. The underemployed older brother of a member of the Institute's corporate board, he had graduated from Harvard College in 1838. Then he spent nearly three decades in desultory pedagogical activities. After an abortive stint as principal of a high school in nearby Brookline, he settled into tutoring boys who planned to apply for admission to his alma mater. They would have to sit a battery of examinations that tested in detail their competence in mathematics, in the grammar of the classical languages, and in the history and geography of ancient Greece and Rome. They would also have to demonstrate that they could compose coherent sentences in both Latin and Greek. Atkinson developed an antipathy to this work. He began looking into studies that documented the state of instruction in England's public schools, which prepared young men to enter Oxford and Cambridge. This led to an invitation to address supporters of Rogers's plan for creating an alternative to liberal arts colleges.

In April 1865, three days before the surrender of the Confederate Army, Atkinson spelled out the case for launching an innovative curriculum.[2] Armed with evidence of the abject state of classical studies at Oxford and Cambridge, he inveighed against the barrenness of "the grindstone theory" used to justify teaching dead languages. In the expanded version of the lecture that he published, we can hear the speaker rising to indignant eloquence as he observes that American boys being readied for college are forced to read more books in Greek and Latin than are required for matriculation at the English universities. Meanwhile, he pointed out, they remain "entirely ignorant of the elementary principles of physics or of any branch of natural history." Atkinson acknowledged that at the time of the revival of letters in Europe, the study of classical literature had opened new career opportunities that had "long been pent up within the narrow bonds of the medieval philosophy." He proposed that "the position of the classics is now reversed": the dead languages were wholly unfit for transmitting the kinds of knowledge currently being produced.[3] Soon he was urging institutions all over the country to make room to teach new subjects by doing away with the study of the classical languages. "No error," he insisted, "is at present more common or more disastrous than the attempt to introduce the new, without any disturbance of the older studies."[4] The vehemence with which he made the case proved persuasive.

When Rogers created a position for Atkinson and designated him professor of English, he put him in charge of overseeing all the subjects that students were to encounter when they first matriculated. The first students who enrolled found that they were to follow a two-pronged curriculum spread out over four years. (The scientific schools at Harvard and Yale offered three-year programs.) One prong, referred to as "non-professional studies," would occupy them through their first two years and continue, though given considerably less scope, in the third and fourth. The other prong, which would begin in year three, afforded a choice among six special branches of scientific or technological study, including civil and mechanical engineering, chemistry, and mining. Two less predictable branches rounded out the options: the Institute created the country's first degree program in architecture, and it offered the opportunity to study "Science and Literature." The latter was a de facto concentration in what it was coming to be called "English." It might have given as much prominence to Darwin and Herbert Spencer as was later accorded in liberal arts colleges to Shakespeare and Milton. Hardly any students showed interest in "Science and Literature," however.

Atkinson enshrined his vision of what the professor of English would be covering in a closely printed eight-page pamphlet headed "English 1868–69."[5] Its implied audience was a body of potential supporters who wanted to see what would replace Latin and Greek.[6] It enumerated many hundreds of topics, most of them referable to locales and events in England and dating largely from periods after the 1660 restoration of the monarchy. He would teach first- and second-year students about literature by employing standard textbooks, and they would be examined on names and dates and conventional ideas about historical periods. Third-years would need to learn from him about law and government and political economy, and fourth-years general science and modern philosophy, with an emphasis on utilitarianism.

There is a striking gap between the bravado with which Atkinson represented the Institute's ambitious English curriculum to the public and the ways in which he undertook his teaching duties. Lecturing before the National Teachers Association in 1873, he proclaimed that "the sovereignty of the world is hereafter to belong to the English language" and insisted that "with this conquering language we possess the world's foremost literature."[7] What we can reconstruct about his pedagogy shows how far his actual practices were at odds with these boasts.

How Atkinson could have managed responsibly to cover even a fraction of the topics enumerated in the eight-page pamphlet is difficult to imagine. How he held students accountable is unknown. The archives hold none of his teaching notes or examinations. His actual practices can be inferred, however, from his published speeches and other writings. He often inveighed against the use of rote memory and against traditional recitations.[8] Instead of hearing students recite, he would simply inform them about things they should know. Even as the total number of students increased, all the students of a given class could be fitted into the Institute's large lecture hall. He held forth separately to all the first years and all the second years on whatever subject he judged was timely on a given day, whether it was Hegelian philosophy or how to read the newspaper.

The Institute's prospectus shows that Atkinson's "English" was directed to recent literature and history, including topics of continuing moment in England, such as trade unionism, Disraeli's speech on disestablishment, and female suffrage. Atkinson lectured in a genial and avuncular style. He was the oldest member of the faculty, and students appreciated his kindness. Concerned to reduce the pressures on the young men, he would entrust them with lists of recommended books that they might wish to read over the summer. Meanwhile, he simply told them what to think about this writer or that issue. He had no intention of doing the sort of work that was incumbent upon the Boylston Professor of Rhetoric across the river at Harvard, who was marking hundreds of essays every week. Instead, the Institute hired a woman to correct the written work Atkinson assigned.[9]

Since students should know something about modern literature, he would inform them about essays by Thomas Babington Macaulay and poetry by Tennyson and Browning. According equal billing to popular writing, he would tell them about the humor of Sydney Smith, the *Proverbial Philosophy* of Martin Tupper, and the poetry of Samuel Rogers, whose life showed what a successful banker might do in his spare time. He protected his students from encountering both the classical languages and any writing in English that would look old-fashioned. He advocated becoming acquainted with literature from "the age that immediately preceded ours," that is, from the time when he himself had been a young man. Nonetheless, England's greatest writer warranted some attention. He would inform students about recent research on Shakespeare's sonnets that revealed what sort of circles a writer needed to move in to be financially successful. While no play is named in the prospectus, mention of Emerson's essay "Shakespeare; or the Poet" rounds out what students ought to know. Emerson's opening sentence might have been readily adapted to justify the pretensions with which the prospectus was constructed: "Great men are more distinguished by range and extent than by originality."[10]

Range is what Atkinson aimed to provide. In order for a budding scientist to be prepared for adult social life and business relations, his education would have to enable him to display an acquaintance with everything else about the modern world. No time was to be wasted reading the classics of English literature. Out on a lecture tour Atkinson explained that "the times of Shakspeare [*sic*] and Elizabeth, or of Milton and the Commonwealth, are grown very remote from us in this nineteenth century."[11] Milton's writings, even more thoroughgoing in their implication with the dead languages than Shakespeare's, and more conspicuously engaged with biblical literature, represented a possible stumbling block in a building where Latin and Greek had been entombed and there was no chapel to be found.

Within two years of creating his prospectus, Atkinson was reporting to the Institute's committee on instruction that he had observed that many students were simply not cut out to be leading professionals. Since they would be going into business and the managerial class, they ought not to be expected to waste their time studying "rhetoric, logic, criticism or philosophy." Nor would they need to know much history. He had therefore decided that his lectures would stick "as far as possible" to materials with which "students were somewhat familiar." He added that the outcomes of the kind of teaching he was providing "are not such as can be very well estimated by a formal examination, or marked on a numerical scale."[12] By listening to his lectures, students would acquire good taste. A few years later, Atkinson announced that, because the amount of time required for scientific subjects was going to continue increasing, his students would now be able to choose to study either history or literature, and they would "be examined only on what they choose to be examined on." It will be enough, he concluded, if the students are asked to turn in brief notes after a lecture. Writing is something that cannot actually be taught; from writing their laboratory reports, students will learn how to write.[13]

Not surprisingly, MIT's continual expansion of what we refer to today as STEM subjects resulted in a continuing contraction of Atkinson's brief. The moment at which the Institute's students were to choose their specialized field steadily moved forward, from the beginning of the third year to the middle of the second year, and soon to the beginning of the second. Eventually, students began studying their special subject in the middle of their first year. As the growth of scientific and technological education began to entail unplanned-for consequences, without missing a beat, Atkinson made fresh use of the principle that had been invoked to do away with the study of Latin and Greek. He turned against history and English the hostility towards ancient classical civilizations that had been lodged in the claim that their literatures were no longer of "any earthly use."

Privately, Atkinson assured President Rogers of his loyalty to the preeminence of technological education and insisted that he be given sole oversight of the English curriculum. "If a question . . . should ever arise between securing the services of some eminent man in the scientific department and expanding the English," he wrote, "I should vote without hesitation for securing the scientific man."[14] Atkinson also sought to rein in a rival, George Howison, who had been hired to teach logic and who proposed to take over the teaching of comparative politics. If this were allowed, "it would completely upset all I have labored for," Atkinson wrote. "There is an intellectual overbearingness and insolence about him which sets me in direct antagonism with him and I greatly resent his attempted intrusions into my department," which "would be the derangement and destruction of all my plans."[15] Rogers proceeded to dismiss the upstart. The University of California subsequently hired Howison to found its philosophy department, where he earned a degree of eminence that placed him in company with Whitehead, Royce, James, Peirce, and Dewey. To this day, the university's prestigious Howison Lecture series continues to feature distinguished intellectuals.

Through the Institute's whole foundational period, as Boston Tech was turning into the premier technological institution that we know as MIT, those ultimately in charge gave oversight of one of the two prongs of the curriculum to an amateur whose professional standing in his field was far inferior to that of his colleagues in the sciences. Atkinson presented students with a deracinated, etiolated idea of "English" that bore virtually no relation to older stages of the language or to other languages. His long continuance in his post reinforced for both his colleagues and his students the assumption that their forward-looking pursuit of scientific and technological knowledge had at last rendered nugatory the old-fashioned study of the humanities.

YALE'S SHEFFIELD SCIENTIFIC SCHOOL, like the Lawrence Scientific School at Harvard, had been founded in the 1840s. Its students took French and German as alternatives to the Latin and Greek required of undergraduates in Yale's Classical Course. Many faculty members in Yale College were made uneasy by the absence of the classical languages in a scientific program that aimed to include some study of the humanities. More profoundly shocking was the fact that among the advanced specialized branches available to Sheffield students there was a "Select Course in Science and Literature." Unlike Boston Tech's "Science and Literature" option, it was popular among the students, and it integrated scientific and humanistic studies. In fact, it offered a complete undergraduate program of the sort that has been available in virtually every college since the middle of the twentieth century.[16]

In 1870 the Sheffield administration launched an "experiment" to expand instruction in the English language and to include subjects not yet available in most classical colleges. When they decided they would hire someone to teach English, a position not found and a subject not offered in Yale's BA program, this further disconcerted the college faculty.[17] They needed a man who would overcome skepticism about whether English could be made to do the sorts of linguistic, literary, and cultural work that the classical languages were alleged to have been doing. To initiate the work, they hired Thomas Lounsbury, a graduate of Yale College (1859) and a veteran of the Civil War. A learned scholar, Lounsbury brought the study of the English language and its literature into the Sheffield School's first-year curriculum. He also expanded the study of English in the "Select Course." During his first weeks on the job, he published a virtual manifesto titled "The Study of English." It set out criteria for how the whole field of linguistic and literary studies might develop. At the end of the academic year the governing board, in its *Annual Report*, pronounced its experiment a success and established the new English studies as a regular component of the school's curriculum. Lounsbury received a promotion, making him Yale's first professor of English. Over the course of the next three and a half decades he demonstrated what it meant to hold that title. His teaching and his scholarship won him many accolades, and he received honorary degrees from Harvard, Princeton, Lafayette, and other institutions.

Lounsbury understood that the study of the English language held out valuable educational opportunities. It provided access to times and places far beyond the everyday experience of young persons. In documents of historic importance, it preserved ideas that had shaped social and political life. It had generated a sizable body of classic imaginative literature. The cultures and civilizations to which English offered access were different from those of ancient Greece and Rome. They seemed at first blush much more familiar. Upon closer inspection, they demanded stretching your imagination.

In "The Study of English," Lounsbury introduced ideas and practices that would inform English studies for more than a century. He began by remarking that this study was "as yet everywhere in its infancy," and he observed that "no satisfactory system of instruction in our literature has yet been adopted generally." He wrote with conviction about what was needed, even as he insisted that knowledge of the subject requires "a life-time" and can never be "complete." There was to be no hurry. Acquiring this knowledge "is necessarily a slow process." Reading actual literature slowly and with care, unlike memorizing names and dates, makes for "a thoroughly honest" process of learning. "Whatever knowledge anyone gets" by reading good literature "becomes an integral part of the man himself, and forms a center about which new accretions of knowledge constantly fashion."[18]

Lounsbury insisted that the teacher should assign the best books. Chaucer was the first author to whom he introduced students in detail. Then he followed up with Shakespeare, Bacon, Milton, Dryden, and Pope, and students made their way towards contemporary writers. Under ordinary circumstances, Lounsbury maintained, "the great authors" need to "be studied in youth, or they will never be studied at all." A "taste for literature must be developed then, if it is expected to manifest activity in later life." By "the great authors" Lounsbury meant especially the best stylists. For style cannot be taught directly. It arises through exposure and generates, largely unconsciously, imitation of those one admires. After all, the goal is for "the student, instead of being a consumer," to "become a successful producer of literature."[19] This was why, in Lounsbury's view, the study of literature is far more valuable than mere training in writing compositions. Experience shows that whatever students learn in composition courses, style cannot be learned through direct instruction. Moreover, because good writing is necessary in many disciplines, administrators operate on a faulty assumption when they create a curriculum that assigns sole responsibility for the teaching of writing to teachers of literature.

At the same time, Lounsbury acknowledged limits to what even an effective teacher of literature can accomplish. The study of literature, he observed, "is capable of indefinite expansion and contraction," and the greatest benefits of reading are acquired in the process of reading itself. He proposed that "a knowledge of English literature can not only be best gained by studying the works of English authors themselves, but it can be gained in no other way."[20]

The article sets out six principal components for how literature should be studied. First, readers should aim to develop sympathy for the author they are reading: "There is nothing really so important." Reading an author sympathetically draws one out of oneself and allows for seeing things as another sees them. This is the great advantage of reading literature composed in the vernacular. By contrast, even students highly accomplished in their knowledge of Latin can rarely read a passage in the language without simultaneously thinking thoughts in their native tongue.[21]

Secondly, readers should pay attention to the author's arrangement of material, from the words in a sentence, to the flow of a paragraph, to the overall result produced by the entire work. Literary works need to be appreciated as a whole, whether a play by Shakespeare, a book of *The Fairie Queene*, or a novel by Walter Scott.

Thirdly, since every writer inevitably refers to things of the past and because literary works contain "references and allusions to the political and military history" in which they are set, students need to look things up. "The study of literature" is inevitably "intermixed with the study of history." The fourth point follows on this: readers will want also to probe how writers use allusions not only to historical events, but to other literary works, the Latin and Greek classics in particular, and to mythology. Once the reading of a work is complete, fifthly, it will be natural to look into the life and circumstances of the author and to the place of the work in literary history. These activities "furnish the best and most legitimate subjects for . . . exercises in English composition."[22]

Lastly, there remains a consideration "so broad, so vast" that Lounsbury aims to give "only the merest outline of what is desirable." This concerns how the words in a literary work are lodged in the history of the language. To do this productively, he proposes, it makes sense that the study of English literature should begin with Anglo-Saxon and proceed chronologically.

Although this sixth point may seem an afterthought, Lounsbury made it foundational for his actual teaching. The language-learning aspect of classical studies had long been considered a fundamental component of a liberal education. Lounsbury endorsed the idea that a competent instructor in English needed to know Anglo-Saxon. He proposed that substituting Anglo-Saxon for Latin and Greek would ensure that students would learn to read slowly, would work on construing passages, and would become attentive to etymology and the dynamics of language change. *The Canterbury Tales*, full of delight in themselves, were useful for the linguistic difficulty that their Middle English posed. Students, by giving their visual and aural attention to apparently unfamiliar words, would transform them into recognizable senses. Reading aloud, or allowing oneself to hear the words in imagination, was a way to assemble what had seemed the pieces of puzzle. The reading pleasure that emerged was like glimpsing the next few steps needed to solve a mathematical problem. But it was never to be forgotten that "we study the language for the sake of the literature, not the literature for the sake of the language."[23] (As we will see in a later chapter, Lounsbury's insistence on this virtually reversed the priority that was soon to prevail at Harvard.)

While these six components of effective literary study line up favorably with the actual practices that Francis March had developed at Lafayette, Lounsbury finally proposed a telling contrast between literature and philology. "Minute and microscopic investigations" of words can be carried out quite apart from literary study. Philology, however great an interest it warrants, "is not literature." Here, we glimpse the scope of philology on its way to being refocused: it was becoming the study we know as linguistics. In the previous chapters, we have seen that in the earlier nineteenth century, influenced by the German practices and perspectives, the range of philology had greatly expanded to include the study of the classical civilizations themselves. But as comparative philology came to be carried out without literary experience in view, its principal concern tended to be discovering various families of languages. For all their inherent interest, philological approaches rarely inspired students the way a Shakespeare play or a Browning dramatic monologue did.

THOMAS LOUNSBURY AND William Atkinson imagined the study of English and its relation to the Latin and Greek classics in utterly different ways. The "English" prong of the curriculum at MIT was meant at best to provide ornamentation to accompany the professional expertise students gained in advanced scientific studies. For a quarter-century Atkinson encouraged students to drive right over the dead languages that his curriculum had buried. He led them down a path that most of them regarded as something to be got over, like the measles, once and for all. Lounsbury, for his part, foresaw a time when "English" would name a study to which college students would bring as much attention and care as was being lavished elsewhere on the Latin and French classics. He taught his students to turn up the roots of a language they too readily assumed they already knew and encouraged them to hone their knowledge of it through the rest of their lives. His teaching and scholarship modeled for dozens of colleges, including Yale's, how an English department could define and enrich a new discipline by cross-fertilizing it with long established ones.

7

An Ardent Desire to Learn

A College for Black People

> Though conscious of the difficulty of learning without a teacher,
> I set out with high hope, and a fixed purpose, at whatever
> cost of trouble, to learn how to read.
>
> —FREDERICK DOUGLASS, *The Narrative of the Life*

THE YEARS IMMEDIATELY following the Civil War seemed to promise large opportunities for young persons to enter the sphere of higher education. More than sixty new institutions of higher education opened, mostly in the East and Midwest. The majority were denominational colleges, meant to provide for local populations, and they typically enrolled fewer than a hundred students. Many would close before the century's end. This chapter and the two that follow will take up, one by one, three newly founded institutions that have survived and flourished: Howard University, Vassar College, and Boston College. Each was dedicated to educating a segment of the population that traditionally had very limited access to higher education: Black people, women, and the sons of immigrants. All three institutions managed to secure a measure of respectability by ensuring that Latin and Greek served as a staple of their Bachelor of Arts curriculum. But in each institution the subject called "English" was constituted differently. The discrepancies illustrate, well beyond what we have seen in the previous chapter, that the broad range of students beginning college without having studied the classical languages ensured that the methods for teaching English would not be standardized. What "English" would be was defined locally, as each college adapted the contours and content of the new subject to the needs, and increasingly to the interests, of the students who were enrolling in it. Black people, especially former slaves whose masters had taken pains to keep them illiterate, benefited from adaptations most of all.

MEMORABLY, *The Narrative of the Life of Frederick Douglass* (1845) tells how its author shrewdly glimpsed that learning to read was his path to freedom. As a young boy Douglass heard his master upbraiding his wife for teaching him the ABCs: "If you teach that n***** . . . how to read, there would be no keeping him. It would forever unfit him to be a slave. He would at once become unmanageable, and of no value to his master." The moment he heard this, Douglass resolved that he would learn to read. He acted on his resolve through the months and years that followed. Yet he found that his skill in reading turned out to be a curse: much of what he read shocked him and left him at an impasse. He remarked that reading "had given me a view of my wretched condition, without the remedy." Still, over time, he learned to love reading, especially the Scriptures. First-hand knowledge of biblical literature liberated him from the self-serving interpretations upheld by the slave-owners. On Sundays he ran a secret Sabbath school for "scholars . . . of all ages" who were "ardently desiring to learn." He looked back on this as the "sweetest engagement with which I was ever blessed," and found he was doing so "with an amount of pleasure not to be expressed."[1] Douglass's teaching of fellow slaves anticipated what became manifest after the Emancipation Proclamation: the importance of literacy for Black people generally. In the generation that followed, while Douglass broadened his contributions to educating his fellow citizens above all through public speaking, as a trustee of Howard University from 1871 until his death in 1895 he took an active part in educating its students.

Writing at the turn of the twentieth century, W. E. B. Du Bois, who taught at the historically Black universities Wilberforce and Atlanta, described a remarkable development that took place "within [the] single generation" that coincided with the last three decades of Douglass's life. Black people, before they could benefit from attending trade schools, needed education in the basics at common schools. But

> Southern whites would not teach them; Northern whites in sufficient numbers could not be had. If the Negro was to learn, he must teach himself,

> and the most effective help that could be given him was the establishment of schools to train Negro teachers. This conclusion was slowly but surely reached by every student of the situation until simultaneously, in widely separated regions, without consultation or systematic plan, there arose a series of institutions designed to furnish teachers for the untaught. Above the sneers of critics at the obvious defects of the procedure must ever stand its one crushing rejoinder: in a single generation they put thirty thousand teachers in the South; they wiped out the illiteracy of the majority of black people.[2]

This progress took place by stops and starts. While literacy remained a foundational consideration and productive participation in trade-school education increased, higher education was still a fraught sphere. In the North, Black men were reminded that they could never escape danger, even and especially if they were educated. In the 1850s, at Central College, an abolitionist institution in upstate New York, William Grant Allen was teaching Greek, rhetoric, and public speaking as integral components of a liberal education. He was the college's—and the country's—second Black professor. When he secretly married a white woman (the first legal marriage between a "colored" man and a Caucasian to take place in the U.S.), he was forcibly driven out of town, ultimately escaping with his bride to England. His life story reminded aspiring Blacks that intellectual achievement and respectable public standing could exacerbate rather than alleviate the white man's fears.

A decade later, after the death-dealing interval that genteel Southern educators referred to simply as an interruption, higher education for Black people slowly began to become an imaginable goal. Thousands of former slaves poured into Washington, DC, homeless, without connections, in need of food and medical attention. They moved into abandoned buildings, stables, and woodsheds. The Missionary Society of the First Congregational Church resolved to take action. They bought land and founded a school to train ex-slaves and others to become pastors, doctors, lawyers, and teachers. Howard University would be open to anyone, Black or white, female or male, young or older, married or single, an immigrant from any country. It included a medical school, a law school, a school of divinity, a normal school for training teachers, and even a college of liberal arts. As was the case in universities generally, the curriculum for enrollees in the professional schools did not require previous studies in the liberal arts. Howard's tiny collegiate department, however, provided a curriculum largely congruent with what was offered in traditional colleges. Candidates for admission were required to demonstrate an advanced knowledge of Latin, Greek, and mathematics. The long-term goal—and it was controversial—was for Black people to be able to enter the upper echelons of cultured society that were marked by knowledge of the classics.[3]

Howard's white founders had studied in leading liberal arts colleges. They were well aware of the widespread prejudice that insisted Black people lacked the intelligence to study college subjects, and they meant to challenge idea that no Black man could learn to read Greek. The university was named for General Oliver Otis Howard, a Civil War hero and the commissioner of the Freedman's Bureau, established by the U.S. government to support former slaves in their transition to a new life. He had studied at Bowdoin and West Point. Among the first faculty members in the collegiate department, Eliphalet Whittlesey, a graduate of Yale, taught rhetoric. Before serving as a general in the war he had been professor of rhetoric and oratory at Bowdoin. At the time of his appointment, he was General Howard's assistant commissioner, working in Raleigh, North Carolina, with refugees and freedmen. Loathing the practice whereby former slaves were being reduced to indentured servants, he had been securing land where free people could farm for profit. When he returned to the classroom, Whittlesey sought to foster something analogous: Black people seeking education as a means of taking charge of their own lives. Even before he introduced training in oratory to the curriculum, the students took it upon themselves to run oratorical contests. They carried out debates, gave speeches, and put on skits. Before long the college began awarding credit for participation in these activities. Meanwhile, among the speeches heard on campus, perhaps the most inspiring and memorable was given by the aged Ralph Waldo Emerson. In January 1874, he talked informally, and without a note, before an audience of 150 faculty and students. His presence and his theme—the importance of selecting one's friends and selecting what books to read—spoke powerfully to students' aspiration fully to participate in learned culture and public life. "In reading Shakespeare," Emerson assured them, "you will find yourself armed for the law, for divinity, and for commerce with men."[4] Shakespeare would be slow to appear in the students' coursework, however. Howard emulated Southern colleges, where, generally speaking, English literature came into the curriculum about two decades after it had become a standard subject in the Northeast.[5]

It took Howard's collegiate department many years to grow and flourish. The first class numbered four students, including a white woman who in time became a teacher in the normal school. For many years thereafter, the Classical Course rarely enrolled more than thirty students. Plenty of work needed to be done to prepare prospective students for a curriculum shot through with Latin and Greek. The university had launched its Normal School precisely to train teachers who would prepare students for its collegiate program. It opened a preparatory department as well. These two programs grew quickly, and by 1872 nearly four hundred students were enrolled in them. By the mid-seventies the collegiate department began offering more science courses and created an alternative curriculum in which students could study French instead of Latin and Greek. This program, denominated the "Literary Course," led to a diploma rather than the BA.

Curiously, for two decades those about to graduate from the collegiate department were required to study a subject that few traditional colleges were offering: American literature.[6] Through their first three years of study seniors had had been taught rhetoric and composition and had had little more than a brush with literature in English. Now, suddenly, they were entrusted with Thomas Budd Shaw's *Outlines of English Literature,* but not in order to acquaint themselves with literature written in the mother country of the early colonists, slaveholders, and other representatives of the dominant culture. They were to direct their attention rather to a recently added supplement written expressly for American students. It provided a lengthy account of a more recent literature, and one largely set in more familiar surroundings. Yet, if not so conspicuously foreign as the literature of the English, American literature was still not entirely their own. The textbook account ignored the existence of Black authors, poets, and orators—even Douglass himself—and thus indirectly signaled Black students about how much work still needed to be done before their distinctive contributions to the culture would be recognized as integral to America's story.

Nonetheless, there was much in that supplement that Howard students could learn to advantage. Its first chapter focused on religious writing and oratory and emphasized the importance of establishing a literary tradition free from models established in England. Its second chapter treated authors widely held in esteem, from Franklin and Irving to Emerson and Hawthorne. Its third chapter, titled "Poetry," placed this genre above anything composed by mere "authors." Poetry, it contended, is "divine and spontaneous," an "overflowing of the soul."[7] Students and faculty alike found it inspiring.

Meanwhile, Douglass inspired Howard students to imagine contributing to the arts and entering public life themselves. From the university's earliest years, he served on its visiting and examining committee as well as the board of trustees, and he modeled academic and cultural interests. He attended local Shakespearean productions performed by Black actors. He recommended the actress Henrietta Vinton Davis, known for her dramatic readings of *Romeo and Juliet*, as "the best colored reader that ever came before the American people." He himself took the part of Shylock in a community reading of *The Merchant of Venice*, and he wrote astutely about the applicability of Shylock's "Hath not a Jew eyes" speech to the situation that Black people occupied in America.[8] Before the end of the century Howard's collegiate department, in keeping with the founders' idea that its students should have access to an education equal to what the best liberal arts colleges were providing, added a knowledge of a Shakespeare play to its entrance requirements. It also began offering an elective course that covered Shakespeare and poets of his era in the first semester and Victorian poets in the second. By the early twentieth century, Howard's dramatic club was demonstrating that Black students could perform Shakespeare and—going one better—that they could develop their own more racially expressive cultural representations.[9]

8

Competing with the Boys

A College for Young Women

Women, like men, must be educated with a view to action,
or their studies cannot be called education!

—HARRIET MARTINEAU, Letter to the American
Women's Rights Convention (1851)

FREDERICK DOUGLASS UNDERSTOOD as well as anyone that the exclusion of women from public life and higher education was deeply intertwined with the exclusion of Black people. Already in 1848, when he attended the Women's Rights Convention at Seneca Falls, he was acting on that understanding. The Civil War then brought increased attention to the connection between the two parallel struggles for legal rights: Union soldiers often marched to the sounds of Julia Ward Howe's "Battle Hymn of the Republic." Meanwhile, although the war effort inspired song and poetry and new conceptions of who deserved to enjoy freedom, for those who were now reaching college age, it put going to college on hold, and not only for men.

In the first year of the war, the wealthy brewer Matthew Vassar, encouraged by his schoolteacher niece, gave half his fortune and two hundred acres of land in Poughkeepsie, New York, to launch a college for women. As news got around that it would be opening, its fledgling administration received more than a thousand letters of interest from families across the Northern states.

From its earliest years Vassar Female College was able to provide far more institutional support for students to imagine their futures than Howard—or, for that matter, scores of other colleges—could. Many enrollees came from affluent Protestant families that had been in the country for generations. They attended an institution with an extraordinary breadth of resources and a clear sense of purpose. Its goal was to provide an education equal to what was offered at the best men's colleges. Richly endowed, the college boasted an art gallery that housed Matthew Vassar's collection, including Hudson River School paintings; a museum of botany and zoology; a cabinet of geology and minerology; a riding school; a music building; a gymnasium; an astronomical observatory; and, climactically, a highly accomplished faculty.

Vassar's handsome academic buildings housed nine "Departments." Here the term was used more or less to refer to subjects under the direction of a professor who had one or more assistant teachers at his (or, in one case, her) disposal. The college had sought to employ women professors, and the very first person hired to the faculty was the internationally renowned astronomer Maria Mitchell. As a young woman she had attended the antislavery conference in Nantucket where Douglass gave his first speech. At Vassar, she became a well-known advocate for women's suffrage and for women's participation in the fields of science and mathematics. From early on, she engaged her students in research, taking a group to Iowa, for instance, to view an eclipse of the sun. Unable to find her like, however, the college settled on male teachers in the remainder of its hiring, rendering its public face more conventional and establishing a strong male presence in all but one department.

By the 1890s, Vassar College (early on the "Female" designation had been dropped) and Wellesley College would be the leading women's institutions in the country.[1] But Vassar's first few years in operation would not have predicted this preeminence, not least because the problems that its English teachers uncovered created an unforeseen amount of chaos and revealed the need to open a preparatory division.

When, in September 1865, Vassar began offering instruction, the faculty soon recognized that a large proportion of the 350 young women who enrolled were ill prepared to do college work. The administration had set as a condition for admission that a young woman had attained the age of fifteen. It was decidedly not in a position, however, to require the academic standards that enabled men's colleges to organize a curriculum that separated students into four discrete classes. Consequently, the administration found it extremely difficult to place each student in courses where she could succeed.

Many young women who enrolled had been educated exclusively at home or had spent only a few years in school. The college therefore was willing to negotiate how much Latin would be necessary. For a second language, it allowed applicants to demonstrate competence in French or German as an alternative to ancient Greek. Applicants also needed to demonstrate competence in "the ordinary English branches, namely, Arithmetic, Grammar, Geography, and Elementary History." One student described the examination on English in a letter home: "they asked what were the principal parts of Grammar, and their meanings, what a sentence was, and its principal parts, and all about the different classes of pronouns."[2] When deficient applicants failed any other subject on which they were examined, the college made provision by creating "Extra-Collegiate Departments" meant to bring them up to speed. But the first instructors encountered so much substandard writing in the English grammar component that the administration decided that failure in this section would mean outright rejection.

As for its English department, the college meant to be an early leader in replacing the old-fashioned rhetorical component of college education with more distinctly literary endeavors. While men's colleges generally prepared students to deliver public orations by emphasizing rhetoric, the Vassar prospectus promised training in reading aloud, the art of poetical recitation, and the practice known as *tableaux vivants,* or charades, all cultivated not merely for amusement but as a preparation to enter public life. The college's president, John H. Raymond, had himself once been a professor of English at the institution now known as Colgate University. Raymond hired Henry Buckham, who held a master's degree from the University of Vermont, to create a program that would stand out among American colleges. Buckham planned to introduce students to the innovative work being done by Francis March of Lafayette College. He would also accustom them to reading poetry. He imagined that by their third year they would be using the textbooks that March had written. These would enable them to learn Anglo-Saxon and to study the history of the English language. All this was to be a prelude to the work of senior year, when they would be reading English literature after the manner of March's method of philological study. As things turned out, none of this materialized. Buckham resigned at the end of the first year. When he explained his reasons to President Raymond, he expressed his disappointment that so many students assigned to his classes had been put into his charge belatedly, weeks after the term had begun. Of the 150 students he had taught, two-thirds were unprepared for college work.[3] The college opened a preparatory school and abandoned Buckham's entire plan for the English curriculum.

The following autumn a new professor of English, Truman Backus, took charge. An open-minded man, he recognized the need for a flexible curriculum adapted to the students' interests as well as their needs. Six women were hired to teach under his supervision, mostly in the preparatory school. Unlike the male faculty, Vassar's women teachers had extensive extra-curricular duties that included living with, supervising, and disciplining the students in their lodgings. This rendered them unusually subject to the students' scrutiny. A student named Mary Mills Badgley wrote to a friend back home in Milwaukee, for instance, that her course on English literature had just begun and she thought she'd like it. Then she hit upon her real news, which concerned her new English teacher:

> Some of the girls have great time [*sic*] here in dressing up. Saturday evening I believe that there were about forty dressed up one as a a [*sic*] negro woman, another as a ghost and others as nuns but it did not entirely please President Raymond, and I expected some of the girls would suffer for it, but they have not as yet. Some of the girls say that one of the teachers here (who is not very well liked) was heard to exclaim when she saw the negro woman. "What horrible thing is this, wherefore is this outrage perpetrated" and the girls say that one of them, one night passed her ginger bread and she said "No, I thank you I have no predilection for gingerbread." and this same teacher has charge of our Literature class, what do you think I shall be when I come from under her charge![4]

Five subsequent letters to Mary's friend are extant; none tells about the upshot.

Not for nothing were the women who taught English at Vassar called "critics." Their academic brief included grading the students' writing, much of it composed on any subject of a student's choice. Backus expected the teachers to provide "minute, personal, and free" criticism, delivered "in private interviews between the teacher and the individual student."[5] These interviews also served as a forum in which education beyond the curriculum could take place.

Through the 1870s, as Vassar's standards for admission became more demanding, the English curriculum stabilized. While students in Howard's BA program were being treated to a heavy emphasis on rhetoric, oratory, and public performance that was tied to their study of the ancient classics, at Vassar the study of rhetoric was geared to enhancing students' experience with the written word. Elocution remained a required subject, but the curriculum emphasized composition, requiring it through all four years. Many students had distinctively literary interests and exercised them as debaters and creative writers. Members of the Philaletheis literary society began putting on modest productions of plays, including *Twelfth Night,* in the auditorium of the Riding School. In 1880 some members formed an offshoot Shakespeare Club.

While students were reading the likes of *Jane Eyre, Aurora Leigh,* and *Little Dorrit* on their own, Backus's English courses assigned the study of Shaw's *Outlines of English Literature.* Students used a version revised by the Englishman William Smith, specially designed for persons who were studying for the India Civil Service examination. Acknowledging that this textbook was held in "high esteem," Backus undertook a thoroughgoing revision himself with American students in mind. Renamed and published in 1874 as *Shaw's New History of English Literature, prepared on the basis of "Shaw's Manual," by Truman J. Backus, A.M., Professor of English in Vassar College,* this textbook achieved considerable popularity across the United States. To enrich his students' experience, Backus sent sophomores off to the library with the names of twelve classic English writers and a list of bibliographical references. Each student was required to produce an essay on one writer, being sure to include her own opinion of the man and his writings. As seniors, Vassar students could then elect one of two English courses, one on English literature, the other an introduction to Anglo-Saxon. The latter was said to be the climax of their English education and to provide a base from which a graduate could go on for further studies.

Backus's treatment of Anglo-Saxon entailed a radical revision of his source. He shortened and simplified Smith's lengthy account of the history of the English language in the Middle Ages. Beyond this, he omitted most of Smith's extensive account of the social and political history of the early medieval period. Smith had referred often to things that he deemed to have been distinctively Anglo-Saxon: the "Anglo-Saxon tongue" and "grammar," "the Anglo-Saxon period"—and "the Anglo-Saxon kingdoms," "church," "verse," "rhythms," "writers," even "literary criticism." He had also taken pains to clarify how the superior "Anglo-Saxon race" interacted with other races.[6]

In revising Smith's treatment of all things "Anglo-Saxon," Backus deliberately curtailed the adjectival use of the phrase. He advocated suppressing it in favor of emphasizing the basic identity between what he called the "Old English" past and the English-speaking present: "For more than fourteen centuries the thoughts and feelings of the English people have found expression in the same language which we now speak." Nonetheless, like Smith, Backus freely referred to the "Anglo-Saxon race." In fact, writing for students in the U.S., he referred to "our Anglo-Saxon race," claiming for it far greater importance than the Roman, Celtic, Scandinavian, and Norman legacies lodged in the history of the English language. He explained that the contributions of "the half-Romanized Britons gradually disappeared" in the "presence of the superior race." "The absorption or destruction" of pre-Anglo-Saxon culture, he went on, "was in accordance with what seems to be an inevitable law regulating the result of the close contact of two unequal nationalities." Writing in the years when the U.S. government was conducting wars against the Sioux, the Cheyenne, the Arapaho, and other Indigenous peoples, Backus sought to clinch this interpretation by pointing to a generally unstated ground on which Anglo-Saxon became a standard component of the English curriculum in U.S. colleges: "That law is operating in our own land to-day, as it guides the North American Indians to the certain fate that must come from their contact with the same Anglo-Saxon race."[7]

Backus's attempt to rename the academic subject called "Anglo-Saxon" as "Old English" did not catch on at Vassar, and the college continued to emphasize the importance of studying Anglo-Saxon. The catalog for 1890–91 lists the four courses offered in the English department: Anglo-Saxon Poetry, Anglo-Saxon Prose, Literature of the Fourteenth Century, and a reading course (presumably tutorial) in "the later English literature," to be arranged with individual students "according to their stage of advancement and also their purposes and aims." The Anglo-Saxon courses were supplemented with auxiliary lectures on English philology. The racial pride with which Vassar and other colleges presented Anglo-Saxon as the foundation for English studies set a peculiar problem for colleges seeking to provide higher education for Black people and for immigrants. The practice of conflating literature from England with Anglo-Saxon racial superiority made some colleges ambivalent about teaching the literature of England so that they had to find ways, as we've seen with Howard, of defining the subject called English quite differently.

BY THE END OF the century Vassar was recognized as a significant player on the national educational scene. In 1893–94, its president hosted the culminating conference of the National Education Association's "Committee of Ten," chaired by President Eliot of Harvard. Having conducted a long and careful study of the variegated standards and practices prevalent in the nation's secondary schools, the committee made recommendations for closing the gaps between what colleges expected of entering students and the skills that applicants were actually bringing to admissions exams. These gaps, as the chapter on Entrance Examinations will show, tended to be larger in "English" than in any other subject. Vassar brought to the discussion a long history of addressing the problem directly and, as we have seen here, some decided views on the importance that Anglo-Saxon should have in constituting college English.

9

Acting English Plays

A College for the Sons of Immigrants

Two plays of Shakespeare will be read during the year by all the Students of the English Department, the Preparatory Department and the College; and will be presented, one during the Christmas Holidays and the other during the Easter Holidays by the Students respectively of the Collegiate and Preparatory Departments.

—*Catalogue of the Officers and Students of Boston College* (1894–95)

IN THE SAME DECADE that Howard University and Vassar College were founded, the Catholic religious order called Jesuits, under the leadership of Johannes Bapst, succeeded at long last in gaining a charter for a college in Boston. It would provide young men, especially the sons of impecunious immigrants, a coherent seven-year program covering the timespan we now associate with high school and college. (Calling the school a "college" reflected European usage, as in France, for instance.) Given that in the United States, high-school education was at a merely incipient stage and that there were relatively few private academies, many institutions of higher education recognized that a large portion of their applicants were not ready to take on a college curriculum; they would need to provide them with a preparatory education. Vassar's preparatory department was something of an embarrassment, a stopgap measure created with the hope of achieving its mission so successfully that it would put itself out of existence. By contrast, the founders of Howard gave priority to creating a preparatory department. Similarly, the Jesuits, ever since they had first opened schools in Europe in the sixteenth century, habitually set out to educate young boys. Ideally, they would take them through a well-designed program that led to a Bachelor of Arts degree. But the founders of Boston College knew quite well that many boys would be leaving to go to work after two or three years. They took the long view. It turned out to take thirteen years before the college graduated its first class of seniors. Given that most U.S. colleges had fewer than a hundred students, all told, that there were twelve graduates meant the college was succeeding.

SINCE THE LATE 1840S, the Jesuits had been attempting to found a school in Boston. They persisted amidst intermittently unbridled resistance on the part of the locals. Irish immigrants were experiencing a vicious backlash in the Northeast, where distrust of idolatrous foreigners and claims that Catholicism was inherently inimical to democratic values were especially strong. In the 1830s a group of American-born Protestant workmen had set fire to an Ursuline convent in Charlestown (now Somerville), Massachusetts. Nativist sentiment reached a peak in the 1850s, as refugees fleeing Ireland's potato famine crowded into Boston's slums. The political party that called itself American and Nativist railed against drunken Irishmen, alleging that they posed a threat to the economic and political security of native-born citizens. Members of the party, when asked what it stood for, were instructed to reply, "I know nothing." But by the mid 1860s, the Irish were already more numerous than the combined number of all other immigrants who had entered the country since the Declaration of Independence.[1]

Prejudice against the Irish had deep roots. It dated back beyond the founding of the Bay Colony to the time when the English, considering themselves bearers of a civilizing mission to untamed barbarians and stubborn pagans, had colonized Ireland. In the 1590s, Edmund Spenser, serving Queen Elizabeth as a bureaucrat in Ireland even as he was composing *The Faerie Queene*, reported that the Irish "Papists" are no Christians but "so blindly and brutishly informed" that "you would rather think them atheists or infidels." Four decades later, when English colonists settled into New England and met with resistance from local inhabitants whom they expected would serve as a ready workforce, they had a tailor-made explanation for that resistance: Indigenous and Black people, like the people of Ireland, were dirty, idle, lazy, and degenerate; races so socially inferior as to require forcible subjection.[2]

The first rector (president) of Boston College, Johannes Bapst, was a Swiss immigrant. He had learned firsthand about the ill treatment of foreigners in the United States. He arrived in New York at age thirty-one in 1848, knowing no English. His religious superiors assigned him to work in rural Maine. He lived among the Penobscot and learned both their language and English. Gradually, his work expanded to include Irish and Canadian immigrants. In 1854, the Know-Nothing Party in the town where he had set up a church blew up the Catholic school. They kidnapped Bapst, stripped him naked, smeared tar all over his body and covered him in feathers. His fellow Jesuits brought him to Massachusetts, where he eventually recovered, and his work in Boston met with tolerant acceptance. Surprisingly, given that he spoke English as an acquired language, he came to be admired for his preaching.[3]

When the state legislature finally granted a charter for a Jesuit school in 1863, it was seeking to mitigate the lasting effects of virulent bigotry. The college managed to operate with a remarkable independence from traditional British influences on American education. Unlike the public schools and liberal arts colleges, it followed curricular plans enshrined in a centuries-old *Ratio Studiorum*. This "Plan of Studies" had swept across Europe in the late sixteenth and early seventeenth century, as Jesuits founded schools from Sicily northward into France and from German-speaking realms westward into the Iberian Peninsula. The *Ratio* integrated the study of literature, history, and drama into the scientific and professional studies of the traditional universities, demonstrating that the humanistic program of the Renaissance could be rendered compatible with the scholastic program of the Middle Ages. But two centuries later the Jesuit faculty of Boston College were suspicious of new intellectual trends and lacked the boldness and imagination of the early Jesuits who, as they had entered Japan, China, and India, sought to adapt the *Ratio* to accommodate other cultures. Instead, they dug in with an insistence on following a once-successful curriculum that in the U.S. could be directed only to a subculture in which Latin was a living language. Whatever academic specialty an individual Jesuit teacher developed, whether in Greek or in chemistry, he had studied the classics for many years. The Jesuits all heard and spoke Latin every morning at mass, they prayed the Latin psalms privately, they conversed with one another in Latin, wrote letters in Latin, and even required students who wished to use the restroom to make their request in Latin. In short, Jesuit teachers were able to think in Latin and aimed to render their advanced students capable of doing likewise. The required yearlong course in philosophy for seniors was conducted entirely in Latin.[4] But even educated outsiders regarded the *Ratio* and the extensive use of a foreign language with suspicion. Harvard's President Eliot proposed that Catholic colleges with their antiquated fixed curriculum could not produce manly adults capable of independent thought. The *Atlantic Monthly* quoted him to the effect that the Jesuit curriculum employed "precisely the method followed in Moslem countries where the Koran prescribes the perfect education to be administered to all children alike."[5]

Although from the start Boston College advertised its program as including English as well as Latin and Greek, its classical program afforded scant attention to literature in English. For three decades, "English" referred to the several subjects taught in the vernacular, from history and chemistry to geography and bookkeeping. Although students made use of an elementary rhetoric textbook and were regularly expected to produce compositions and often to compose poems, they did not take courses on English literature. But, almost from the beginning, each year the whole school had been involved in studying and performing two Shakespeare plays. Only in the 1890s, when Timothy Brosnahan, who as a young teacher had fostered students' interest in writing poetry, became the college's president, did English literature fully enter the curriculum. Now, in addition to learning poems by heart (e.g., Shelley's "Ode to a Skylark," Milton's "Lycidas") and writing a weekly composition, students began studying Thomas Babington Macaulay's style as exhibited in his essays on Milton and Addison. They were analyzing purple passages from Shakespeare and the rhetorically sophisticated speeches delivered by the fallen angels in Milton's Pandaemonium. They were reading and discussing, and sometimes seeking to imitate, lyrics by Wordsworth and other classic poets.

In introducing the study of English literature into the *Ratio Studiorum* curriculum, the Jesuits had faced a peculiar problem. They needed to defend their educational work against two competing critiques, each antithetical to the other. To a nativist public, a Catholic college had to show that its members were loyal to the nation and that its curriculum was academically comparable to what respectable liberal arts colleges offered. To the authorities in Rome, whose local bishop in the U.S. would grant an imprimatur to their textbooks, Jesuits needed to show that, when they began teaching literature in English, they were not thereby initiating their charges into the dominant Protestant culture. The *English Reader* that Jesuits used for introducing students to poetry and prose commenced with lengthy excerpts from Cardinal Newman's *Idea of the University*. Newman lavished high praise on the sui generis achievements to be found in English literature: "the style of Shakespeare, or of the Protestant Bible and Prayer-Book, or of Swift, or of Pope, or of Gibbon, or of Johnson!" The phraseology and diction of these writers, Newman observed, "have become a portion of the vernacular tongue." "So great a work of man" is this literature, Catholics will never be able to reverse the fact that "English literature will ever *have been* Protestant."[6] Belated and at times besieged, Catholics in the English-speaking parts of the New World, although they would hear the words of English literature with the ears of native speakers, learned also to process it with an outsider's eyes.

Although the Jesuits were tardy in designating English literature an object of college study, their tradition of making drama a vehicle of education had long since opened the unusual practice of performing plays. The *Ratio* prescribed dramatic performances as a staple of education. Preparing a production and performing it enabled students to bring their mental, bodily, and imaginative capacities into play all at once. The first known performance in a Jesuit school was given in Messina, Sicily, in 1551. As upwards of three hundred Jesuit schools sprung up in Rome, Seville, Innsbruck, Munich, Vienna, and other European cities, Latin plays were typically acted in all of them. Music and dance, even ballet, enhanced the entertainment. The productions fostered and exhibited an integration of what the students were learning.

At Boston College, beginning in 1867–68, well before it was common practice in other colleges,[7] and then for many decades, each academic year the entire student body and the faculty came together to put on a classic play in English. The absence of women students occasioned some bowdlerizing. Already in the 1860s students acted *The Merchant of Venice*, *Richard III*, *Coriolanus*, *I Henry IV*, and *Julius Caesar*—all performed with the female roles omitted. In a performance that took place in 1893 Lear's three daughters were transformed into three sons (Godfrey, Botolph, and Cordelius). Occasionally, a non-Shakespearean play was given: *The Rivals*, for instance, and *The School for Scandal.*[8] Notably absent from the plays acted by the end of the century were the Shakespearean romantic comedies and *Othello*. Both racial and sexual subject matter seem to have been judged beyond the bounds for adolescent boys. We can confidently infer, however, that to perform in a play the students secured a measure of acquaintance with Shakespearian language. They needed and got training in articulation and phrasing to carry across the meaning of the words. They learned to consider what each speech contributed to the scene in which it was lodged and to the play as a whole. Mounting the play was no mere extracurricular activity. It afforded students their most intense literary and educational experience.

The absence of *Othello* from the list of plays the students performed suggests something that Catholics may have been unwilling to acknowledge. Students of Irish descent had far better prospects than Black people had for entering into the country's prosperity. Catholic colleges, eager to defend their mission against the charge that loyalty to the pope rendered their work incompatible with American values, did not call attention to precedents and parallels between the experiences of former slaves and those of unwelcome immigrants. But with the spread of allegedly scientific claims about the inferiority of certain races, including Black people and the Irish, the parallels were operative in the larger culture. Nearby at Harvard, Louis Agassiz was influentially promoting a theory of polygenesis. Elsewhere other academics were seeking to provide scientific proof that some races are inherently inferior, both bodily and mentally.[9] The whole business cast an unacknowledged shadow over the growing prominence of Anglo-Saxon in the English curriculum of the established colleges, where it was presented as the earliest form of the students' native language and the source from which a distinctly English literary tradition had sprung. Howard University and Boston College did not teach Anglo-Saxon. In this regard, the prominent women's colleges (Smith, Wellesley, Barnard, and their predecessor, Vassar) were different from other colleges that served previously excluded populations. When it came to appropriating the whole history of the mother country's language and its literature as the students' rightful legacy, the new women's colleges, innovative as they were, simply lined up with the traditional men's colleges.

PART III

LITERATURE IN ENGLISH AS A FIELD FOR STUDY

10

Entrance Examinations

If you wish to kill a study, make it the subject of academical teaching.

—GRANT ALLEN

LONDON, 1880S. The *Pall Mall Gazette* is running a series of letters from prominent persons debating whether Oxford University should found a School of English. Various luminaries—Walter Pater, John Ruskin, Max Müller, Matthew Arnold, and others—have been invited to participate. The respondents all hold the nation's literature in high esteem, and most are not sanguine about turning it into an "academical" subject. Several objections recur: Instructors will not be able to organize the subject in a logical progression, the way those who teach mathematics take students through a series of steps that build one upon the other. If "our" literature is to become an object of study, its beauties will be spoiled and readers will be robbed of its pleasures. Literature cannot be examined, only facts about literature. Grant Allen, known for his writing on science and for his fiction, calls attention to the many people who, having studied the classical languages, "cordially hate and dislike the literature of ancient Greece and Rome." The "reason," he writes, "is clear; because it was made to them in childhood and youth a symbol of drudgery and an instrument of torture in the horrid form of licensed vivisection known as public examinations." His letter concludes with unblushing insolence: "May we never live to see examination papers set . . . on Wordsworth's 'Ode on the Intimations of Immortality.'"[1]

By the time this virtual symposium was taking place, English literature had already been turned into an academic subject. Participants in the symposium took no notice of this. Young Englishmen who had attended the best schools and matriculated at Oxford were familiar with "our" literature. The "our" here meant not simply "we English," but "we" of a class that did not deign to notice that the study of English literature had been taking place in dissenting academies, mechanics institutes, coaching schools where applicants prepared for the India Civil Service examinations, various colleges that prepared candidates to take the University of London's examinations for the BA, and at universities in Scotland and Canada.[2]

Meanwhile, in the United States, the president of Harvard was busy explaining the grounds on which the study of English now warranted widespread support in universities. Although Charles Eliot had been slow to build up Harvard's English department, he had come to think about English literature quite differently from the ways in which his counterparts in the esteemed English universities thought about it. He presented it as the inheritance of everyone who is a native speaker of the language. He promoted the idea of a bond with the mother country that entitled the U.S. to piggyback on the civilizing mission that the Empire assigned itself. "English," he declared, is "the tongue of nations which are preeminent in the world by force of character, enterprise, and wealth." Given the state of modern scholarship, people now learn "more about the Jews, Greeks, and Romans through English than through Hebrew, Greek, or Latin." English literature surpasses that of the ancients in its aesthetic achievements and provides a more timely and useful cultural legacy than the classical languages.[3]

TWO DECADES BEFORE the debate about whether English would be taught and examined at Oxford, there had emerged in the U.S. a new context in which a knowledge of the language would be examined. When Eliot became Harvard's president in 1869, his was one of 563 postsecondary institutions in the country, enrolling some 52,000 students. Within two decades, as attending college came increasingly to be seen as a preparation for entering the workplace, there would be nearly a thousand such institutions, enrolling more than 156,000 students.[4] Demonstrating a degree of competence in employing the vernacular became a sine qua non component of the examinations required for admission to college. Many colleges began to consider the English exam decisive and denied admission to anyone who failed to pass it. The stakes in the

English entrance exam were higher than they were in any English examination that a student had taken in secondary school or might take in college.

For decades, every college had offered its own entrance examination. (Not until 1892, with the meeting of the Committee of Ten, would colleges begin to work together to create common entrance requirements.) Typically, each college specified in its annual catalog how much Latin, Greek, and mathematics an applicant was expected to know. For instance, this is how, in 1869, Bowdoin College spelled out what applicants would need to demonstrate: besides a knowledge of Latin grammar, Virgil's *Bucolics, Georgics,* and six books of the *Aeneid,* seven orations of Cicero, and writings by Sallust; besides Greek grammar, four books of Xenophon's *Anabasis* and two of Homer's *Iliad,* etc.; along with arithmetic, algebra, and several levels of geometry. Generally speaking, catalogs mentioned only in passing that applicants were assumed to have a knowledge of English grammar. Even Harvard did not ask for a sample of a student's writing until after the new freshmen had matriculated.

As the number of applicants to college multiplied and colleges curtailed the scope allotted to the classical languages, some institutions found that seriously testing their applicants' knowledge of English gave them an opportunity to be more selective. One of the earliest to require a detailed English test was Vassar, which from its start (as we've seen) had encountered great difficulty in placing enrollees in English classes at the appropriate level. Vassar's annual catalog early on added its English exam to the specimen examinations covering the traditional subjects it had been listing. The exam required responses to prompts like these: "What is grammar?" "Define a phrase, and give the various kinds of phrases with illustrations of each." "State the several offices of the various parts of speech." However accomplished an applicant's performance in the examinations on traditional subjects was, if her work on the English exam was deficient, she would not be admitted.

Another newly founded institution devised a still more exacting test for ascertaining whether an applicant's knowledge of English was sufficient to predict success in college. When Cornell University first opened its doors in 1868, although it enrolled the largest entering class of any American university up to that time (412 students), it soon decided to restrict admission to high-school graduates who could demonstrate a knowledge of English that rivaled what an accomplished college senior knew about Latin. Cornell published in its annual

Register and Catalogue a specimen examination on English grammar. The *Register* counseled applicants that "although perfect answers to all the questions are not indispensable, a near approach to perfection is required in all cases."[5] It warned further that, typically, about 15 percent of applicants were rejected, above all on account of deficiencies in their knowledge of English grammar, and that many students were admitted only conditionally.

A handful of sample questions shows that Cornell was setting decidedly advanced standards. Here are some questions that can be answered briefly:

> Use the word *iron*, (*a*) as an adjective; (*b*) as an [*sic*] noun; (c) as a verb.
>
> What is meant by an *exception?* give several instances of exceptions to rules of grammar.
>
> What is meant by one word *governing* another?[6]

And here, a question that would take longer to answer and for which applicants could draw on their knowledge of other languages, French as well as Latin and Greek, and even Anglo-Saxon or German:

> Give the meaning, formation and derivation of the following words: virtuously, autobiography, hospitable, journalist, circumvolution, disenthrall, inconsequent, interlineation, dissatisfy, quadrennial, worthlessness, contemporaneous.

And here, a question that, given that perfect answers are nearly "indispensable," must have intimidated many applicants. For the more accomplished applicants, it posed a challenge that made for a bit of fun:

> Turn into grammatical prose the following verses, placing the words in natural order, and supplying ellipses:
>
> Meanwhile the south-wind rose, and with black wings
> Wide hovering, all the clouds together drove
> From under heaven; the hills to their supply

> Vapor, and exhalation dusk and moist,
> Sent up amain; and now the thicken'd sky
> Like a dark ceiling stood; down rush'd the rain
> Impetuous, and continued till the earth
> No more was seen; the floating vessel swum
> Uplifted, and secure with beaked prow
> Rode tilting o'er the waves; all dwellings else
> Flood overwhelm'd, and them with all their pomp
> Deep under water roll'd; sea covered sea,
> Sea without shore.

The source of the passage is not identified, nor is an identification asked for. Experienced readers would recognize here the description of the biblical flood. More experienced readers, noting the blank verse, even if they have not read *Paradise Lost,* may well have been able to divine the source. What the examiner is looking for, however, requires first that the applicant isolate the main verb in each of the clauses, around which the accompanying words will be rearranged to create the "natural order." Other skills were required as well; for instance, the ability to recognize that "their" refers to the "clouds," that "supply" here is a noun, that "vapor" is the direct object of "sent up," and that "dusk" (meaning "darkish" and "gloomy," *OED,* 1 and 2) and "moist" contribute to the idea that this vapor will replenish the clouds as they drop the rain, so that the five words following "Vapor" constitute something akin to an appositive. Far from settling for the sort of information about literature that students fed with Shaw's *Outlines of English Literature* needed to produce, this exercise puts worthy applicants to work making intelligent use of their native language. And while it does not presuppose knowledge of any particular literary work, it goes well beyond Vassar's English examination in testing an applicant's literary experience and sensibility. By including the passage from an epic poem, it gave knowledgeable exam-takers the opportunity to engage with highly sophisticated writing from the past, a curious foretaste of what they might encounter in college. The instructions enhanced the possibility that adroit applicants would take pleasure in playing with Milton's fustian. Above all, the exam-makers valued the importance, beyond the ability to reproduce information, of achieving understanding. Had the participants in the *Pall Mall*

Gazette's virtual symposium been interested, this examination might have stimulated them to imagine a future in which English literature could be rendered an object of study without spoiling its beauty.

IN 1872–73, Harvard began a campaign to promote the study of English in secondary schools. Its annual catalog announced a stricter requirement that would provide an index with which to judge each applicant's intelligence and understanding: newly matriculated students would now be expected to read prose aloud. Applicants were advised to practice by reading Goldsmith's *Vicar of Wakefield*. Prizes were to be awarded to the best performers. This procedure soon gave way to something more ambitious—and, given the rising number of applicants, more practical. The university established a highly articulated system of written examinations that tested fourteen different subjects. For the first time "English Composition" joined the many other subjects that were tested *before* admission could be granted. The catalog described the requirement as follows: "Each candidate will be required to write a short English Composition, correct in spelling, punctuation, grammar, and expression, the subject to be taken from such works of standard authors as shall be announced from time to time. The subject for 1874 will be taken from one of the following works: Shakespeare's Tempest, Julius Caesar, and Merchant of Venice; Goldsmith's Vicar of Wakefield; Scott's Ivanhoe, and Lay of the Last Minstrel."[7]

The inclusion of literary works was new, and its implications would be wide-ranging. The examiners set the texts, which were to vary from year to year, to promote a greater range of literary experience among high-school students generally. Candidates for admission would now be expected to be familiar with several books announced in advance. In the entrance exam, just one of the books would serve as the basis for an essay. The aim was simply to elicit writing samples on a common subject, the better to judge among applicants comparatively. When the examination for 1879 was given, the examiners, although they acknowledged they had gone too far in "tempering justice with too much mercy," failed 157 of the 316 applicants.[8] The admissions committee, chaired by LeBaron Briggs, expressed dissatisfaction with the exam itself on many counts, and yet acknowledged that they had been unable to conceive a better one. But they supplemented it with a second exercise that asked for corrections of faults in excerpts drawn from essays composed by previous applicants. A few years later, before admitting an applicant, they began taking into account all the prose that each applicant produced while writing on the fourteen different subjects on which he was being examined.

Harvard's examiners gave a good deal of thought to what could be learned from the exams. They observed that students commonly assumed that the only course in which good writing mattered was composition and that many secondary-school teachers seemed to think an essay that had no "faults" in grammar, spelling, punctuation, or paragraphing was to be praised. Applicants and their teachers alike needed to understand that a vigorous style trumps accuracy and that intelligent thought, not an absence of errors, makes for good writing.

The seriousness with which the Harvard English faculty took the English examination is manifest in various essays that they published about its workings and results.[9] (These were distributed to more than two hundred high schools.) In a report on "The Harvard Admission Examination in English," Briggs called attention to how important it is for examiners to apply appropriate standards when deciding which essays warrant passing marks. The report reproduced in their entirety two student essays on the story of Viola in *Twelfth Night*. Of the first, Briggs acknowledged he was "ashamed to print it as part of a successful examination." He explained that he included it to reveal how lenient the examiners need to be and how much more important an applicant's ability to write is than his knowledge of specific details. He quoted a second essay, which manifestly lacks "vigor," to show how weighted down a student's prose can be when his high-school hours have been given to producing translations from Latin.

Briggs also quoted extensively from essays on *Pride and Prejudice*, chiefly to manifest how pervasively "the fancied necessity of infusing morality somewhere" compromises students' writing.[10] This, he speculated, must be in large measure due to encouragements on the part of their instructors to suppose that the purpose of reading is to deduce a moral from every story. Here is the first paragraph from an essay quoted at length to illustrate the writer's "vicious morality":

> What a strange paradox of character Darcy at first seems? You hardly can account for it. It may seem unnatural when first you think of it. But think. Know you not many of your friends whose actions seem to be inconsis-

tent. Aye, look you at your own. Think how often you astonish yourself, as well as those who know you, by your various actions and then look at Darcy.

"None but a cynic can fail to sympathize with the writer of this theme," Briggs remarked, for the grief that lies ahead of him as a student at Harvard, where no one will suffer such "Gush." Illiteracy, even immorality, will be overlooked, "but the blatant moral oratory of a man who thinks no better of himself cannot be lived down in a four years' course."[11] Briggs concluded his essay, without rancor or complaint, by acknowledging that the chief characteristic of admissions essays is their utter dullness.

The practice of setting texts as a basis for securing writing samples spread to other institutions. Notably, it reached the University of Michigan almost immediately, and with far-reaching effects. In the early 1870s, President Angell had begun having faculty members inspect the state's secondary schools. He then created a list of feeder schools that could send their graduates directly to the university with no need for an examination. Meanwhile, the university continued to hold oral entrance examinations for students from other schools. For the English component of the exam, applicants were expected to demonstrate a detailed knowledge of the chapters on punctuation, capitals, figures, versification, poetry, and the study of the English language as set out in a standard rhetoric textbook. By 1878, applicants to the university's Department of Science, Literature, and the Arts needed to pass a new written examination on specified books they had studied in high school. That year, applicants were expected to choose from the following subjects: "The Story of Brutus, from Shakespeare's Julius Caesar; The Story of Amy Robsart, from Kenilworth; [or] The Story of Tiny Tim, from the Christmas Carol." It proved possible for the university to create this requirement because most applicants came from the state's public schools, which shared a sufficiently common curriculum. The requirement ensured an important step forward: secondary-school students would now be reading whole literary works. But, as at Harvard, the examiners were less interested in ascertaining whether examinees could reproduce information than in gauging the overall quality of each person's writing. The annual *Circulars* regularly reported that "a large proportion of those who seek admission to the University are found to be very deficient in their preparation in English."[12]

The requirement that high-school students read long narratives—whether these were dramas by Shakespeare or novels by the likes of Walter Scott and Charles Dickens—in time effected a massive educational change for the better. A well-written literary narrative is an intricate human creation, the result of thousands of choices and decisions made by its author. Reading such a work involves not only extensive use of memory, but associative thinking, reflection, and contemplation. It builds new circuits in the brain and promotes new neural connections that lead the reader to personal insights. It occasions making reasoned judgments. Sometimes it promotes empathetic connections. It requires and develops stamina.

Within a few short years, the English examination given at Michigan would become more far reaching and rigorous. Applicants were expected to analyze the grammar and rhetoric of several passages. They were advised to prepare for the exam by making regular use of a good dictionary and rhetoric textbook, by using annotated editions of whatever masterpiece they were studying, and by writing at least one original essay every week for two years. In the mid-1890s, applicants were also advised to be well versed in English classics and to be in the habit of "memorizing . . . notable passages, both in prose and poetry," as "all-important for the development of a correct taste in language and literature"; to be reasonably familiar with "the lives and character" of the authors they were reading and of "the history of their times"; and to cultivate a "good knowledge of the chronological order and leading characteristics of the principal modern English writers."[13] It was impossible of course to test the full extent of an applicant's preparation. The admissions exam in English required only "two essays of not less than two hundred words," one of which was to concern a set text and the other to be written out of personal experience. But the advice about how to prepare for the exam betokened a large change in what constituted the study of English in college, where courses on literature were multiplying. The actual exam permitted applicants who had not yet developed a capacity to demonstrate rich understanding of the text to get by with a show of basic information. Still, the requirement that high-school students read whole literary works and be able to write about them proved to be a decisive turning point. It ensured that the study of literature in English would hereafter be considered fundamental to the subject, and that writing about literary works would become a standard practice. In the early 1890s the National Educational

Association's Committee of Ten put its stamp of approval on the idea that every high school should require four years of English study.

The admissions instruments administered by most colleges before the 1890s suggest that, when it came to examining literature, the Englishmen who argued that it could not be properly done were not merely attempting to preserve the status quo. They had good reason to expect that it would result in diminishing the pleasures to be had in reading literature and would render its study a mere duty. The study of literature in high schools and colleges did not immediately move away from the methods by which students had been examined on the information provided in manuals. Gradually, some institutions developed testing instruments that were mutually beneficial to both the test-takers and the evaluators. Cornell's specimen entrance examination on the language provided a model for how such an instrument could work to the advantage of both the evaluators and the applicants. It enabled the admissions committee to gauge what each applicant had learned about the workings of English, and it gave applicants an opportunity to learn something on the spot as they made an unexpected use of that knowledge. In chapter 14, we will consider how Cornell's instructors went on to devise English literature examinations with the mutual advantage of both exam-takers and exam-makers in mind.

THE PRACTICE OF setting entrance examinations on literary works could be deployed for other purposes as well. At the very moment that Oxford was laying plans for its new English School (it opened in 1894), the newly founded Stanford University in California introduced a variation on the kind of English entrance exam that made writing samples available to those who evaluated applications for admission. The university's founding president, David Starr Jordan, took an active part in recruiting students and in creating the English examination. A noted ichthyologist, Jordan had been educated at Cornell, and was subsequently mentored by Harvard's Louis Agassiz. He brought to California an active interest in the field of eugenics, which led to his publication of a widely influential volume titled *The Blood of the Nation: A Study of Races Through the Survival of the Unfit*. This interest manifested itself in several English entrance examinations that concerned *The Merchant of Venice* and posed questions about characters whose position as social outsiders contrasted with that of the principals.

The young men and women who made application to be part of Stanford's second entering class were required to write about a dialogue between Portia, the wealthy heiress whose late father has set up a demanding test for anyone who would woo her, and the Prince of Morocco, whose purpose in coming to Belmont is to sue for her hand. The passage differed in two respects from those typically given elsewhere. It afforded prominence to a relatively minor character, and it italicized several words and phrases to be commented on. Morocco's first words call attention to his unusual appearance: "Mislike me not for my complexion, / The *shadow'd livery* of the burnish'd sun."[14] The Prince goes on to propose that if a suitor who is "the fairest creature *northward* born" could be brought onto the scene, an "*incision*" into each man's body would show "whose blood is reddest." Having thus defended his "complexion" and challenged an imagined rival, he ends his opening gambit by proclaiming "I would not change this hue," and by offering Portia a position of royalty, "Except to steal your thoughts, gentle queen." Portia's reply explains that if she were free to choose among suitors, "Yourself, renowned prince, *then stood* as fair / As any comer I have look'd on yet." Applicants were expected to identify the play, to describe the situation, to name the speakers, and to gloss the italicized words and phrases.

We don't have evidence about how the applicants responded to this prompt. Nor do we know just what Jordan and other evaluators may have been looking for. What is clear, however, is that the examination put applicants on notice that they needed to attend to issues of cultural and racial differences; and it did so by highlighting a dramatic context that precisely concerned marriage and thus the possibility of racially mixed offspring. Over the next few years Stanford's entrance exams continued to feature *The Merchant of Venice* and brought to the fore ideas of race and racial hierarchy that were of utmost interest to the university's president. Applicants were asked, "By what line of argument does the Prince of Morocco persuade himself to choose the golden casket?" Other exams varied the focus by posing questions about Shylock: In his speech denouncing Antonio's Christian behavior, what is to be made of Shylock's reference to his "tribe" and his "sacred nation"? . . . "Was Shylock treated unjustly? Give reasons for your answer." If these writing prompts were given with a view to eliciting, indirectly, information about each applicant's ideas about race, this was left unspoken. In any event, the exams were not incompatible with the goal of testing students' knowledge of English. It would be of interest, however, to have from Stanford's evaluators the sort of report that Briggs and the Harvard admissions committee provided about what they had learned from the required writing samples.[15]

11

Taking Notes

What professors say they teach is often different from what students hear, or what they write in their notebooks, or what they say they remember learning through the haze of alumni nostalgia.

—CAROLINE WINTERER, *The Culture of Classicism*

"I GOT TEN TIMES more from my father," a distinguished graduate of Princeton once remarked, "than I got in college."[1] The father, the Rev. Joseph Ruggles Wilson, was a teacher of rhetoric and oratory in theological seminaries in the Carolinas. The son, Thomas, had always loved hearing him preach. The two of them talked endlessly about how to train ministerial students who were to hold forth from the pulpit. Tommy (as he was called) dreamed of one day being an influential public speaker.

In 1873 the elder Wilson, who had been a leading figure in the Presbyterian Church of the Confederate States of America, sent his son to Davidson College, a Presbyterian institution favored among Southern families. Tommy found the instruction there far inferior to what he was accustomed to receiving from his father, and he went back home. After what we would now call a gap year, in hopes of finding a curriculum that would prepare him for a career in public service, he enrolled at the College of New Jersey in Princeton. Again, dissatisfaction set in. This time it had to do both with what he was getting in college (plenty of lectures) and with what he was not getting. Rhetoric, oratory, and English literature occupied but a tiny space in the curriculum. At this point the young Thomas Woodrow Wilson's ambitions might more readily have had him imagining that one day he would be president of the United States than that he would become president of his university. He nonetheless stuck out the four years, graduated with distinction, studied law, earned a PhD from Johns Hopkins, and, after brief teaching stints elsewhere, returned to his alma mater as a professor of Political Science. A commanding lecturer, he became one of most popular teachers in the college. In 1902 he was named president of Princeton University and set about pursuing thoroughgoing reforms in the undergraduate curriculum.

Since the 1840s, critics of the curriculum at the College of New Jersey (its official name until 1896) had been advocating that the time given to the classical languages be reduced in order to make room to study the English language and its literature. Nothing much changed until the 1870s. Various holders of the Holmes Professorship of Belles Lettrès passed through a revolving door, and the position sometimes remained vacant. Then, in the same year that Wilson began his abortive sojourn at Davidson, Princeton appointed an adjunct professor of rhetoric and of the English language to provide for the increasing number of students enrolling. The Rev. Theodore Whitfield Hunt, AM, had graduated from the college in 1865 and stayed on for two years as a tutor. Then he headed to Europe for studies that introduced him to philology. Returning to his alma mater as an adjunct, his first assignment was to teach large lecture courses on rhetoric to the freshmen and sophomores.

Hunt attempted to move rhetoric in the direction of literary study by teaching it as "rhetorical science." He employed this phrase in the title of an article that he published during his first year of teaching. "We hold most tenaciously to the doctrine, novel as it is," Hunt wrote, "that there is no such thing possible as rightly teaching the science and the art of Rhetoric without a thorough knowledge of that science and art, as expressed in literary forms."[2] Hunt simplified this mouthful by telling students that "rhetorical science" would be emerging as the gateway to the study of English literature. His article had nothing to say about orations.

Through much of the U.S. the esteemed place of the orator had been eclipsed. Colleges were downplaying the traditional rhetorical training that had made giving an oration at commencement the highest honor a student could attain. As established a place as rhetoric had held for centuries in Western education, most colleges now gave it scant scope, and it is doubtful that many students regarded it as their favorite subject. Increasingly, professors of rhetoric understood their principal responsibility as teaching composition. At Princeton, despite the presence of an associate professor of elocution, freshmen had declamations only a few times a year. Practice in public speaking took place principally during the first of the three academic terms when, on Saturdays, the student body, the faculty, and the president assembled in the chapel to hear seniors perform oratorical exercises. As for Hunt's two rhetoric courses, each met for only a single hour a week and at an inauspicious time. At four o'clock on Friday afternoons, the sophomore class, about a hundred strong, listened to him lecture. On Saturdays, the freshmen, in addition to being required to attend the seniors' exercises, had to attend either a lecture by Hunt or an exercise presided over by the teacher of elocution. If a clock was visible in the lecture hall, we can imagine that every student, even the note-takers, directed a good bit of attention to the movements of its hands.

The textbook that Hunt assigned, *A Manual of Composition and Rhetoric,*[3] had been written by a local hero. John Seely Hart graduated from the college in the 1830s and then built a reputation writing textbooks. Princeton brought him back in the 1860s as an occasional lecturer, and he served briefly as the Holmes Professor.[4] Hunt's students found that "Hart's rhetoric," as it was known, dealt almost entirely with written discourse. Its distinction lay in its copious provision of examples. Hunt held students responsible for what was lodged in five chapters, on diction, sentences, figures, versification, and poetry, respectively. Tommy Wilson found himself impatient with all this. An entry in his diary reads as follows: "Spent most of this morning studying Hart's rhetoric which is an immensely stupid book. Some of his ideas are extremely crude."[5] That same year, the college founded its first newspaper, the *Princetonian,* and Wilson discovered there an apt outlet for his criticisms.

Dissatisfied with Hunt's rhetoric course, Wilson joined the American Whig Literary Society and became its speaker (i.e., president). Here he could craft and deliver orations and take part in debates. He found the standard much beneath what he had known back home, and he kept up frequent correspondence with his father about this. In his spare time, he read the great orators: Daniel Webster, Edward Everett, and, above all, Edmund Burke. He would sometimes find a private spot to practice reading a whole oration aloud.[6] Princeton's rhetoric curriculum be damned, he would become a commanding public speaker.

A VISIT TO THE Princeton archives, twenty-first century. You enter the reading room through glass doors. The archivists working on the outside can watch what goes on within. Inside you find individual tables, laptops on most of them, and various archival materials that readers have requested. Here and there someone is taking notes by hand on a bright orange piece of paper. The staff supplies these papers, a conspicuous hole punched near the middle of each one. Orange papers with holes, the only papers visitors may carry into or out of the room in an era of tightening security. The archivists have delivered to my table an old narrow college notebook, its bright red spine at the top. The front and back covers are multicolored. The "Finding Aid" promises that this exercise book will contain a student's notes taken in Theodore Hunt's sophomore rhetoric course, the one that met late on Friday afternoons once a week. You open it to find two pages, vertically arranged. On each page you see printed blue lines, eighteen on the top page, eighteen on the bottom. Only on the lower half is the handwriting neat, even handsome, and easy to read. The script on the top page is upside down. When you turn the notebook over, you see writing in a different hand. It is a record made by some other student in a different course.

As you flip rapidly through these pages, there's suddenly a reason to stop. A page looks altogether different. Instead of running discourse, the writing is set out in columns, sideways. There are numbers and, apparently, surnames. *This is a scorecard from a baseball game—what's that doing here? This wasn't written in the lecture hall.* From this point on, the pages are almost entirely blank, just a few more class notes and the other half of the scorecard recording the visitors' outputs. The writing on these scorecards is in another hand. One gives a date, April 21. In addition to listing the names of the players, it provides the surname of the umpire: *Duffield.* Curious. The Finding Aid names "John F. Duffield" as the note-taker.[7] *Who was this guy?* A little sleuthing seems in order.

Various wags have remarked to the effect that lecturing is simply a mindless process that transfers, through the instrument of a fountain pen, what is found in a professor's notebook into the students' notebooks. But notebooks filled up by students in a lecture hall are not transcripts. Like scorecards, they record information while something is unfolding. Duffield's notes preserve an imperfect and subjective record of what he was hearing in Hunt's class. Evidence of industry mixes with occasional evidence of distraction. His notes tell us what, at a given moment, he wrote down. We can see where he crossed something out, or made a correction, or squeezed in a few words between the lines or in the margin. Occasionally, we spot a blank space where something is missing, a surname, an unfamiliar technical term, or even a key word needed to make sense of ones before and after it. As is the case when we look into any notebook, we can be sure that we are missing a good deal. This is the nature of note-taking: it omits taken-for-granted features of the surrounding context.

Perhaps most researchers who look into a student's notebook do so to learn about the instructor's approach to a subject. But the student is not merely a recorder, and the notebook is not simply a window. Students' notes bring us closer to their own hidden internal intellectual processes, to attending, choosing, reflecting, digesting. They give imperfect access to how two people—the one speaking, and also the one recording—were thinking. Any extant notebook or textbook with annotations in the margin someone saved. But for what purpose? a memory of an especially beloved professor, or of a favorite course? a memento from college? background possibly helpful in future courses? a blueprint for use when one becomes a teacher? We wonder, *Who was this note-taker, and what did he go on to do? How did the notebook finally make its way, probably after many years of benign neglect, into the safety of an official repository?* Someone realized that the notebook had accrued historical value. Someone else, specially trained in the science of preservation, cared for it, cataloged it, gave it a number and a place on a shelf, made it available to anyone who could offer a respectable reason for looking at it. Someone put in place rules for allowing access and for denying it, including rules that protect privacy. *Have other researchers taken an interest in this notebook?* Every interaction between researchers and carefully archived material enlarges its significance.

ATOP MY TABLE in the archives a second old notebook has joined the first. The Finding Aid indicates that both notebooks were created during Hunt's sophomore rhetoric course in 1873–74.[8] This was Hunt's first year teaching and the first time he gave the course. Some archives hold multiple sets of notes on a given professor's course, all from different years, which facilitates exploring changes over time. This pair of notebooks, created by two students sitting in the same room, hearing the same lectures at the same time, enables us also to compare how John Duffield and now William Van Lennep, both from Princeton's class of '76, processed the lectures. Their notes yield evidence that they were conscientious and that they each experienced, not necessarily at the same moment, difficulty understanding what the lecturer was getting at. The notes thus provide a point of entry into curricular culture in the long and awkward transitional dance that had begun with studying rhetoric and that gradually issued into reading actual literary works.

Before probing what the notes can tell us about how Hunt's course contributed to and retarded the study of literature at Princeton, to enrich our sense of context, it will help to know a bit more about the note-takers. Van Lennep and Duffield were seniors during Thomas Woodrow Wilson's freshman year. They heard Hunt's sophomore rhetoric lectures three years before Wilson did.

John Fletcher Duffield was born in 1857, the son of Princeton's professor of mathematics, the Rev. John Thomas Duffield. The *Nassau Herald* for the class of 1876 (a forerunner of Facebook) tells us that he was called "Duff" and that he was a Presbyterian. As a junior and senior he played on Princeton's baseball team, which competed against other colleges and some early professional teams, including the Athletics of Philadelphia. He was honored as a commencement orator at graduation in 1876. Four years later he received an MD degree from Columbia. He practiced medicine in the New York City area and served for many years as the class of '76 historian. He died in 1912, at age fifty-four. His widow entrusted her late husband's college notes to the Princeton archives. It turns out that the notes that begin at the opposite end of this rhetoric notebook had been taken by John's brother George, class of '73, while listening to sermons on the life of Christ given by the college president, James McCosh.

William Bird Van Lennep, our other note-taker, was four years older than John Duffield. Born in Istanbul to missionary parents, he prepared for college at the Sedgwick Institute in Great Barrington, Massachusetts. His father had attended Amherst College and held a doctor of divinity degree. The *Herald* tells us he was called "Van" and that he was a Presbyterian. (Even as late as the 1870s, this latter point may have been not merely informative but reassuring to the dominant group.) Van belonged to the glee club and the crew team. Occasionally he played on the baseball team as a ringer. Like Duff, Van studied medicine after graduation. He took his degree at the Hahnemann Medical College in Philadelphia, with the highest honors in his class. Afterwards he continued his studies in Paris, Vienna, and London. Returning to Philadelphia, he practiced as a surgeon and served on Hahnemann's faculty as a teacher of pathology, anatomy, and surgery. He was one of the founders of the American College of Surgeons and published widely in the field of homeopathic medicine.[9] His notebook was accessioned by the Princeton archives in 1933, a decade and a half after his death.

Right from the start Van Lennep seems to have had it in mind that he would be saving his notebook after the course ended. He wrote his notes, as Duffield did, into a bound volume with a red spine and multicolored face. This one opens like an ordinary book. Pasted on the front cover is a rectangle with his name and "Princeton, 76." Inside, in his own hand, he has written, "Please return to Wm. B. Van Lennep." The notes start with a title page identifying "Rev. Theodore Hunt A.M." as "Adjunct Professor of Rhetoric & the English Language in Princeton College." The page also states "for the Sophomore Year 1873–74, of the Class of '76." The facing page includes a penciled note in the margin, manifestly written later: "Grade 90." (Princeton used a scale rising up to 100, with anything below 50 a failing mark.) At the top of the page Van Lennep has noted that he anticipates a biennial examination at the end of the academic year. Here he lists what students will be responsible for: "'Hart's Rhetoric.' 5 Chapters i.e. 'Diction.,' 'Sentences,' 'Figures,' 'Versification,' and Poetry. French [*sic:* "Trench" was the surname of the author of another textbook] on Words. 5 first Lectures. Lectures on the 'Art of Composition.' Lectures on Philology."

The rhetoric section of the biennial exam had been newly instituted. The 1870–71 *Catalogue of the Officers and Students of the College of New Jersey* printed a full copy of the 1869–70 examination: it shows that while students were expected to answer detailed questions on Latin, Greek, chemistry, ethics, political economy, modern history, science and religion, and metaphysics, there were no questions on rhetoric, the English language, or English literature. Until this year rhetoric, a merely ornamental course that met only one hour a week, had been deemed too trivial for inclusion. The new lecturer, known to have just returned from prestigious studies in Europe, would be offering an innovative approach to what had long seemed to students a tired and trivial old subject.

The reverse side of Van Lennep's first leaf provides a table of contents for Hunt's lectures. One heading here is "Rhetorical Science." (It seems unlikely that the students knew about the article that Hunt was writing for publication. But with increasing frequency they had been hearing the word *science* used to confer prestige upon various curricular practices.) Following the contents page there are 165 numbered pages of notes. The writing is so neat throughout, the crossings out and corrections so rare, that Van Lennep may have first made notes on other papers during the lecture and then copied them into this notebook afterwards. The notebook concludes on page 165 with the words "*Grand Finale.* Thus endeth Soph Year."

Duffield also identifies himself at the head of his notebook and adds "Sophomore Year." Comparing his notes with Van Lennep's, we see that for each class both note-takers divided the day's notes into two parts. Their notes on the second part, the "Lecture proper," are generally more alike than those recorded under the earlier heading "Analysis." This suggests that Hunt preserved something of the older recitation system by beginning with a measure of analytical interaction between instructor and students. For a class that Van Lennep heads "A Liberal Culture," his notes under *Analysis* are set out in numbered points, each delivered in a complete sentence. Duffield's notes in the *Analysis* section show that while Hunt was going on about "mental culture," he heard Hunt say something about "Shakespeare and Burns." Only Van Lennep's *Analysis* makes it clear that Hunt presented these writers as exceptions to a general rule that the best writers had extensive formal education. (That Duffield later got the point can be seen in his notes on the lecture proper.) Van Lennep's notes show where Hunt was going with all this. He was emphasizing the importance for educated persons, whether businessmen, doctors, or lawyers, to have "general culture." This points to a tacit understanding between Hunt and the students that his lecturing aimed at enriching their capacities for life after graduation. The quality of their notes shows that, at least implicitly, both Van Lennep and Duffield understood that the actions required in taking careful notes enhanced the whole process of their learning.

That Hunt casually mentioned particular writers by name suggests a purpose that would come into focus for the students only later, when his lectures would include telling them directly about what there will be to read in life after graduation. Hunt often named authors who were thought to be the best writers. (Shakespeare is the only one to be read beyond mere "portions." Chaucer, Spenser, Milton, and Dryden come in for mention.) In the first part of the course Duffield was recording the names of more authors than Van Lennep did. Later, in notes on a lecture about Celtic writers, Van Lennep got down more names than Duffield, including Swift, Goldsmith, and Burke. By this point he seems to have understood that recording the names of writers had some value but was not as important as noting down that Sheridan's writing shows "the true Irish character." If Hunt spelled out what he meant by that assertion, neither note-taker recorded it. (Sometimes Hunt's lectures seem to have offered little more than might be extracted from Shaw's *Manual.*) Still, the students were learning about what there was to read; and the likes of Van Lennep and Duffield were being equipped to think about what books they might want to acquire for their personal libraries.

While in some lectures Hunt freely dropped the names of writers, in others—on rhetorical science, on philology, on the history of languages, and even on "The Study of the Best Orators"—he rarely mentioned anyone by name. Strikingly, however, both note-takers record that in his lecture titled "The Study of Philology," he singled out professors from other colleges who were promoting a philological approach to language. "We are glad to notice," Van Lennep records him saying, "an interest in the study of philology at Harvard through Professor Child, who is very high in this branch; Yale college is fast approaching through Prof. Whitney. Lafayette said that in proportion to her age there was no culture superior to that of the English."[10]

Here we can see that even an industrious and intelligent note-taker is not able to make everything clear. The point about Lafayette seems cryptic, and Van Lennep perhaps thought Hunt was referring to the French hero of the Revolutionary War. (Duffield accurately recorded that Hunt mentioned Lafayette College's Francis March by name.) The phrase "very high in this branch" sounds like rough paraphrase. Duffield's notes suggest a richer idea about what was going on at Yale by Hunt's mention of a second philologist, Hadley. (James Hadley was professor of Greek; Whitney, professor of Sanskrit and instructor in modern languages. Whitney kept up a voluminous correspondence with March.) More importantly, Duffield noted that Hunt went on to quote one of the brothers Grimm to the effect that "English will be a universal language."

Some of the surrounding notes help make sense of all this. Hunt had been talking about the history of college education in the United States. Both note-takers paraphrased his points in ways that suggest that they did not fully understand his drift. Here is Van Lennep: "In early history the classics and English were separated. This is not generally abandoned but is going out. The study of English is likely to go to the other extreme—no classics. Everything seems to call for it. There is a tendency to shut ourselves up within the language we are studying."[11]

And here is Duffield: "There used to be no English Department in our colleges, used to teach Latin & Greek & not English. The Scientific world has demanded the study of English. We are bound to be thoroughly English in our culture. The tendency is to shut ourselves up in the element of the language, to the exclusion of all else. Here is the function of comparative Philology. Instead of isolated study of a single language."

Duffield's notes on the previous *Analysis* part of class, though still more fragmentary, show that before this lecture there had been talk about "comparative philology" as a "new science, vital to [the] English student." "More than the grammar of the Language needed, we need to know its genius, origin, application, & power, all with special reference to prose composition." Clearly, Hunt knew about what March had introduced into the curriculum at Lafayette. Not ready to do that sort of work himself, he was nonetheless convinced that studying comparative philology—and the English language itself—was the wave of the future.

Talking about what was going on elsewhere, praising developments that would transform the old study of rhetoric into a new study of language and literature—Hunt was not telling students what their rhetoric course was doing, but what a college education in the future was going to be like. His point was to bring everything (and there was much more, about unwelcome criticism of the classical languages, about the superiority of German scholarship, about the importance of studying Anglo-Saxon) back to the topic of "prose composition." Although the biennial examination would now be including questions on rhetoric, it was not going to be asking students to name famous authors or to tell what was going on with language and literature in other colleges. It would be asking them about words, sentences, and figures of speech. The students were taking notes for reasons other than simply preparing for an exam.

Meanwhile they would be writing prose compositions. Hunt wanted them to be ready to live in a world where science, business, and emerging middle-class values would show that they had studied Greek and Latin in vain. "We must become more distinctly English," Duffield wrote in the *Analysis*, "or [we will be] less acceptable & influential to the people." (Probably Hunt meant, and Duffield understood, that college graduates needed to use the English language well. Whether and to what extent this might have been thought to entail imitation of English nationals is unclear.)

How, we might wonder, did students like Duffield, Van Lennep, and their cohort feel about what Hunt was telling them? His lectures were informing them about an education they were not getting. Was he trying to provoke envy for the students at Harvard and Yale? or perhaps covering his own sense of inadequacy by referring knowledgeably to what was going on in the "leading institutions"? Hunt was manifestly new to teaching. He was aware that Princeton's curriculum was out of date and out of touch. He told the students that it was "not right that the best students of English should be Germans" (Duffield). For one hour a week, late on a Friday afternoon, he was in no position to introduce the kinds of studies that they needed. A rhetoric course that could be called "scientific" might sound more respectable in the changing academy. Studying "comparative philology" and Anglo-Saxon, however, was unlikely to yield the kinds of pleasures that students found in reading literature. Nor would these subjects prepare students for the world in which they would have to make their way after graduation.

Tommy Wilson must have had plenty of company in finding the two rhetoric courses taught by Hunt useless. Perhaps Duffield eventually assessed his sophomore course similarly. In any event, during the spring he seems to have found what he regarded as a better way to spend his Friday afternoons than to attend Hunt's lecture. The largest difference between his notebook and Van Lennep's is that, once the third term began on 21 April, his note-taking petered out.

Whether or not Duffield secured permission to absent himself from the required rhetoric course, the many blank pages in his notebook point to an otherwise hidden context in which Hunt was giving his course: the extraordinary popularity of baseball at Princeton. It was becoming America's pastime. When the Princeton nine made their way to New England to play Harvard and Yale, they had the support of their fellow students, who gladly paid a subscription to make the road trip possible. While Hunt busied himself with telling the students that their studies were not up to what their contemporaries were getting at those institutions, students from Princeton were keen to show their New England rivals that, in what counted to them most, they were the equal of the "leading institutions." Princeton's administration soon began supporting athletic activities in ways that they had never supported the literary societies. It created both a Faculty Committee on Outdoor Sports and an official advisory committee on athletics made up of alumni. In the 1890s Van Lennep would act as an advisor along with Duffield's younger brother Henry. Thomas Woodrow Wilson, who as a student had been head of the college's baseball association, would serve on both committees.[12]

DURING WILSON'S undergraduate days, the study of literature at Princeton was in great flux, much of it stirred up by students. We can see this in detail because, as it happens, an unusual number of student notebooks are extant from the years just after Duffield and Van Lennep graduated. The university had finally managed to hire, in James Ormsbee Murray, a professor of belles lettrès who from one year to the next conscientiously revised his courses. Unlike institutions that began offering elective courses in English, Princeton now introduced a required two-year English literature course for juniors and seniors. But the administration put a strict limitation on its scope. Murray lectured one hour a week to the whole junior class and one hour a week to the seniors. At first his plan was to cover writers from Chaucer to Burns and Byron. In May 1877, the newly founded *Princetonian* (Wilson was its managing editor), published a piece that voiced telling criticisms of the course. "From time immemorial," the anonymous writer began, "the editors of College magazines have beguiled their leisure time by picking flaws in the College curriculum."[13] He went on to complain: "One hour a week for two years is inadequate for obtaining any idea of the authors of our language. Could all this time be given to reading their works, it would not suffice. One week is devoted to Spenser, and perhaps a student who attends his other recitations could read one book of the Fairie Queen [*sic*]; such must be his knowledge of Spenser's poetry." (This was in fact just how much time Murray was dedicating to Spenser.) Then the writer turned a surprising—and more damning—criticism against his teacher:

"In fact, however, the time must be employed in committing names and dates. This is a fruitless method of study."

Murray had inherited the idea that students of literature were to be examined on names and dates. He knew quite well that one hour a week left little time for students to be reading more of *The Fairie Queene* than the story of Una and the Redcrosse Knight. The writer for the *Princetonian* proposed an immediate remedy for the problem: "let there be an elective course in English, during Junior and Senior year, equal to Latin and Greek." This, he explained, would not disturb the weekly required English course. It would add to it. He avowed that the new course would begin to bear fruit immediately in the students' own writing and in their debates. Beyond this, he made a prediction—and this was probably the sticking point: "That such a branch would be popular, needs no proof." More than any other subject competing for space within the traditional classical curriculum, English, casting a shadow over the classics, represented a threat to their dominance.

Murray felt himself grappling with the complex relations between what he referred to as "intrinsic study," carried out for its own sake, and "educational study," which had a more utilitarian purpose. He held intrinsic study in esteem and urged that young readers need the opportunity to experience prolonged engagement with excellent writers, because it trained them to teach themselves as they read.[14] Begrudgingly, he also acknowledged the necessity of employing conventional mechanisms for marking students and expected them to learn names and dates. But his lectures did not prepare them to be examined on the sort of matter that could be found in handbooks.

One student's notebook reveals something about how Murray examined his students. William Reed Barricklo, in the midst of his notes from the senior course in 1877–78, suddenly wrote down the words "Subjects for Examination," almost as if the lecturer had just casually reminded the students of its existence. Barricklo recorded the names he heard Murray list for them to study: "Dryden and Swift (first term notes), Gray, Cowper, Hume, Johnson, Burns, Byron."[15] The notebook shows that Murray had been lecturing on many more writers than he expected students to write about in the exam. It also suggests that Murray came to believe that assigning less work could result in studying with greater care and with pleasure. In fact, a student's notebook from a subsequent year shows that Murray abandoned his original plan and concentrated instead almost exclusively on Shakespeare and Milton. He was unusual among U.S. lecturers on the Bard in that he lectured on particular plays: *The Merchant of Venice, King Lear, The Tempest,* and *As You Like It.*

Another notebook, kept by a classmate of Wilson as they sat through Murray's lectures, reveals how radically he departed from his plan for seniors to hear about many authors of the eighteenth and early nineteenth centuries. Fifty-two of the ninety-seven pages in William Wilder's notebook are devoted to the life and writings of John Milton.[16] The notebook shows that during the first two terms Murray gave only fourteen (numbered) lectures, the first two rounding out the study of Shakespeare that had occupied the third term in junior year, followed by eight and a half on Milton. In "Lecture the Ninth," just before the Christmas recess, Murray proposed, apropos of *Paradise Lost,* that one ought not try to read the epic unless there was time to read it in its entirety. Students were probably relieved to hear this. But to reinforce their assumption (if not everyone's resolve) that someday they would read this famous work, Murray used this lecture and "Lecture the Tenth" in January to describe the epic in detail. He laid out the whole story-line from Book I through the final Book XII, where Adam and Eve must leave the garden. While he offered no sweeping generalizations about the meaning or the aesthetic value of the poem, he did not scruple to mention that Alexander Pope charged Milton with having made God sound like a "school divine," nor to add that he himself felt disappointed that Milton's God "lacks all warmth and tenderness." The notes also show that for other works by Milton, including some of the prose, Murray referred to particular pages in books that students were expected to be reading and copies of which they likely had to hand in the classroom.[17]

On February 12, after briefly considering Dryden and Restoration drama, Murray concluded the course with "Lecture the Fourteenth," on Pope. (In the third term, the seniors' courses no longer met. Seniors spent their time preparing for both oral and written examinations in all their subjects.) Although no copy of a final examination for the English course is extant, Barricklo's notebook and Wilder's both show that Murray had found a way to make knowing names and dates count for a relatively small portion of a student's grade for the course.

The better to reduce the weight given to demonstrating a knowledge of factual data on the year-end examination, Murray created an unrelated essay assignment for juniors. It came due during the term. Students were to work up, independently, an essay on a subject discontinuous with their study of English literature. As the field of literary criticism of the sort familiar to us was only just coming into its own, Murray was well aware that students had no training that would enable them to write critically about literature.[18] There was, however, an analogous precedent for his writing assignment. Colleges (including Princeton) typically awarded prizes at commencement for the best academic writing conducted apart from the curriculum. Any student who wished to enter the competition could work up an essay on some topic set in advance. To encourage independent study and to have another basis for evaluating his students' performance, Murray crafted his assignment on this model and set multiple topics to choose from. On the first page of Wilder's notes from junior year, he recorded that an essay would be due on January 10, on one of five topics: (1) Communism in America; (2) The Danger of Monopolies; (3) Hawthorne as a Novelist; (4) Poetic Justice; and (5) Greek Mythology.[19] When we turn the notebook around and page through Wilder's notes on the senior course, we find that, similarly, an independent essay was due on February 5, one week before the final lecture on Pope. The topics to choose from included "The Influence of Jefferson on our Political History," "The War with Afganistan," and "The 'Solid South.'"

BY THE LATE 1870S, then, Princeton had begun to make sweeping changes in the teaching of English. Besides the pressure that students were putting on the faculty for more literary study, the two professors of rhetoric and of belles lettrès, Hunt and Murray, were pushing the administration to purchase the latest editions of books in which students could read substantial amounts of English literature. Hunt went on to acquire for the library an important collection of books in and about the early history of the English language, and he began teaching Anglo-Saxon to graduate students. He made a name for himself as a key figure in defining what college "English" was to be when he published an article in the inaugural issue of the new Modern Language Association's journal (*PMLA*). It called attention to the widespread practice whereby most colleges were still devoting ten hours to foreign languages for every one hour allotted to study of English. Titled "The Place of English in the College Curriculum," Hunt's essay proposed that English should occupy a "prominent place" in every college student's program. It set out a vision of an expansive curriculum that would awaken a desire for a broad and deep knowledge of a new field yet to be plowed and cultivated. Hunt had written it not from the position of a "leading institution" but from that of an onlooker eager to get into the action.[20] Some months later President McCosh made an abrupt about-face. In debates about the elective system he had been the principal antagonist of Harvard's President Eliot, insisting that the classical curriculum not be disturbed. Now he informed the trustees that, while Princeton had long required Latin and Greek and had then made room for some French and German, since English is the medium through which students acquire knowledge, it must be regarded as having the "highest value."[21]

By 1887, although Princeton still had not established an English department, English courses were the most popular electives in the college.[22] Juniors could elect a survey from Chaucer to Pope with Hunt, or study Old and Middle English with him. Seniors could choose to study Gothic. Or they could elect Murray's survey of literature from Cowper to Tennyson, or take his Shakespeare elective and read *Othello, Macbeth, The Winter's Tale, Merchant of Venice,* and *Much Ado About Nothing.*

By the early 1890s the course offerings in English were more numerous. Freshmen were studying discourse and English philology and using a textbook written by Yale's Thomas Lounsbury. They also had on hand Hunt's own *Principles of Written Discourse* (1884). Sophomores studied English prose style using a textbook written by Francis March. Other textbooks by Hunt, *Representative English Prose and Prose Writers* (1887) and *Studies in Literature and Style* (1890), served as staples in advanced elective courses. Concurrently, all juniors and many seniors studied literature with Murray. He was now offering two electives for seniors, the one on Shakespeare and another on Victorian and American literature. The latter introduced students to Tennyson, Browning, Arnold, Carlyle, and Thackeray, and then to the Americans: Irving, Hawthorne, Bryant, Longfellow, Lowell, and William Prescott, author of remarkable narratives about the conquests of Mexico and Peru.

In 1893 the administration hired Bliss Perry away from Williams College and named him Professor of Oratory and Aesthetic Criticism. In addition to teaching rhetoric and elocution, Perry began offering elective courses on genres, one on poetry and drama, another on fiction. Courses on oratory were now required each year: elocution for freshmen, declamation for sophomores, and written orations (some of them delivered orally) for juniors and seniors. Composition was also required in all four years. The college encouraged students to write competitively and began awarding many more literary prizes than ever before. Two prizes were awarded to students for literary work done outside the curriculum.

In 1896, when the College of New Jersey celebrated its sesquicentennial and changed its official name to Princeton University, Professor Woodrow Wilson gave the keynote address. He titled it "Princeton in the Nation's Service." Six years later, he was named the university's thirteenth president and launched a major restructuring of the academic administration. The university would now, like other institutions, have departments of instruction based on separate academic disciplines, including a belatedly established Department of English with a head who reported directly to him. Wilson named his old rhetoric teacher, who had come to be known familiarly as "Granny Hunt," to the post. Wilson doubled the size of the faculty, hired top-notch recruits, and began a program of sweeping educational reform. Concerned to make each student's experience better than his own had been, he put in place a distinctive system of small group discussions called "preceptorials" that would supplement lectures, each overseen by a preceptor who had earned a PhD degree. Students now had a common two-year curriculum of general studies, followed by a concentration in one particular discipline of their choice. These conditions made it even more likely that students themselves would contribute something genuinely distinctive to their college's long-delayed attempt to answer the question "What would 'English' be?"

12

The Study of Masterpieces

What the universities can mainly do for you—
what I have found the University did for me, was, that it taught
me to read . . . so that I could go into the books . . . and
try anything I wanted to make myself master of.

—THOMAS CARLYLE, *On the Choice of Books*

"THE MOST DELIGHTFUL FEATURE of the history of college education in America," a recent Harvard graduate remarked in the opening paragraph of his first book, "is the constant expansion of the curriculum. . . . Never more rapid has been this enlargement and improvement than within the present decade."[1] The year was 1878, and the author had spent two years gathering information about the curricula, libraries, finances, and administrative workings of more than three hundred institutions of higher learning in the United States. His enthusiasm for the expanding opportunities to study new subjects owed a good deal to what he had experienced as a student. But his survey also turned up a pocket of stasis: "most colleges"—and he had reason to include his first-hand experience at Harvard here—"offer very meager opportunities for the study of the origin and growth of either our language or our literature." He observed, nonetheless, that at the University of Michigan students were able "to devote considerable attention" to English literature.[2] He offered no specifics. What he left unreported is worth looking into.

In the mid-1870s seniors at the University of Michigan could elect a course on English literature the likes of which were available almost nowhere else. (In chapter 14 we will see that students at Cornell had similar opportunities.)

The instructor had students reading in their entirety several well-known works from the sixteenth through the nineteenth centuries.[3] The course would soon metamorphose into a seminar called "Study of Masterpieces," in which students themselves did most of the teaching. Its design was the work of Moses Coit Tyler, Michigan's professor of English from 1867 until 1881. Tyler developed practices that inspired three interrelated breakthroughs in the history of teaching literature in the U.S.: the inauguration of English entrance exams that got high-school students throughout Michigan reading whole literary works; the creation of courses in which undergraduates studied aesthetically accomplished works in their entirety; and the formation of seminars in which students themselves did much of the teaching. The university's archives hold an ample collection of materials that enable us to see the kinds of work students did in the seminars.

The University of Michigan offered rich soil for the risks involved in teaching English literature differently from the ways it was treated in other colleges. Founded in 1817 and administratively restructured in 1850, the institution began to launch educational innovations that would make it the prototype for American research universities on the German model. Faculty were hired for their expert knowledge, without regard to their religious affiliation. Teachers experienced greater freedom to experiment than their counterparts in eastern institutions enjoyed. Instead of subjecting students to daily recitations, they provided them with lectures and laboratories. The policy proved controversial, and for a short time the university's regents managed to undermine it. But in the mid-1870s, the newly appointed president, James Burrill Angell, revived it. He also initiated a procedure that fostered a high-school curriculum that would prepare students throughout the state for entrance into the university. His plan became a model in devising standards for secondary schools, and it led to a process of regional accreditation that other states then followed. In this way Michigan consolidated the idea that a high-school education was a necessary and, under certain conditions, a sufficient prerequisite for entrance into college.[4] (Tyler contributed to Angell's plan by devising the kind of admissions exam we have seen in the chapter on entrance examinations, whereby applicants were required to write about particular literary works that they had studied in high school.)

MOSES TYLER WAS BORN in Connecticut and raised in Detroit. He enrolled at the University of Michigan in 1852. That year the chair of rhetoric and English literature lay unfilled. He withdrew and started over at Yale, where the requirement that he follow the traditional curriculum had little to do with the education he provided for himself. Tyler read widely in classic literature, copying out excerpts and making copious notes in his commonplace book. He found in a fellow student, Andrew Dickson White, someone who shared his interests in literature and history. The two would become life-long friends. After graduation White moved to Ann Arbor to serve as the professor of English and history at Michigan. He held the position for only a few years before serving abroad in the diplomatic service during the Civil War. In 1868 he became the founding president of Cornell University, where, included among the many innovations he contemplated, there was to be a School of English.

Meanwhile, Moses Tyler was jumping from one activity into another. He studied theology at Andover, served a short time as a minister, and suffered a nervous breakdown. He went to Boston, where he found a cure in a physical fitness regime. He married and soon had a young family. He left them behind while he went off to England to teach "musical gymnastics." There he lectured and published essays, interpreting American civilization to the English.[5] When he returned, he moved his family to Michigan, where he had been named White's successor. When he began teaching, his method was at first so conventional that no one could have predicted the university would soon be singled out for leading the country's way forward in English studies. Restlessness quickly set in, and Tyler moved to New York, where he edited the *Christian Union* in 1873–74. Then, just as suddenly, a year later he decided to go back to his old job at Michigan. This time he went right to work.

The breakthrough in the teaching of English literature that Tyler wrought at Michigan, assigning students to read literary works in their entirety, owed something to his own long quest to find a worthy anchor for his sustained attention. It was an era of innovation and technological advances: rail travel, instantaneous communication by telegraph, steam-powered printing presses and cheaper means of making paper. Teachers and students, the populace more generally, knew what it was to let one's mind wander and to flit about from one thing to the next. Lurid newspaper coverage of violence and fraud, pulp magazine stories of robberies and great escapes, Beadle's Dime Novels—they all fed readers' hunger for sensation. Tyler, longing amidst all this to write something that would prove lasting, accepted an offer from the publisher G. P. Putnam's Sons to write a survey of American literature. Soon after he began, he recognized that there was such a dearth of relevant secondary material about the colonial period that he would have to read every document for himself. As he did, he wrote out what he found in each one. In March 1878, in the midst of his teaching duties, he wrote Putnam's that dashing off a superficial survey was impossible. Instead, he was working tirelessly on a two-volume *History,* "never stopping except for university duties, sickness, rest, and other inevitable interruptions. The subject has constantly grown upon my interest; and I have no greater satisfaction in life than to be engaged upon it."[6] The experience of immersing himself in a project that fully engrossed him inspired related experiments in his teaching. He began to take pleasure in putting together courses that would engage a young person's imagination, sustain interest, and offer intellectual and affective pleasure.

When Tyler had first taken up his position, like instructors elsewhere, he had expected students to recite information that they had gleaned out of textbooks. Restless and dissatisfied, one year he had them employing the popular *Manual* by Shaw; the next, a manual by Thomas Arnold; then still another by Henry Morley. He liked Morley's, but it assumed knowledge about European and English history that left students needlessly puzzled. He decided to make a thoroughgoing and friendlier revision. While carrying out the task, he hit upon an idea that would dramatically change the principal way that literature was taught. Manuals made literature something remote, something to be studied from outside. At best, they might be useful as reference books. Why not have students read literary works for themselves and make their own notes on them?

Because libraries in the U.S. could offer few resources for studying older literature, Tyler decided to retain most of the information found in Morley's handling of the centuries before 1700. But since students could easily get hold of more recent literature, he decided his revision would radically reduce the amount of information about eighteenth- and nineteenth-century literary works; he would have students make their own "direct study" of them. Eager for them to feel the power that comes from teaching oneself, he assigned each student to study a different writer, first by reading his works and then by making use of the library. They were to have "the pleasure and gain" that derived from reading literature for themselves and to experience "the exhilaration of original research."[7]

From this experiment, "Study of Masterpieces" emerged as a seminar. It met twice each week for a total of three hours. Every week Tyler assigned the reading of a literary classic (say, De Quincey's *Confessions of an English Opium Eater* or Pope's *Rape of the Lock*). One student worked up a detailed knowledge of it, wrote a substantial essay about it, and then read the essay to the group. Another member delivered a prepared critique of his classmate's essay, and then the whole group participated in a discussion to which each person was required to contribute. The basic idea was to place excellent writing at the center of attention and to occupy the students fully in a communal task of discovering the grounds of that excellence. The instructor's work was to choose the readings, establish the protocols, make the assignments, and then (for the most part) stay out of the fray. This design rendered "Study of Masterpieces" and a second-semester companion seminar, "Study of Shakespeare," the most sophisticated and demanding courses on English literature to be found anywhere in the country. They were nothing like what Tyler himself had experienced as a college student. Their design owed a good deal to what he had experienced while writing his book on early American literature.

Besides teaching, Tyler had been doing a good deal of creative and scholarly writing. He published a lightly veiled satire on contemporary controversies about physical fitness called *The Brawnville Papers.* More substantially, he completed for Putnam the two-volume *History of American Literature During the Colonial Period.* In 1881 President White invited him to chair Cornell's history department. He accepted the position, moved to Ithaca, and became the nation's first Professor of American History.

BUSY AS TYLER had been during his last years at Michigan, to free him for this work, the university hired a new assistant professor of history and rhetoric, Isaac Newton Demmon, a man of some experience. During the war Demmon had been a private in the Indiana Regiment. Afterwards, in two Ohio colleges, he taught ancient languages and what was called "Greek Science." He then moved to Michigan and became the principal of Ann Arbor's high school. At the university, he taught rhetoric to the freshmen and sophomores and a required Anglo-Saxon course for students in a Bachelor of Letters program. When Tyler left in 1881, Demmon inherited his courses.

Demmon was no Tyler, but he had strengths as a builder and consolidator. He put his best efforts into developing the university's outstanding collection of Shakespeareana. He appreciated the originality and brilliance of Tyler's design for the seminars. When he took them over, he had Tyler's rules for how each meeting was to proceed printed in a pamphlet. He headed it with an epigraph taken from Carlyle to sum up the rationale by which students could responsibly become one another's teachers: "What the universities can mainly do for you—what I have found the University did for me, was, that it taught me to read."[8] Demmon then filled out most of the pamphlet's thirty pages with extensive bibliographies of criticism tied to each book the students were going to read. A first-rate bibliographer, he kept abreast of recent scholarship and provided regular updates. He stabilized the seminars and kept the process fresh by introducing students to the latest contemporary critical perspectives.

For "Study of Masterpieces," Demmon retained nearly all the titles that Tyler's students had been reading. He also left in place the two interlocking principles that determined the order in which students would encounter them. The syllabus divided the readings into two principal parts, first prose works, then poetry. Each half was organized chronologically, from oldest to more recent. The chronological component thus gave students two opportunities to be developing, indirectly, a sense that literary history and every genre, far from being inert, were unfolding processes into which each new generation inserted itself.

Because each title illustrated a different genre, every week called for adjustment. The course began with political satire, Thomas More's *Utopia.* Demmon insisted that the students read the whole work carefully, twice if they could make the time. They should formulate their thoughts about it and then begin to look into what critics had to say about it. They should get some idea about how *Utopia* compared to similar works, such as Francis Bacon's *New Atlantis* and Plato's *Republic.* Another week was devoted to Milton's *Areopagitica,* a prose tract condemning pre-publication censorship and written as if it were an address to Parliament. In the U.S. this work had long been held to contain the foundational argument for freedom of the press. Burke's oration reflecting on the French Revolution—serious thoughts seriously and eloquently expressed—came next. A week later, students would encounter the baffling humor of Carlyle's *Sartor Resartus,* with its challenge to all old knowledge and beliefs, a valuable prompt for free-wheeling discussion. George Eliot's novel *Silas Marner* followed, an outwardly simple tale, wrought in a strikingly realistic mode and full of subtleties to be discerned by attentive readers.

When the course doubled back for direct study of poetry, students read the first book of Edmund Spenser's allegorical *Faerie Queene* and then Shakespeare's sonnets. The most ambitious undertaking of the whole semester came next: *Paradise Lost,* ten thousand lines in blank verse to be processed as best as one could (along with some secondary literature) in seven days. Milton was the only author to make two appearances. In the following semester's seminar Shakespeare's dramas would occupy the entire time.

To represent the period after England's civil war, Dryden's *Absalom and Achitophel* was next up, another allegorical narrative, this one dressed in biblical clothing, the better to serve its mock-heroic purposes. This reintroduced political satire, now cast into the heroic verse that became the gold standard for decades to come. Demmon replaced Pope's *Rape of the Lock* with *An Essay on Man,* a poem that popularized the sorts of optimistic philosophy that had swept through Europe in the eighteenth century. Then, to make the transition from Classicism to Romanticism, Wordsworth's *Excursion,* a lengthy poetic piece lodged in an even longer poem, illustrating the sort of rural setting and poetic diction that came to be called "Wordsworthian." Finally, a story set in a woman's university where men were forbidden to enter: Tennyson's *The Princess,* another narrative in blank verse, picking up the various strands of humor that had run through the readings. Whatever the students learned about the authors and from the readings, the course showed them that masterful prose and poetry has been—and can be—lodged in many different kinds of writing. It prompted them to develop standards for judging aesthetic worth and habituated them to adjusting their standards by imagining the different audiences and circumstances to which any given work is addressed.

We know a good bit about how "Study of Masterpieces" worked in practice because librarians preserved copies of Demmon's pamphlet and several appreciative students saved their notes and seminar papers. By the mid-1880s English courses had become so popular at Michigan that Demmon agreed to oversee, simultaneously, three different sections of the seminar. It exposed numerous students to professional literary scholarship and required of them writing that incorporated, and in some measure imitated, that scholarship such as it was. (It tended to be historical, impressionistic, and evaluative. Literary critics were not yet constructing meticulous arguments that enlisted close textual evidence to produce interpretative readings. That practice began to emerge in the 1920s.) The protocols were not meant to provide pre-professional training in what would come to be called "close reading" or to prepare students to become teachers of English. In selecting a dozen students for a given seminar, Demmon did not give preference to those whose previous courses had been heavily skewed towards literary study. Any accomplished student who had successfully completed six prerequisite courses would be considered, and many whose principal interests lay outside the humanities eagerly enrolled.

The university's librarians recognized the historic importance of Michigan's seminars. One copy of the pamphlet includes a note explaining that Tyler first organized "The Study of Masterpieces" as a supplement to other English courses and that he had conceived it as a "systematic and critical study of representative pieces in each age of our literature."[9] A note pasted inside another copy explains that the purpose of the pamphlet had been to provide in "outline" what could be accomplished simply "by suggestion—the highest quality of scholarship." Suggestion, when given at the right moment, is said there to surpass anything that could be done "by actual teaching." An ample archival collection of students' notes and papers shows that students learned the importance of teaching themselves and one another. Many went on to professional careers in fields that included library science, biology, law, medicine, teaching, university administration, and finance.

A detailed account of how Demmon typically proceeded on the first day of class may be seen in a notebook kept by Edwin Goddard (class of '89).[10] It shows that the freedom to read independently entailed first committing to a collaborative framework. Goddard began by recording the requirements for the essays. Paraphrasing and freely quoting, his account of the protocols runs like this: *The essay should be no longer than can be read in its entirety within forty minutes.* (This meant that students were required to devise for their presentations abbreviated versions of the full papers now housed in the archives, many of which exceed forty pages.) *The scope of the essay is to be "comprehensive." It should treat both form and substance. It should make clear the circumstances in which the work had been composed and describe the work itself in brief outline form. It should judge whether and to what extent the work conforms to various criteria by which art is judged: unity, proportion, clarity, and "variety in style & propriety in diction."* Goddard's notes for the second week record advice for the student who was to present a critique: *Read the masterpiece thoroughly and carefully before reading the essay. Know that while all critics "discover faults," good ones never deal with them in a "frivolous or unkind spirit." They approach what they have been assigned to criticize in a "generous spirit" and they "bestow praise where clearly due."* The student who wrote the paper was to provide the critic with a copy a full week in advance. The critique was not to exceed fifteen minutes.

Goddard also made notes on the rules for participations in the discussions. Again, paraphrasing and quoting: *Above all, know the work thoroughly. When you speak, do so ex tempore. Don't think that expressing disagreement with something that has been praised shows your originality. To "make a contribution of your own," decide ahead of time what you want to say. Don't write it all out, and certainly don't read from notes. "Prepare what you will say beforehand but leave how to the moment." Be specific, and illustrate your points with "aptly chosen quotations."* Goddard's notes also show that when Demmon finished spelling out the protocols, he gave his students advice for life as well as for writing: *"Be satisfied only when you have done your best & when you have done your best be satisfied."* This guidance about how to participate in discussion makes sense of the fact that the extant notebooks show that after the first two or three meetings students stopped writing class notes. Taking an active part in the weekly discussions required being fully present in the moment. Abstracting oneself to write down information to be rehearsed in a final examination had no place in the seminar's design.

IF YOU WERE TO visit the archives in Michigan's Bentley Historical Library today, you could call up a large box containing a miscellaneous collection of writings by Mary Elizabeth Clark (1846–1933). You would find these materials as challenging as a massive, partly assembled jigsaw puzzle from which some undetermined number of pieces have been lost. Random fragmentary remains. Class notes. Several essays. Extensive notes on reading done outside coursework. Notebooks with passages copied out from serial publications and from books, their sources sometimes unidentified. Paraphrases of ideas gleaned from her reading. Most materials are undated. Some offer information that would enable us to place them in a chronology. Others belong to a particular course about which we know no more than what the notes might suggest. We have no way of knowing what may have been lost, suppressed, or purposely destroyed. Out of context, full of gaps, yet often richly suggestive of an intellectually engaged life, these writings reveal a resourceful person fashioning for herself what, in the twentieth century, would be called an "English major." For her, it was a prelude to her entry into medical school.

Mary Clark had a checkered college career. Both her parents had emigrated from England, and the family ran a prosperous farm in Lapeer, Michigan, about seventy-five miles north of Ann Arbor. Her mother, Rebecca Beech Clark, was an organizer of the Dryden Ladies' Library Association.[11] (The nearby town of Dryden was named after the poet.) When Mary first enrolled in the university in 1875, she was twenty-nine years old and well read. She had been accepted into the Department of Medicine and Surgery. (Michigan began admitting women in 1870. It was no different from dozens of other universities in that it admitted applicants to medical school with no previous college experience.) She left before the second year. Two years later, she re-enrolled, this time to pursue a Bachelor of Letters degree. In 1885 she would finally receive it. Then she re-enrolled in the medical department. Another two years after that, she received her MD degree.

Unlike the other students whose notes and essays are in the archives, Clark studied with both Tyler and Demmon. In 1878–79, Tyler taught her a pair of elective courses in which students "directly read" English literature from the time of Chaucer down almost to the present. Demmon had taught her rhetoric, and she had read *Julius Caesar* with him. She had taken his Anglo-Saxon course, which was required for sophomores. When in 1884, following another hiatus in her studies, she re-enrolled and took "Study of Masterpieces," she had already read some books on the syllabus and was familiar with the distinctive features of the course. The first thing that she wrote in her notebook was that the seminar was meant to free students from textbooks and recitations and to enable them to make a proper use of books.[12]

Clark's papers are held in a single box, and the contents are of interest for what her writings show about how she employed that freedom to make independent use of her reading. Into a commonplace book, she copied both long and short quotations from her reading, not always identifying the sources. Many passages derive from Disraeli's *Curiosities of Literature.* Others come from a book about the relations between church and state. A host of entries concern the importance of educating young people and the purposes of education. A prominent entry comes from Milton's *Of Education.* There are extensive notes on plays by Molière, and, strikingly, many pages of notes on Oliver Cromwell, whose "history," she remarks, "is of interest to any country loving and desiring liberty." She included here a lengthy passage from his *Letters and Speeches* as compiled by Carlyle, whose *Sartor Resartus* was the book she was assigned to write on for "Study of Masterpieces."[13]

Clark used the back pages of her seminar notebook for copying out passages from her outside reading. Here, she lodged material from a long periodical article that caught her interest because, as the excerpts show, it engaged questions about the relative intellectual and imaginative capacities of men and of women. The article, which had first appeared in the *Edinburgh Review* for 1850 (Clark was three years old in 1850), reviews Charlotte Brontë's novel *Shirley,* published under the pen name Currer Bell. Clark first inscribed a passage from the long introduction, where the reviewer points out that "no women have yet attained the highest eminence in the highest departments of intellect. No Shakespeare, no Bacon, no Newton, no Milton, . . . no Burke." She spotted here the very authors that she had been reading in "Study of Masterpieces." The review made its way into ample praise for Currer Bell's earlier *Jane Eyre* before it filled page after page of mostly damning criticism of *Shirley.* Clark reproduced a segment that treated an episode that led the reviewer to insert, amidst his complaints about the failings of "the authoress," a long quotation from the second volume of the novel. It concerns what Clark refers to as a "Remarkable tirade about Miltons [*sic*] Eve." The criticism is not directed toward the tirade, which the reviewer grants to be an "eloquent rhapsody," but at the improbability of its being "uttered in a quiet conversation between two young ladies," because that "destroys half our pleasure." Clark does not comment on this nor on the reviewer's often misogynistic perspective. (In fact, she rarely commented on passages she copied out.) Still, her decision to record this section of the article suggests an interest in the history of reading Milton's epic, a history of which she knew herself to be a part.

Mary Clark lived in Ann Arbor into her late eighties, long enough to see the university's reputation grow and flourish. The archives now safeguard her papers not least because she herself came to understand that these material traces of her education belonged to a larger social history.

THE SEMINARS ENROLLED some students who were not especially adept at writing about literature and some who, although they were more accomplished, often enough produced work that shows they were out of their depth. Henry Pratt, for instance, liked to make knowing pronouncements. In "Study of Masterpieces," he was assigned the heaviest lift. Writing on Milton's epic, he delighted in pointing out "manifold mistakes and faults" in a work that he nonetheless presented as in some respects "the most remarkable poem that has ever been written."[14] In "Study of Shakespeare" his love for doling out praise and blame was directed more towards the characters than towards the playwright. His forty-one-page essay on *I Henry IV* could have been much shortened. Heavy with personal opinion, its handling of each character builds to a moral judgment, whether approbatory or derogatory. Shakespeare, Pratt told his classmates, "endeavors to bring out that the Prince was not a debaucher with no sense of honor or propriety, but a spirited hot-blooded young man, who had a certain amount of wild oats, to sow and was then sowing them."[15] Falstaff's vices Pratt deemed forgivable, because he is so frank and high-spirited. As for Bolingbroke, his wrongdoing had justly led to his comeuppance. Pratt may well have saved his essays in the first instance with the assumption intact that the purpose of reading literature is that it enables us to learn moral lessons. But years later, he sent them back to his alma mater, explaining that, having "recently dug up in my attic . . . some relics of my college days,"[16] he wanted them to be passed along to the archives. He had by that time little reason to think that essays that once made him proud were to be valued for their contents or style. After graduating, he had gone on to study zoology at Harvard, earned a doctoral degree from Leipzig, and then taught biology for many years at Haverford College. Long experience led to his recognition that the seminars he had taken at Michigan were unusual among college courses, and of historic importance.

Like Pratt, Edwin Goddard (the student whose copy of the protocols we have considered) enrolled in the seminar with no thought of its involving preparation for his future career. He had specialized for three years in mathematics. As he entered senior year, he recognized that his university offered him an opportunity he was unlikely ever to have again, and he sought to broaden his reach in the humanities.

The paper from "Study of Masterpieces" that Goddard deposited in the archives treats Shakespeare's sonnets. Its qualities suggest that, despite the rigor called for in the protocols, Demmon was not assigning the essays with a view to training scholars; the protocols simply guaranteed that the students would be exposed to scholarship, the better to stretch their thinking and to allow them to envision working to a higher standard. Goddard's essay, hand-written in clean black ink, grapples with questions that the sonnets raise about their relation to the poet's biography. This put his fellow students in touch with a preoccupation of late nineteenth-century critical writing on the Bard. Attempts at rearranging the sonnets to reveal previously hidden episodes in Shakespeare's life were multiplying with increasing speed. As students in the seminar learned about the chaotic disagreements this practice was generating, they likely developed a healthy skepticism with which to deal with pretentious critical pronouncements. "It is astonishing," Goddard reported to his classmates, "with what sublime audacity each critic asserts his view as *the* one in the light of which all the fog and cloud of mystery melts away as before a summer's sun."[17]

When after graduation Goddard took a job teaching math at the public high school in Saginaw, Michigan, his colleagues there were impressed with the uses he was making of his education, and they invited him to describe how a literature curriculum might best be integrated with a high school program in which students were studying many different subjects. Goddard's address to his fellow teachers evinces a thorough understanding of how Michigan's seminars were made to work. He took the occasion to imagine for them a rich program that would integrate the study of literature with the writing students were doing in various subjects. He advocated ridding the high-school English curriculum of textbooks, arguing that they render literature a remote object of study and that they are written in a style much inferior to that found in actual literary works. "If pupils are allowed to study that which is inferior," he observed, "the standards which they form will be low."[18] He urged teachers to put into students' hands styles of writing that inspire imitation. Complete books that draw readers into connected narratives, he explained, will transport the imagination into realms beyond everyday experience. After a few years in Saginaw, Goddard returned to his alma mater, first to teach mathematics there and then to study for a law degree. He spent the last thirty-five years of his working life as a professor of law.

AN ESPECIALLY ACCOMPLISHED essay from "Study of Masterpieces" is dated "Nov. 3, 1896," two decades after Tyler had begun experimenting with having students experience entire books through "direct study." It concerns *Areopagitica,* and its excellence owes something to the maturing not only of the seminar but of English studies generally. (By the 1890s bright students in many colleges were producing equally adept writing.) Still, the excellence that this essay exhibits owes much to the writer himself. Shirley Wheeler Smith enrolled in the Bachelor of Letters program in 1893 and went on to make a distinguished record. While he was continuing his studies towards an MA degree, he was hired by the university to give instruction in English. A decade later, after several years working in financial services for an insurance company, he was named secretary of the university, a position that he continued to hold even after he was promoted to vice president and chief financial officer. (That Smith was a "he" seems surprising now, but the name "Shirley" was originally given only to males. It was Brontë's novel that popularized it as a chic name for girls.)

As an undergraduate Smith took courses mostly in history, politics, and sociology. When he was assigned Milton's most famous prose work in "Study of Masterpieces," it must have seemed a near-perfect fit for his interests. His twenty-five-page essay is more concise than other extant seminar papers, and it is clearly addressed to sophisticated readers. The culmination of its first paragraph expresses what Smith found attractive about the writer and intimates that the tract has continuing value:

> For the ordinary man it might perhaps be satisfaction enough to know that he could write anything the government wanted him to at any time, or write anything *he* wanted to sometimes, but there was one man at least

> who wanted to be able to say or write anything he pleased and whenever he pleased. This man was John Milton and the Areopagitica is his protest against a pre-licensing government.[19]

The essay highlights the tract's distinctive emphasis on the importance of good books and intelligent reading. It also wrestles with the seeming anomaly whereby, even as Milton proposes that these activities foster the public good, he makes his case in long, involved sentences that require close attention to be followed. When Smith quotes a critic's remark that Milton "begins anywhere and leaves off not when the sense closes but when he is out of breath," he quips, "I daresay [that this sentence] has appeared in every essay read upon the subject since the Masterpiece course was established."[20] Aware of the seminar's long-standing reputation and attuned to its focus on genre, he goes on to explain that he himself finds the arguments in *Areopagitica* ultimately unconvincing, not in themselves, but because Milton decided to frame them in the cold diction of a constitutional lawyer. He suggests that the case against censorship might better be made by a passionate personal appeal. Finally, Smith confides to his fellow seminarians his personal experience in preparing for his presentation:

> I would not have it understood by anything I have said that I found the reading of the book a task. The author's ponderous, Latin style took close attention and even that wasn't enough to get the meaning for me in every case. But I found on the second reading that I got much more pleasure and benefit from the work than I had at first, with every indication that these results would continue to increase with further perusals. I suppose that this is one of the great tests of a classic.[21]

More effectively than the other surviving papers from the seminars, Smith's genuinely tested the masterpiece assigned to him.

WHEN MOSES TYLER invented Michigan's English seminars, he sought to unsettle the idea that literary studies should produce the certainties to be found in the study of subjects like mathematics. His decision to have the students teach one another provided an opportunity, first, for them to discover a range of interpretive possibilities and, then, to infer that no one interpretation ought to drive out all others. His provision for a discussion in which everyone was required to take part meant that students would also have to grapple with the fact that some interpretations are better than others. These were precisely discoveries to be made, not doctrines to be delivered by authorities. This goes as well for Tyler's decision to have the students reading "masterpieces," as Goddard, who became an apostle for the practice, and as Smith, who demonstrated how it was to be carried out, fully recognized. Against the human tendency to let one's mind wander, and in a prosperous era when innovations and novelties constantly offered opportunities for distraction, Tyler understood that everyone faces a fundamental question about what constitutes a worthy object of attention. For those able to give several years of their lives to advanced schooling, he put together a set of possibilities that led to engagement with writing of the highest caliber. That is, he fashioned a concentration for students who, whatever their other interests and purposes were, sensed that they wanted to give a significant part of their college years to learning how to read great literature. His curricular positioning of "Study of Masterpieces" and "Study of Shakespeare" at the apex of a student's literary education made for what amounted to an inchoate English major, avant la lettre.

PART IV

WHAT CONSTITUTES AN ENGLISH MAJOR?

13

The Idea of a Major

As the student enters his second or third year in college he is confronted by lines of elective study. . . . Nine students out of ten in this situation say to themselves . . . , "I can study literature for myself . . . ; the study of literature would be delightful, but it would require a good deal of time, and under the circumstance would be an indulgence." This . . . is the thought of many students at the critical moment in their college lives.

—CHARLES W. HODELL, "The Study of English Literature from the Standpoint of the Student" (1895)

IN A BOOK ABOUT the English major it may seem odd that the word *major* has scarcely appeared up to this point. Its near absence is appropriate. *Major*, as a term designating the principal subject that someone studies in college, had little currency before the twentieth century. Mathematics and the classical languages long exerted a firm hold in the standard liberal arts curriculum. But it would not be accurate to think of these subjects as constituting a student's major. *Majoring* in a subject implies a student's freedom to choose it. Even as late as the 1890s, when students had achieved a good deal of freedom to take charge of what they would study, most colleges and universities did not require undergraduates to elect a special subject. The term *major* came gradually into play to name a feature of postgraduate training, where it proved useful because the students took courses in more than one subject.

Tellingly, the earliest known appearance of the word *major* in an academic context appears in the 1878 *Register* of Johns Hopkins University, the first institution in the United States founded precisely to provide postgraduate education: "The major course must be followed in any subject which the candidate offers as one of his two chief departments of work."[1] The *Oxford English Dictionary*'s entry for *major* observes that the term referred first to "a student's special or principal subject or course" and was then extended to refer as well to "a student specializing in a particular subject." When Johns Hopkins opened in 1876, fewer than thirty persons had earned a PhD from a U.S. university. (Yale, having granted 23, accounted for about 90 percent of them.[2]) While studying for an advanced degree, students typically took courses in multiple subjects or "departments." Hopkins, created on a German model, expected its faculty to produce professional scholarship and required its postgraduate students to develop a well-focused specialization. Its president, Daniel Coit Gilman, hired renowned scholars who wrote learned articles, founded scholarly journals, and trained their successors to be professionals by requiring them to pursue two "Major courses," each in a different "department" of study.

"Major courses" entailed significantly more intense study—and time—than others. They did not fit into a predetermined temporal frame such as a semester or an academic year. Unlike the locution "The Classical Course" or "The Scientific Course," which named a whole undergraduate program of study, Johns Hopkins's "Major *courses*" referred to only part—the most important feature—of a graduate program. Students also took "Minor" courses in "departments" closely related to the "Major" ones, for instance a mathematics minor along with physics and chemistry. In addition, for interest and enrichment, students could engage in an occasional study of some other subject, including English.

Given the importance that the concept of a major would eventually have in American colleges and universities, it is of interest that at Hopkins the term *major* also designated a component of undergraduate education. Devoted as the university was to finding, admitting, and supporting postgraduate students who would aptly match the abilities of its faculty, it managed to accommodate a tiny handful of students seeking a bachelor's degree. It admitted only demonstrably serious candidates who had at least as much training as a sophomore in the traditional colleges, persons who, although they would not be required to do it, seemed likely to continue on to a PhD degree. In 1880, three young men were awarded the AB, and a university *Circular* printed a brief explanation of what they had done to qualify for it. Like the postgraduate students, these undergraduates had the advice of a faculty mentor as they pursued two "*major courses,* implying . . . a real mastery of the subjects, and three others, *minor courses,* which [were] studied well but not so extensively."[3] One of the degree recipients had, for example, taken Latin and history as major courses, and German, French, and physics as minor ones. The students had satisfied other requirements as well, not necessarily by doing coursework. No undergraduate was to be "honored with the degree" without a knowledge of at least one ancient and two modern languages, nor without a sufficient knowledge of mathematics; and he needed to demonstrate that he had developed powers of observation through work in scientific laboratories. These requirements could be satisfied in various ways, at each student's own pace. They could be fulfilled by doing classroom work. Or a student, having worked up a subject on his own, could be examined by a faculty member other than his teacher.

One or more of the three AB graduates in 1880 may have studied some English, a subject that was regarded as lacking in sufficient importance to be a major or even a minor in the PhD and AB programs. The English department had only three courses on offer. The principal one focused on Old and Middle English, studied in relation to the histories of other languages; it could serve as a supplementary study for a graduate student pursuing work in comparative philology. Because a knowledge of Shakespeare was a mark of educated persons whatever their specialty, the department offered two courses for enrichment, both devoted to the Bard's plays. The difference between the two serves to illustrate that "courses" at Hopkins were not standardized according to how many class hours students attended or the amount of work that was expected. One Shakespeare class met only twice a week, the other, daily. Six students took the one, seven the other. All thirteen were specializing in other subjects altogether.

IT TOOK MANY YEARS before the terms *major* and *minor* made their way into general usage. When President Gilman went out on the lecture circuit to speak about innovations in higher education, he accommodated his audiences by referring to the "dominant" or "principal" or "comprehensive" subjects that students pursued, and to "subordinate" or "subsidiary" subjects.[4] This distinction became operative in some institutions sooner than in others. As late as the mid-1890s, the idea that students would single out a special subject still required explanation. We know this because in 1893 the Chicago-based journal *The Dial* began publishing, from prominent colleges and universities, ample accounts of how they were organizing the study of English. After a year and a half, eighteen reports had been amassed. Mention of an undergraduate "major" appeared in only one. The report from Stanford began by explaining an unusual curricular practice whereby every undergraduate, at the beginning of sophomore year, was required to declare a "major subject." Nothing was said about the circuitous route by which the term *major* had made its way from Johns Hopkins to the newly opened university in California.

When in 1890 Leland and Jane Stanford were making plans for a new university to be named after their deceased son, they offered the presidency of the institution to Andrew Dickson White, then president of Cornell. Like Gilman, who had been his classmate at Yale and was his lifelong friend, White had an estimable reputation for his successful educational reforms. Among his innovations was the creation of Cornell's successful English program, more than two decades before Oxford established its English School. White declined the Stanfords' offer and recommended his protégé, David Starr Jordan, who had been a member of Cornell's pioneering class of 1872. At the time, Jordan was the president of Indiana University. He had devised there eight different paths to the AB degree, including one for those who wished to make English language and literature their "specialty." Jordan accepted the post at Stanford and introduced there the idea that undergraduates should give one-third of their college studies to a single subject. He borrowed from Johns Hopkins the term *major* and thereby made the workings of a practice designed for graduate education, and de facto operative at Cornell, the central feature of the entire undergraduate curriculum. (And, as we have seen in the chapter on Entrance Examinations, Jordan took a surprisingly active role in deciding which applicants to Stanford would be admitted.)

A railroad magnate and U.S. senator, Leland Stanford bestowed enormous and enviable resources upon his university. Unsurprisingly, when its report appeared in *The Dial,* readers were treated to more than a little bragging about the effects of its founder's munificence. Stanford had been able to open its doors with an entire faculty in place and without the baggage of an inherited curriculum. In no time, its newly hired English professors devised a highly articulated rationale for studying vernacular literature as a "major subject," and they were offering nearly as many English courses as Harvard, which had the largest English faculty in the country. Stanford undergraduates who chose English as their major had to take, with advice from a faculty member, collateral courses in one or more languages (Latin, French, and German). In some cases, they also had to study history. They were otherwise free to choose electives in any other subjects. The Stanford report in *The Dial* declared that the results were already "far superior" to what went on in a "conventional college curriculum," because students "elect for the most part only such subjects as they have taste or talent for, and professors have the pleasure and inspiration of working with earnest and enthusiastic men and women." It added that, beyond this, by making the English portion of its admissions examination rigorous, the university was able to avoid altogether offering a composition course of the sort required for first-year students in other colleges. This eliminated "the drudgery of correcting Freshman themes,—work really secondary and preparatory, and in no sense forming a proper subject for collegiate study."[5] (That year only 40 of some 150 applicants had passed the examination.) Sophomores who declared for English began by making a careful study of nineteenth-century prose writers. Later they would undertake to study poetry and older literature. Before they could elect courses on Shakespeare, Spenser, Milton, and classic authors of the eighteenth century, they were required to take courses on Anglo-Saxon and on Chaucer, and they were advised to study ancient and modern literatures in translation. For juniors and seniors, the department provided an array of other electives, including ones on the Romantic poets and on American literature. As students neared the culmination of their major, they could elect a seminar on philology or paleography.[6]

The Dial's GATHERING OF accounts of how English was being taught and studied across the country created a virtual symposium. The collection of eighteen reports marked the culmination of a variegated process by which the study of English had become an integral feature of higher education in the United States. The enthusiasm with which the various departments were describing what they were doing—the eagerness with which they were sharing information and displaying curiosity about what was going on elsewhere—was unprecedented. In 1895 an associate editor of the journal, William Morton Payne, reprinted the reports from what he labeled the country's "leading institutions" in a volume titled *English in American Universities.* He presented them as evidence that, among the various subjects made available to students by the spread of the elective system, English was likely the single greatest beneficiary. He also observed a growing consensus about the boundaries of the field: most English departments had come to regard "the art of [oral] rhetoric" and "the science of linguistics" as autonomous subjects to be housed in other departments. Nearly everywhere, teaching literature and composition now lay at the heart of an English professor's work.[7] As we will see in the chapters that follow, some of the most successful departments hired separate sets of instructors to teach composition and to teach literature, on a model that we've seen established at Lafayette College. Departments that implemented this practice acknowledged that literature was already a vast field that required faculty as devoted to it as their colleagues in other disciplines were to their fields. They also recognized that writing—which puts one's thinking onto paper—was an inestimably valuable tool for learning in almost any subject and that, rather than passing off composition to the English department, instructors in many different disciplines needed to be working with their students' writing.

Having realized that with the expansion of elective studies students had made English a widely popular subject, Payne decided to include in the published collection a student's contribution titled "The Study of English Literature from the Standpoint of a Student." The task was entrusted to Charles W. Hodell, a Cornell graduate student who had not attended one of the "leading institutions." This is of interest because Hodell's undergraduate experience rightly suggests that many colleges that receive no direct consideration in this book were already following the lead of those institutions by expanding their English offerings.

Hodell's essay sounds like an outpouring of a lively, alert, and rather naïve convert to English studies. It draws a picture of undergraduates everywhere attracted to the "delight" that literary studies have to offer. Without a hint of irony, Hodell puts forward the hyperbolic claim that the vast majority of college students seriously consider pursuing literary studies. Perhaps only ingenuously, he allows that students think they can just read, say, *Twelfth Night* or *Paradise Lost* on their own, without having had much literary experience and training. Yet he acknowledges something that has continued to weigh on students well into our own time: most students, he observes, dutifully choose to study more utilitarian subjects.[8] How was it then that Hodell chose differently? and on what basis did he think he had something to contribute to *The Dial* symposium "from the standpoint of the student"?

Hodell knew what he was doing when he chose to work on a postgraduate degree at an institution known for its innovations in organizing English studies. He hailed from Indiana and had attended DePauw University in his home state. At the time he happened to enroll, DePauw had just installed a requirement, on the model of the state's flagship university, that each student select what it called a "major." Previously, its students had been able to choose among four different paths that led to a bachelor's degree. None had involved any serious study of literature in English, even though, curiously and incoherently, the college's entrance examination expected applicants to have read *The Merchant of Venice*, *Julius Caesar*, and two books of *Paradise Lost*. But by 1888 when Hodell began his studies, the college had adopted, and was busy adapting, the kinds of curricular reforms that David Starr Jordan had initiated at Indiana University.

Compared with the elaborate arrangements for coursework described in *The Dial* reports, the workings of and rationale for DePauw's English major were unusually transparent. The college's new curriculum prominently included a required "major" and a "minor." The coursework was heavy. Students were to take twenty-four courses through their four years, each course meeting for four hours a week through long eighteen-week semesters. The major was to consist of six courses, and those courses had to be taken in six different semesters. The idea here was a gradual and in-depth assimilation of knowledge: the time that had been spent in each course was said to make for an increasingly valuable breadth and depth in one's acquaintance with the subject. All first-year students were required to take an introductory English course, whatever their major was to be, and any student who wished could elect a course in Anglo-Saxon. Those who then chose the English major took five lecture courses covering English literature chronologically, from Chaucer's Prologue, the first book of *The Faerie Queene*, and *Hamlet*, on through the periods when they would be reading works by Browning and George Eliot. The five sequential courses offered auxiliary sets of collateral readings among which students could choose, as long as they were willing to be examined on them. All five required writing papers on literary works. As seniors were completing the major, they could, with their instructor's permission, also take an additional advanced course on the lyric or on drama.

Acknowledging the presence of an English major at DePauw before more prestigious institutions had one might well prompt looking into the history of English studies in dozens of colleges that do not directly figure in the origin story told in this book. Clearly every institution, even if like DePauw it drew inspiration from a "leading" institution, developed the contents and shaped the contours of its own English major in accord with its own particular situation. In the chapters to follow, we will examine, one by one, English studies in three English departments whose reports appeared in *The Dial.* Cornell, before other colleges encouraged students to pursue a single subject as central to their education, cut a Gordian knot when it opened up the possibility for students to make English the principal subject they studied. By contrast, Harvard long forbade its departments to design a concentration or major, freeing students to create their own specialty by choosing whatever courses they wished. Meanwhile, just at the time when *The Dial* began publishing its reports, Wellesley College initiated a thoroughgoing revision of an ambitious far-flung curriculum that had lacked coherence. This made it possible for its young women students to study one or two subjects in depth. Almost immediately Wellesley's English department proved dramatically successful in attracting students to a thoughtfully structured "major."

The range of possibilities that we will see amidst the similarities and differences in organizing English studies, even among only three departments, suggests that there are myriad ways that an effective English major may designed. Already in the period we have been considering the number of excellent literary works that might have been studied meant that mastery of the subject was impossible. In our time, the exponentially greater accumulation of excellent writing in English now available around the globe invites a veritable renaissance of English studies.

14

English as a Special Subject at Cornell

To read any one good production of an author, even superficially, is far better than to read all that has been written on and around and about it.

—HIRAM CORSON, "Syllabus of a Course of Lectures on the English Language and Literature" (1873)

IN THE SUMMER OF 1864, shortly after the Civil War had officially ended, the New York State Senate was busily deliberating about what was to be done with funding received from the Morrill Land-Grant Act. Most senators advocated opening many small colleges to serve local regions. Two senators argued for creating a single institution that would have a more far-reaching impact. "I would found an institution," Senator Cornell declared, "where any person can find instruction in any study."[1] In making his case he had the support of Senator White, who was known to have a well-informed interest in reforming higher education. Andrew Dickson White had spent extensive time in Europe, both as a student and, during the war, as a diplomat. He argued persuasively in favor of creating a modern, scientific, coeducational university that would offer instruction in a host of subjects from agriculture to zoology. Ezra Cornell saw in him just the man to share his vision. That their position prevailed had far-flung implications for the distinctive answer a new university would give to the question "What would 'English' be?"

Chartered in 1865, from its inception Cornell University had many advantages. The institution derived its initial funding from the fortune that its eponymous cofounder had amassed in the telegraph business. When the Morrill Act granted Ezra Cornell's new university nearly a million acres appropriated from the Cayuga Nation, he purchased a large portion of it for himself. Other land-grant colleges sold their allotted scrips almost immediately. (Brown University received less than forty cents an acre). Cornell held his land until he was able to sell it for nearly five dollars an acre. He then donated the proceeds to his university, making it the richest of all the land-grant colleges.[2] He named White the university's first president and entrusted him with the work of hiring a faculty that would make good on his ambition that any and every respectable subject was to be on offer. Alert to the wartime national urgency, White had left his position as professor of English and history at the University of Michigan to enter public service. Back home in New York, as Cornell's first president, he established nine different "faculties," each constituting what was sometimes designated a "College," sometimes a "School," and functioning pretty much as what we're now accustomed to thinking of as an academic department. At the outset White did not deem that "English" warranted a distinct school in its own right. He had something more fundamental in mind: he planned that English would be a required subject in every undergraduate degree program, occupying the place in higher education long held by the classical languages. The students' native language would be the principal vehicle through which they received practical training in speaking and writing. The study of English literature would enrich their knowledge of general culture.

Before the university opened in 1868, nearly 500 young men, each at least fifteen years old, applied for admission. (Women were first admitted in 1875 and needed to be at least sixteen.) In its first year of operation 412 students enrolled, far more than could be found in most colleges. In accord with the general principle that Cornell students were to have "complete . . . liberty in the choice of studies," applicants were able to choose one of three different Courses (uppercase "C") leading to a bachelor's degree.[3] Freedom of choice had its limitations, however: all three Courses would entail substantial English study. Successful applicants for the Bachelor of Arts degree, whose entrance exam had demonstrated an advanced knowledge of Latin and Greek, would continue studying the classical languages and, through all four years, take English courses (lowercase "c") devoted to rhetoric, oratory, elocution, and literature. Students enrolled in the Course leading to a Bachelor of Philosophy were required to continue with Latin, to add a modern language, and to study English for ten of their twelve trimesters. Applicants for the Bachelor of Science degree were not expected to demonstrate knowledge of any foreign language. Once admitted, they would take introductory courses in French and German and, for their first seven trimesters, courses on the English language and its literature. Each degree program ensured that its students would likely spend at least as much class time with English as any other subject. Within a short time, however, these ambitious plans for the study of English would be markedly curtailed.

FROM ITS INCEPTION, besides requiring undergraduates in the degree Courses to take English, Cornell offered two alternative programs in which students could freely choose English as their principal focus. With the approval of the faculty, a student could design an idiosyncratic degree program consisting of sixty courses in various subjects and receive, upon completing them, an appropriate bachelor's degree. Or, without seeking a degree, a student could pursue a single subject and work towards a license certifying proficiency in that "special branch." The second option proved the more popular, and for decades a large proportion of those who availed themselves of this possibility chose to study English. By 1880 the university began allowing students in all the degree Courses to choose what was now called a "Special Study." This was what we routinely consider a major, and Cornell made this opportunity available well before other institutions did. The majority of undergraduates pursued specialties in the sciences. Among humanities subjects, Anglo-Saxon and English literature proved popular choices.

In the university's earliest years, the large number of required English courses had meant that the first professor of English, Homer Sprague, was instructing hundreds of students. He brought to the work a wealth of experience. At Yale, where he edited the literary magazine and graduated the year before White, he had been class valedictorian. Afterwards he had taught law and literature, been principal of a Normal school, and, as a committed abolitionist, had served as a Union officer in the war. White's plan had him teaching rhetoric, oratory, vocal culture, and an abundance of literary works. Freshman were to study several leading English writers; sophomores, literary periods; juniors, masterpieces; and seniors, selected topics.

And there was more. To supplement Sprague's literature courses, and to attract the general public, White hired celebrated literary figures as nonresident professors, including Harvard's James Russell Lowell. Each came to campus for a trimester to give a dozen lectures. The university's lavish provision of what was now called English proved to be too much, conspicuously so for Sprague, who resigned after two years, and also for the students. The vast majority would never have freely chosen to study the subject so extensively.

Sprague's resignation occasioned a thoroughgoing reconsideration of the original plan. In searching for a new professor of English, White's high standards meant that he was willing for the position to remain vacant until he found the right man. He thought he had identified him in the person of the eccentric Hiram Corson, but the trustees put up resistance. Going back to the drawing boards, White secured permission to hire two professors for what was to be a School of Letters, in which students could work toward a newly conceived Bachelor of Literature degree.[4] He divided the school into two "departments," one to be overseen by a professor of Anglo-Saxon and English literature, the other presided over by a professor of rhetoric and general literature. This division was similar to the arrangement that had been worked out at Lafayette. There it had been instituted to free Francis March from having to mark the underclassmen's compositions, and it enabled him to give his time to teaching language and literature and to his own writing. To serve as professor of rhetoric, White hired Charles Chauncey Shackford, a graduate of Harvard who had been in charge of a school for girls. Shackford would be responsible, every year, for responding, either orally or in writing, to hundreds of writing exercises, essays, themes, orations, declamations, and undergraduate theses. Meanwhile Corson, encouraged by White to bide his time, moved his family to Ithaca and felt relief at last when he was offered the chair from which he would direct the study of language and English literature.

The trustees had balked at White's proposal to hire Corson because he had not attended college and possessed no degree. In his early twenties he had been Daniel Webster's secretary. Then for several years he worked in the copyright department at the Smithsonian, where he made use of the Institution's resources to read widely and deeply. He married Caroline Rollin, a scholar in her own right, and together they ran schools for girls and taught them literature. Corson emphasized the importance of reading literary works aloud. Caroline began translating Henry Wadsworth Longfellow's prose romance *Hyperion* into her native French, and she and the poet began corresponding with one another.[5] Longfellow had emerged as the most popular poet writing in English, possibly on both sides of the Atlantic. Hiram, who had a flair for the dramatic, began reading Longfellow's poems at public gatherings. Audiences are said to have found his voice at once sweet and powerful. When they heard an American odyssey in dactylic hexameters reminiscent of classical poetry, they thrilled to the tale of Evangeline's quest to find her lover. *The Song of Hiawatha* proved even more popular. Corson went on tours, reading Longfellow and classic English writers to enthusiastic gatherings in Washington, Philadelphia, and New Jersey. He accepted a post at St. John's College, Annapolis, and began trying out college teaching. When he was hired by Cornell in 1870, he immediately began creating new possibilities for the study of the English language and its literature.

OF THE TWO PROFESSORS hired to teach English, Corson proved far more influential, both on campus and especially beyond it. After publishing conventional textbooks (an elocutionary manual and a handbook of Anglo-Saxon), he would go on to write several books on literary works and pedagogy. These included *An Introduction to the Study of Robert Browning's Poetry* (1886), *An Introduction to the Study of Shakespeare* (1889), and an idiosyncratic manifesto, *The Aims of Literary Study* (1894). It was as a performer, however, that Corson was at his best. All through the years, every Saturday morning when the university was in session, he gave public readings. Ithaca's townspeople were invited to attend, and they came in flocks. As Saturday was a regular school day, his students were there as well. Corson read British and American authors alike. He especially enjoyed performing works by Chaucer, Shakespeare, and Browning. Sometimes Poe found a place on the program. On Tuesday evenings he gave readings for the Cascadilla Literary Club. One week the highlight might be Coleridge's "Kubla Khan," the next Elizabeth Barrett Browning's *Aurora Leigh*. Another time he read excerpts from *The Scarlet Letter, The House of the Seven Gables,* and *The Marble Faun*. Attendance increased, and the readings were moved to larger quarters. He added poems by Bret Harte and John Greenleaf Whittier to his repertoire. He brought Harte to the campus to read his poetry himself.[6] And Corson resumed his practice of going out on the road. He gave readings in Baltimore, Philadelphia, and Syracuse. When he read in London, he received praise for having avoided interlarding his speech with Americanisms.[7] During a later trip to England in 1882 he introduced the poetry of William Cullen Bryant into British literary circles, and he became a charter member of the Browning Society.

As a teacher, Corson gave the university's trustees good evidence that White had known what he was doing in hiring him. He offered students eager to pursue studies in English literature more possibilities than they could have found at just about any other institution. His classes met every day of the week. He imagined a new way to organize a required undergraduate literature course. It would introduce a range of older literature, above all works by Chaucer and Spenser; students would learn from this a good deal about the dynamics of language change. Then, if they wished, they could go on to elect more courses, including ones that treated more modern writers. Corson prepared an innovative "Syllabus of a Course of Lectures on the English Language and Literature." Students had never seen anything like it. It summarized the leading points to be taken up in each class. It listed the best and the most accessible editions of the works they were reading. It gave bibliographical leads to philological, historical, biographical, and critical materials; these were to be regarded, however, as purely auxiliary. Students were to make use of such materials on their own time, and only after they had thoroughly read each literary work for themselves. Corson believed students deserved credit for being able to read literature on their own intelligently and that they would come to class eager, on the basis of this, to test their impressions. In the classroom he read aloud from the day's assigned text to illustrate what they should be aiming to be able to do themselves.

Having largely educated himself, Corson freely broke with pedagogical practices employed elsewhere, above all the nearly ubiquitous practice of assigning students to learn about literature from a manual. He knew what it was like to work up a knowledge of literature on one's own, and he felt free to teach almost anything. He launched the direct reading of literary masterpieces before Moses Coit Tyler introduced the practice at the University of Michigan. And long before Harvard or Yale offered a survey of British literature, he dreamed up a course that, through some forty-two classes covering literature from Anglo-Saxon times to the present, offered a broad overview. While instructors at other colleges were only beginning to invent English courses on this or that subject (say, a period, or an author, or a genre), he accommodated students who wished to go on studying literature by implementing a rigorous four-year curriculum that, in the third year, focused on Chaucer, Spenser, and long poems. For seniors he offered a yearlong Shakespeare course as the climax of their studies; students took it at the same time as they were reading a good bit of Shakespeare in a general literature course with Shackford. Corson read aloud from the plays, with such explanations of the development of the plot as would be necessary. Visitors from the town were welcome to attend the classes, and many who had leisure of a weekday morning took advantage of the offer.

Corson's teaching worked against the dominant ways in which English was being brought into the curriculum elsewhere. White had always insisted that Cornell's instructors would have considerable freedom in how they conducted their courses. They would not find themselves caught up in the widely used marking system for generating each student's rank-in-class at graduation, and students would not be "marked" every day on how well their recitations showed they had mastered a small allotted task. Corson considered it a distraction to hold students accountable for mere information—about writers, titles, dates, literary periods, footnotes in editions, and (worse still) the conventional reputations that had accrued around individual authors. That would keep them from doing what he called the essential work of learning to read sympathetically for oneself. He avoided larding his lectures with facts that students would be expected to give back in examinations. He maintained that lecturing about literature is no better than lecturing about music, and he encouraged listening for the rhythms in literary works. He selected books that experienced readers found moving, believing in the ability of every student to engage privately and personally with a good poem or story. He encouraged his charges to pay attention to their own lively impressions, inchoate as they might be, some of them puzzling, some perhaps exhilarating, some merely silly. He counseled them that, even when they felt puzzled or bored, to keep reading on, because initial impressions offer a starting point for vicarious experiences that may ultimately yield synthetic insights.

To foster reading of this sort, Corson advised students to cultivate what Wordsworth called a "wise passiveness." He encouraged slowly gathering impressions without knowing what will come of them; allowing what is indefinite to marinate in semiconsciousness; and suspending the sort of judgment that translates a writer's concrete language into an abstract statement. Poetry, Corson wrote in *The Aims of Literary Study*, challenges the common assumption that what we know is "confined to the conclusions of the discursive understanding." He emphasized that literature, like music, invites affective as well as intellectual engagement. When asked how a teacher can best secure a student's full response to what's most alive in a poem, he answered, by eliciting a full "interpretative vocal rendering of it."[8] Literary masterpieces, he contended, ask for as much training and exercise of the speaking voice as musical masterpieces do of the singing voice.[9] As an educator, he looked for ways to undermine the precedence that examiners routinely granted to questions that called for purely cerebral responses. Nonetheless, almost as soon as his teaching at Cornell began, Corson had had to knuckle under to some of the realities of his having gone into harness. New as he was to the obligation of enforcing high standards, he wrestled with the practical difficulties inherent in having to assess his students' literary knowledge.

Cornell's administration placed considerable weight on written examinations. Students took an exam in virtually every subject at the end of every trimester. Beginning in 1871–72, the university's annual *Registers*, in addition to the specimens of the entrance examinations that we encountered in chapter 10, printed samples of trimestrial examinations from a formidable panoply of fields and disciplines. By publishing samples that encompassed subjects from architecture and the Icelandic language to military science and veterinary medicine, the fledgling institution called to the attention of interested parties the unprecedented range of programs it was already offering. The examinations disclosed what the faculty expected students to know, and they exhibited the university's high standards. They also gave students access to the kinds of questions they would need to answer and to the formats they were likely to encounter.

Today, in addition, these specimens afford us something extremely rare, because few institutions have preserved copies of examinations from the earliest courses called "English." In the 1870s, Shackford and Corson contributed to the annual *Registers* more than twenty examinations from at least ten different courses they had taught. A veritable bonanza, these examinations render evidence about what some of the earliest college English courses offered in the U.S. were like.

It makes sense to consider Shackford's materials first. His examinations were fairly conventional. He taught traditional subjects—rhetoric, oratory, and elocution—to students of all four years. He gave a general literature course to seniors that covered genres with an ancient pedigree: epic, lyric, tragedy, comedy, orations, and the like. Two early exams that come from the same rhetoric course that Shackford taught in different years contain prompts that notably differ from one another. Therefore, an industrious applicant who consulted the printed exams in advance could learn not to expect exactly what he had seen in a single specimen. Still, Shackford's exams became more predictable. (Cornell's practice of printing specimens ended abruptly after a few years. Making samples readily available inhibited instructors from recycling effective questions.)

All Shackford's exams made use of numbered prompts. Typically, each prompt assumes one of two forms, either a question or a briefly stated topic. The exams from his rhetoric and composition courses generally begin with warm-up prompts that ask for information; for instance, "Define Pleonasm, Circumlocution, Redundancy, and Tautology."[10] But the majority of prompts require a demonstration of understanding. "Illustrate how derivatives are formed, by taking a noun-root, a verb-root, and an adjective root."

A more demanding examination that Shackford created for first-year students concluded a trimestrial course that featured the "new science" of "philology." In an address to the whole university reprinted for many years in the *Register,* President White's old classmate Daniel Coit Gilman had proclaimed that Science had at last displaced Letters as the heart of a liberal education. He encouraged the teaching of "the new science of comparative philology," because it "is giving fresh vigor to linguistic research and leading to most instructive lessons in respect to the history of mankind, the development of races and the progress of civilization."[11] This would be a splendid way, Gilman proposed, to revivify the old curriculum that for too long had dominated in colleges. Shackford's philology exam began with a question that might have occasioned an extensive essay, "Why is the English language classified as belonging to the Indo-European family?" Its other prompts include "State Grimm's Law of Phonetic change"; "Give some examples of words radically the same, but of different form, because entering the language from different sources"; "State the successive stages of English from Anglo-Saxon to modern English with the dates."[12] The sheer number of questions in an exam such as this likely proved overwhelming. Probably, although the printed page says nothing about it, students were given some choice about how many they were required to answer. This consideration brings us to a significant innovation that Shackford implemented on the model of an examination given by Corson.

Seniors in two standard Courses took Shackford's ambitious yearlong general literature course. The lectures first took up lyric, epic, and dramatic poetry and then moved to comparing ancient and modern orators. They continued with an introduction to literary criticism and built to consideration of the philosophy of literature and aesthetics. Shakespeare, more than any other author, featured in the lectures. The first two exams that Shackford drew up for this course illustrate that he had designed general literature as the capstone for the students' literary education: it would broaden literary concerns beyond what had been encountered—historically, geographically, and culturally—when studying literature in English. In the earlier exam this ambitious aim generated twelve demanding prompts. They included "1. Poetry as one of the Fine Arts"; "6. The Tragic and the Comic Element,—how manifested in the Drama"; "9. The distinguishing characteristics of the Hindoo, the Hebrew, the Persian, the Greek, and the Latin poetry," and "12. The Tendencies in Literature at the present time."[13] The questions are rich enough that students would have been hard pressed to answer all of them.

The following year's exam expanded the list to twenty-nine topics, incorporating the twelve posed previously and adding new ones. Some take the form of an imperative: "Rhythm, its origin, nature and necessity." Others are questions as broad as "What is Realism in Poetry?" and "How does Shakespeare idealize his characters?" Some questions require concrete knowledge of particular works: "How does the opening of Macbeth contrast with that of Hamlet in movement, tone, general effect, and diction?" Others entail detailed cross-cultural comparison: for example, "Compare the method of Shakespeare with that of Schiller in dialogue." Then, at the end of the long list, a single line suggests a ground for deducing that students were not expected to answer all twenty-nine questions: "To each student five topics [are] assigned."[14] This procedure must have been announced in advance. It enabled Shackford to hand out a list of topics for review. When in the actual exam students were assigned only five topics, Shackford could expect to read answers that went into some depth. As we will see, Corson had further purposes in mind for this sort of exam.

THE SPECIMEN EXAMS devised by Corson and printed in the *Registers* belong only to the earliest phase of his long career. Aware that teachers of college English needed to demonstrate that literature could be responsibly examined, Corson submitted to the university's insistence on written examinations. But he sought to undermine the precedence that examiners routinely granted to questions that call for purely cerebral responses. "*Examinations*" he proclaimed, placing the whole sentence in italics, "*are the bane of literary study.*" He attributed this to a widespread determination to confine interest to what is "definite" and "matter of fact."[15] Over the years, as his long beard grew whiter, he unashamedly declared traditional examining was at cross purposes with his pedagogical goals and methods.

From his earliest years on the faculty Corson constructed exams that gave his students an opportunity to learn something new in the moment of writing them. One early specimen for advanced undergraduates shows how he got students reviewing a full trimester's work and then probed them in some depth about a well-focused portion of what they had been studying. This exam belonged to a course that covered literature from Chaucer's era down to the time that Shakespeare began writing plays. It prints forty-five topics that had been given out in advance. A headnote provides a reminder that each student was receiving "four or five connected questions" to be answered within a single essay; and the instructions advise that "the literary merits of the Essay, as well as the correctness and fullness of the answers given, will be taken into account."[16] Each set of five topics was to contain a mix of potentially interrelated prompts. Some topics would require more factual knowledge than others. Some would require reasoned judgment. But writing on the set as a whole demanded creating an organizing structure. This procedure introduced the possibility that different students would receive different sets of topics. It gave students room to exercise discretion and meant that any subset of examinees who had been given the same topics would invent different ways of interrelating them. It got students using their imaginations—and likely resulted in more interesting reading for the examiner. I offer here an imaginary example that constellates five actual questions and topics that had been given out in advance:

—What qualifications did Chaucer possess for becoming a great national poet?
—State the plan of the Canterbury Tales. To what extent was it carried out?
—In what kind of verse is the Canterbury Tales written?
—Give the plan of the Faerie Queene and state what are regarded as the artistic defects of the plan.
—What are the distinguishing characteristics of Spenser's verse? Describe the Spenserian stanza."[17]

Corson must have spoken in the classroom about matters that would bear on answering these questions. To answer them in a single essay demanded a student employ ingenuity to develop a coherent synthesis. Demonstrating "fullness" required bringing forward knowledge built up before the exam through independent study and then developed during the exam period while organizing and writing the essay itself.

The most demanding specimen of Corson's term examinations comes from an advanced elective course. Like the exam on English grammar devised for the university's entrance exam, it puts the examinees to work using what they have previously learned. Probing almost relentlessly for specific knowledge, it presupposes study well beyond the stage when one reads a literary work without reference to what has been said about it. Headed "Critical Reading," this exam concerns only a single work, Milton's "Lycidas," a pastoral elegy of 193 lines. The prompts fill the best part of two printed pages that test for detailed knowledge of the poem's language, and test as well for related knowledge that enhances appreciation of the poem as a whole. The exam begins with general questions: "Give the occasion of the poem, and analyze its structure." "Explain as minutely as possible the ecclesiastical allegory running through it." Then the questions become highly specific. With respect to the phrase "sad occasion dear," students are asked for other examples where Milton or other writers place a noun between two adjectives that modify it. Subsequently, students are asked what a certain critic has said about the use of "dear" and what a certain editor proposes about the etymology of this word. Dozens of questions focus on particular words and lines, asking for glosses, allusions, etymologies, derivations, illustrations of language change, or how "the force" of this and that word has altered from Milton's time to the present. These are occasionally interrupted by questions that move quite outside the poem, as when, for instance, with respect to Milton's phrase "walked the waves," the examinee is asked, first, "after what class of intransitive verbs was it common in Elizabethan English to omit the preposition?" and then told to "Give examples from Shakespeare."[18] Elsewhere comparison with other elegiac poems is required, with Virgil as a predecessor, for instance, and with Tennyson as a successor. If there were persons resistant to the idea that English could be made a sufficiently difficult subject to warrant a place in the modern university, this examination might have stimulated them to imagine a future in which English literature could be transformed into a respectable subject for critical reading. The exam predicted the industry and rigor that Corson would expect from students in other advanced courses.

The year 1880, as we noted near the outset, marked a decisive turning point in the history of Cornell's curriculum and in the workings of the English program. Students were encouraged to take advantage of the traditional motto whereby "any person can find instruction in any study" by choosing a "Special Study" as the principal focus within their degree-work. (Most undergraduates elected one of the sciences.) Corson and Shackford continued to teach required courses within each of the traditional Courses. But students who elected English literature as a "Special Subject" would now begin in their first year with Anglo-Saxon and continue in the second with a course on medieval language and literature. Juniors, seniors, and students who came to Cornell chiefly for English took a series of courses covering the fourteenth through the nineteenth centuries, inclusive. These courses included examinations, but ones that would rarely ask for a rehearsal of the historical, biographical, or bibliographical information that Corson taught them to regard as merely "adventitious." In the class meetings themselves he sought to accomplish what he regarded as the real work. He brought the students into direct relation with the essential character of masterpieces and aimed at helping them develop a sympathetic appreciation of Chaucer and Milton, Wordsworth and Browning. By reading aloud and highlighting what he found to be alive in the words, he meant to inspire the independent reading that henceforth they would be doing on their own.

As it happened, not long after Shackford's retirement in 1886, all the courses that Cornell students took in junior and senior year became entirely elective, and Corson developed a more concentrated English program. It required juniors and seniors who wished to specialize to devote at least nine hours per week to literary work. Corson went on to create four advanced seminars: two on prose (sometimes fiction, sometimes nonfiction) and two on poetry (eighteenth century and nineteenth). Accomplished undergraduates enrolled in them along with graduate students. When in the 1890s *The Dial* invited Corson to describe how English was being taught at Cornell, he climaxed his account by characterizing his current seminar. The students were reading all of George Eliot's novels and presenting papers that "bear chiefly, almost exclusively, on what is understood by their authors to constitute the life, the informing spirit, the moral proportion, the *motives,* of the works treated."[19]

That already in the previous two decades Corson had gone about inventing a virtual English major owed a good deal to the university's foundational commitment to enable "any person" to study "any" respectable subject. When Cornell first opened, President White had envisioned a grandiose array of English studies as a required and auxiliary component of every undergraduate's education. This was unusual but not unique. As we have seen in earlier chapters, at just the same moment, the subject was gaining momentum elsewhere. The Massachusetts Institute of Technology required incoming students to take an ambitious two-year program described under the heading "English, 1868–69." Yale's Sheffield School hired Thomas Lounsbury to teach English language and literature to all of its students. Meanwhile, at the University of Michigan, Tyler, White's successor, would soon be implementing the practice called "direct study" of "masterpieces" and putting in place a virtual English major. It was Cornell, however, which as early as 1880 listed "Literature" among the "Special Subjects," that first promoted "English" beyond its previously auxiliary status and fully recognized it as a respectable university subject. University policy made it theoretically, and Corson made it practically, possible for a student to earn a bachelor's degree in English.

15

A Concentration in English Studies at Harvard and the "Harvard Annex"

If I am offered only the alternative of absolutism or *laissez faire*, I choose *laissez faire*. Out of chaotic nature beautiful forms do occasionally proceed. But absolutism kills in the cradle. It cannot tolerate a life that is imperfect, and so it stifles what it should nourish.

—GEORGE HERBERT PALMER,
Possible Limitations of the Elective System

WHEN ACADEMIC DEPARTMENTS called "English" began to appear in North American colleges, for the first time in history adolescents were able to make the formal study of vernacular literary works the respectable object of their sustained attention. At the oldest college in the United States, Charles W. Eliot's presidency (1869–1909) oversaw the gradual unraveling of a fixed curriculum, the creation of new disciplines, and the transformation of the institution into a modern university. By the 1890s, Harvard's English department was the largest and most influential in the country. But Eliot himself deserves little credit for that preeminence. For many years, he enforced two policies that precluded the possibility that Harvard students would join the likes of their peers at Cornell and Michigan, where the English departments were fostering the study of vernacular literature. First, he credited an old-fashioned idea of what English study entails. This was made manifest in the brief he created for his English department, which rendered it merely a handmaiden to other subjects. Second, he put up resistance to attempts by the several departments to group courses into a coherent curricular path. To his way of thinking, grouping constituted an insult to the manly freedom that the free elective system guaranteed. "Groups are like ready-made clothing," he insisted, "cut in regular sizes, they never fit any concrete individual."[1] It was not until the second decade of the twentieth century that Harvard's administration allowed departments to offer what the college would refer to as a "Concentration."

Eager as Eliot was to set an elective system in motion, he was never in a position like that of presidents of newly founded institutions who hired an entire faculty ab ovo. The Harvard he inherited had a required traditional curriculum and a large faculty already in place. Eliot proceeded to hire dozens of more specialized instructors. As he made room for new electives, he pared down requirements in traditionally prescribed studies. He nonetheless made one conspicuous exception, and it defined "Harvard English" in merely instrumental terms. When students finished their first year and a large range of electives was open to them, Eliot saw to it that they still faced—as sophomores, juniors, and seniors—a formidable battery of prescribed composition courses. These were fundamental to his belief that a Harvard education necessarily included training for public speaking and writing. The continued existence of required composition courses may seem to us to have served as a major. But—and this is crucial—the courses did not constitute a major, precisely because students did not freely choose them.

In the early part of his presidency, Eliot personally hired every new faculty member. Busy as he was recruiting specialists who would outflank the entrenched instructors that he inherited, he tended to take for granted members of the old guard. This included the accomplished scholar Francis Child, Boylston Professor of Rhetoric and Oratory, who had spent more than two decades reading thousands of undergraduate compositions every year. But when in 1876 the new Johns Hopkins University attempted to hire Child away, Eliot, in order to hold on to him, appointed him professor of English and freed him to teach electives on language and literature.

All the composition courses were now gathered together and designated as English courses. Meanwhile, Eliot named Adams Sherman Hill as Child's successor in the Boylston Chair. Hill was assigned the work of overseeing the writing courses and Child was exempted from teaching them. First-year students continued to take traditional rhetoric and composition, and sophomores had prescribed theme-writing. Juniors and seniors had courses called "forensics." This was a technical rhetorical term. It referred to persuasive oratory of the sort used in a court of law and in debating. Typically, in U.S. colleges, the professor of rhetoric taught forensics, and he required students to compose persuasive arguments to be delivered in speeches. At Harvard, the subject had generally been taught by philosophy professors, and forensics students wrote lengthy argumentative essays, not orations. When all the writing courses started to be called "English," the genial philosophy professor who had been giving instruction in forensics, George Herbert Palmer, continued to teach them. As we will see, Palmer eventually made an intervention that helped pave the way for the number of literature courses to multiply.

Child had been exposed during his education in Germany to philological methods for studying literature. He believed that the way to embark on English studies was to attend to the language. In the years just before Eliot became president, he had offered Anglo-Saxon as an elective. His students used textbooks written by Lafayette's Francis March. He gradually added two other electives. One covered the history and grammar of English. The other employed Edwin Abbott's *Shakespearian Grammar* as its textbook and included the study of three Shakespeare plays. In time the grammar course would evolve into a yearlong elective covering six or seven plays in their entirety, each one handled thoroughly, scene by scene, with attention riveted on the language. Child presented the Bard's words as the source of his power, above all when familiar words (e.g., "kind" or "virtue") were put to unfamiliar uses. In the classroom, he continued the traditional practice of calling on students to recite memorized passages. He worked hard to teach them how to handle the meter, and he assigned them to get by heart excerpts from each work they studied, running to a total of about six hundred lines per year. When he provided philological commentary, his students could feel a certain excitement that a writer who used their own language was being treated on a par with Latin and Greek ones. Although Child himself never wavered in his support for study of the ancient classics, students became aware that their study of vernacular literature was a mark of a new dispensation, and they felt fortunate to have entered it.

Extant class notes taken by Child's students show that he did not lecture. His goal was to make certain that every word in a literary work could be understood in its context. Students typically wrote glosses on words and phrases into their own copies, using blank pages interleaved within the textbook.

Browsing through their notes today might give the impression that the classes were so thoroughly trained on linguistic minutiae that they must have been insufferably boring. The notes offer no evidence that Child devoted a sustained patch of lecturing to anything like a theme, a character, or a plot, or that he had any inclination to generate an interpretation of a play as a whole. He put select words under a magnifying glass, and it was for each student to pull it back and generate a picture of the whole. The object was to learn to read slowly, at a deliberate pace; to cultivate practices of attention that would enable you to notice a subtle, telling nuance and give you confidence that you could unravel a textual knot on your own; and ultimately to develop a taste, through long practice, that enabled you to read the plays with pleasure.

In his midterm examinations, Child expected students to explain particular words and phrases and to write out passages that had been assigned for memory. But three-hour final examinations required short essays on assigned readings done outside class as well—for example, from Edward Dowden's popular *Shakspere Primer.* ("Shakspere" was the standard Harvard spelling of the surname well into the twentieth century. In the pages to follow, except when reporting a course title or reproducing a quotation, I will employ the spelling that is generally in use today.) And there were questions about the playwright's biography, a subject that rarely came up in the classroom. Eventually, Child put a rotation in place, so that a student could study Shakespeare for two years running. Typically, in one year he taught *King Lear,* both parts of *Henry IV, Julius Caesar, All's Well That Ends Well, Macbeth,* and *The Tempest;* in the next, *Hamlet, Romeo and Juliet, Henry V, The Winter's Tale, Antony and Cleopatra,* and *Othello.* (Notably absent here were the lighter comedies.) With this rotation largely intact, Harvard's English 2 (Shakspere) would become the country's most influential course on the Bard. It remained so after Child's death well into the next century.

While Child was Harvard's only English professor teaching literature, Eliot hired young instructors and tutors, on short-term contracts, to do the spadework in teaching composition. This allowed A. S. Hill a measure of freedom to develop new courses. He devised an elective called "Advanced Rhetoric and Themes." Admission was open only to demonstrably accomplished upper classmen. He also supervised a modest elective called "Oral Discussion" that provided a forum for debate.[2] Eventually, he was allowed to begin giving an elective on relatively recent vernacular writing. He gradually expanded it into a pair of courses on eighteenth- and nineteenth-century literature. At this point it became theoretically possible that a student who elected Child's two-year Shakespeare rotation and Hill's guided tour through more recent literary culture could spend fully one quarter of his college years studying English literature—this, in addition to taking the prescribed writing courses. But the pickings among English electives remained scarce, and students regarded Hill as a dull teacher.[3]

LARGE CHANGE SOMETIMES takes place gradually in small increments and then, suddenly, announces its arrival all at once. The year 1887 witnessed a decisive change of direction for the Harvard English department. A new circular boldly declared that its faculty would hereafter be teaching "Group One" and "Group Two" literature courses. Group One courses—Anglo-Saxon grammar, Old English literature, Chaucer, Spenser, the English Bible, Shakspeare, Bacon, and Milton—would continue to feature the well-honed procedures that Child employed in the Shakespeare rotation. This involved "a minutely critical examination of a limited number of works which illustrate the growth and development not only of English literature but also of the English language." The Group Two courses were to "cover the field of English literature from the beginning of the Seventeenth Century to the present time." They would provide "a general acquaintance with the life and works of each author taken up, and with his position in literary history."[4]

Two former tutors, now hired onto the faculty, were assigned to teach the first Group Two offerings. These would be considered "half-courses" and would meet either twice a week for one semester or throughout the year but only once a week. Both courses sported a title that attested to the centrality of Shakespeare for the study of English, even though none of his works appeared on either syllabus. Barrett Wendell's English 14 was called "The Drama (exclusive of Shakspere) from the Miracle Plays to the Restoration." Its final examination gave evidence, as we observed in chapter 1, that Harvard was now examining students on literary works in ways that required them to use logic and imagination. LeBaron Russell Briggs's English 15 was called "English Literature (exclusive of Milton) from Shakspere to Dryden." When the dean's year-end report announced the "enlargement of the instruction offered in English literature,"[5] he designated the Group Two offerings "the most noteworthy" development in the college's curriculum. The courses attracted large numbers of students; they filled the temporal gap between the periods covered by Child and by Hill; and they gave a first inkling of the department's ambition to expand the possibility of studying literary works from any and all periods.

AN ACRIMONIOUS CONTROVERSY centered on Harvard's free elective system offers a context that helps to explain how Eliot's policy against grouping courses unraveled. An increasing number of colleges were offering students more elective opportunities, and criticism heated up among educators across the country who feared that their curriculum was catapulting towards the extreme they believed Harvard represented. The critique that touched Eliot most closely had been leveled in 1885 by the president of Princeton, James McCosh, a Scotsman who loved a good debate. McCosh contended that granting students "unfettered choice" yields injurious results. To illustrate what he took to be at stake, he chose an example that defined a conspicuous difficulty inherent in attempting to launch the study of English: "Literature is so wide and varied," he observed, "no one can master it all."[6]

U.S. English departments differed considerably from one another in how they were organizing their literature offerings. McCosh's critique put a finger on how arbitrarily they were making decisions about what materials counted in the new discipline. On what basis did a department (or an individual student, for that matter) decide which literary works ought to be read? Which might (or might not) be covered in electives? Which writers, which genres, periods, methods of study and critical lenses were to be brought forward, and how were these components to be meaningfully arranged? (It was obvious that over time, as an exponentially larger number of valuable literary works would become available, the problem that McCosh had isolated would intensify exponentially.) McCosh insinuated that the randomness with which colleges were presenting literary works in English epitomized an inherent weakness in the free elective system itself: while hundreds of electives were becoming available, allowing "unfettered choice" among them meant that many students would find that their four years of coursework added up to nothing in particular.

Into the breach stepped George Herbert Palmer, professor of philosophy, and close colleague of Child and Hill, with whom he had taught writing courses for many years. As much a critic as a defender of the free elective system, Palmer took on the role of neutral mediator. During the 1886–87 academic year, drawing on strategies for argumentative writing that he employed when teaching young writers, he published an irenic two-part essay under the bland and ambiguous title "Possible Limitations of the Elective System." The limitations he had in mind turned out to refer, negatively, to rules meant to minimize abuses wrought amidst "unfettered choice" and, positively, to practices that would help students channel their personal interests productively. The better to reinforce a common ground among his readers, Palmer depicted both Harvard and its critics as responsibly avoiding two extremes. These he designated as "absolutism" and "*laissez faire.*"[7] Absolutism expressed itself in micromanagement. It belonged to the old days, before students had a share in shaping their own education, when colleges prescribed a uniform curriculum and *grouping* referred to keeping each entering class studying the same subjects together. The real genius of Palmer's strategy lay, however, in his decision to employ the term *laissez-faire.* It named a style of leadership that critics thought Eliot was promoting. By suggesting that some space lay between Harvard's practices and a laissez-faire system, Palmer gave Eliot some maneuvering room and nudged him away from doubling down on his policy against grouping courses.

As a mediator Palmer demonstrated wide sympathies and enjoyed unusual credibility, both in his own institution and abroad. A learned classicist and a talented writer, he had made a fine prose translation of the *Odyssey* and was attracting large audiences to public readings from it, just as Child was doing with Shakespeare. He collected valuable materials associated with the poet George Herbert, after whom his parents had named him, and published a three-volume edition of Herbert's works. And he was a beloved teacher, known as the "Dean" of teachers for inspiring many students to enter the profession. His intervention in the controversy did not stoop to defending Eliot by calling attention to Harvard's numerous required courses in composition. Instead it credited his readers with a genuine concern for students' welfare and displayed a generous understanding of the critics' complaints. At the same time, Palmer expressed a concern that bore directly on Harvard.

In a recent lecture titled "What is a Liberal Education?" (1884), President Eliot had begun promoting the idea that there was a reciprocal relationship between the language in which university education was henceforth to be conducted and a body of literary works in English that was larger, more diverse, and more aesthetically accomplished than any other in world history. He was encouraging large lecture courses that would include ones on the "most splendid literature which the world has seen."[8] Palmer saw clearly that the unfolding transition from the old culture of recitation to a culture of lecturing tempted instructors to become showmen and that some students were seeking out amusing and diverting lecturers. This posed a timely challenge for the English department in particular, because it was about to launch the new Group Two offerings. Palmer had been a lecturer himself, and readily acknowledged that lectures made for a genuine improvement over recitations. But he pointed out that in lecture courses the instructor generally does the bulk of the work, and he was unafraid to assert that a "pure lecture system" is a "broad road to ignorance." It leaves students "entertained or bored." "Learning," he continued, "is not acceptance; it is criticism, it is attack, it is doing. . . . One who will grow wise must perform processes himself, not sit at ease and behold another's performance." Dismissing the idea that the young have a "vicious" desire to enroll in "soft" courses, Palmer urged that students want to be engaged and need to be challenged. "The goal," he wrote, "is to get students not to want such courses."[9] This was something he thought Eliot, who sought to fill up large halls with lecture courses, needed seriously to consider.

Palmer did not single-handedly convince Eliot to modify his policies. Rather, he called attention to vulnerabilities in the actual operations of Harvard's free elective system. He helped to make space for his colleagues in English to begin grouping their courses in ways that students would find educational. The English department now proposed that each course on offer would lead to one or more of three outcomes: (1) scientific knowledge of the origin and development of the English language and literature; (2) acquaintance with English literature; (3) proficiency in English composition.[10] Sandwiching the new Group Two agenda (2) between the traditional ones, this proposal discreetly downplayed a startling innovation—making literature from any and every period or locale fair game for study—and endorsed its legitimacy. Child, for his part, was a genial and open-minded person. Although he himself remained committed to directing meticulous attention to the language that appears in older classic texts, he readily tolerated the expansion of the field. He also respected the innovative approaches that younger instructors brought to teaching literary works. As for prescribed composition courses, however, he remained skeptical about their worth.

IN THE MID-1880S, Harvard had only two English professors to make good on its president's extravagant claims for the greatness of English literature. Granted, Eliot had been willing to hire recent graduates, on short-term contracts, as tutors. But he took a risk when, instead of attempting to hire away established specialists from other institutions, he appointed Briggs and Wendell as instructors in English. Different as they were from one another, both had teaching experience elsewhere and both became major contributors to making Harvard's English department the most celebrated and influential in the country.

Barrett Wendell (class of 1876; AB, 1877) fell into a job at his alma mater haphazardly. He hadn't studied literature as an undergraduate and never earned an advanced degree. He was well read, however, and had been one of the founders of the satirical *Harvard Lampoon*. After graduation, he dabbled briefly in legal work and was meandering along a desultory path when a chance encounter with Hill led to a job marking undergraduate essays. He found the work tedious and thankless. Assigned to do some teaching of women off campus (more on this momentarily), he developed his own versions of theme-writing and forensics and began dreaming up innovative ways of teaching composition that he hoped to use one day at Harvard. Once given the chance to teach literature, he took instinctively to the dual tasks of the script-writer and the lecturer. Eccentric, sporting a red beard and spats, he walked around the lecture hall twirling his watch chain, and through Harvard Yard brandishing his walking stick. He spoke in a high staccato voice and affected a way of speaking that students often mistook for Anglophilia. He presented himself as an amateur, not a scholar. Shamelessly pontificating, he took delight in saying things that would shock his students. Increasingly, he enjoyed playing the gadfly and flaunting unconventional opinions, the better to expose the dangers he saw lurking in "modern" ideas of "social justice" for the working classes. His colleague from the philosophy department, George Santayana, remarked of Wendell's teaching of composition that it showed he could be "a useful pedagogue," and of his lectures on literature, that he taught students "nothing except what to think about what you happened to know." Yale Professor William Lyon ("Billy") Phelps, who studied and taught with Wendell in the early 1890s, remarked—insisting in an ambiguous tone that it was "the highest possible compliment to Harvard"—that no other institution in the country would have retained him on its faculty.[11] But the Group Two drama course that Wendell created in 1887 was Harvard's first on a single genre and proved to be astonishingly influential. (The Harvard archives hold more than ten sets of notes recording what transpired in the lectures.) He went on to teach the university's first course on American literature and managed to introduce an alternative to Child's Shakspeare course. And, fulfilling the dreams he first conceived elsewhere, he developed the writing courses for which he is sometimes remembered today.[12] Still, making a show of his amateur status amidst scholars as he did, he had to wait until 1898 to be promoted to professor.

LeBaron Russell Briggs (AB, 1876), unlike his eccentric and fiercely independent erstwhile classmate, was a company man through and through. After graduation he was hired as a tutor in Greek, earned a graduate degree (AM, 1882), and taught—to women off campus—a greater range of subjects (Anglo-Saxon, theme-writing, forensics, and literature) than Wendell. He rose quickly up the ranks in the English department (instructor, 1883; assistant professor, 1885) and into an overlapping administrative career that began when he was named the department's third professor and the university's first dean of students (1890). Soon he was serving as dean of the Harvard faculty and president of Radcliffe College for women, all the while continuing with his teaching. An affable man with a prodigious memory, Briggs was said never to have forgotten a face or a name. T. S. Eliot recalled "Dean Briggs" as the teacher who introduced him to the poetry of John Donne. For years it was widely assumed that Briggs would be named Harvard's next president. (Charles Eliot liked the job, however, and just kept going.) In the same year that Wendell taught Harvard's first course on the drama, Briggs taught the first course on seventeenth-century literature. It turned out to be significant for the booming popularity of English at Harvard that both instructors had had their formative teaching experience off campus, where their students had been women eager to pursue literary studies. In time, the nearby flourishing of random English courses for women provided a second context for the unraveling of Harvard's policy prohibiting departments from grouping their courses.

HARVARD DID NOT admit women as students. (It did not fully admit women until the 1970s, but that is a different, though related, story.) In the 1870s, a local philanthropist gathered a group of women from Cambridge and Boston, and together they founded the Society for the Collegiate Instruction of Women, which in 1894 would be chartered as Radcliffe College. Fully aware that in the nation's high schools young women were surpassing the achievements of young men; ready to counter the oft-repeated claim that women are both physically and mentally too weak for the rigors of study; and eager for liberation from the assumption that higher education was unnecessary for carrying out the duties of wives, mothers, and educators of small children, in 1879 the founders secured quarters near the college campus. They proceeded to arrange for Harvard faculty members to repeat their lectures for the women. President Eliot, no friend of women's education, acceded to the arrangement, because the Society would be adding a handsome supplement to the salaries of Harvard professors. The women would not be allowed to earn a bachelor's degree. They could work towards a "certificate." Given an inevitable randomness among the courses that turned out to be available, however, they had the freedom to choose among them, and this would prove telling.

At the "Harvard Annex," as it was called, the study of English started unspectacularly. The first English courses were taught by Hill, who repeated his Harvard lectures on composition. Hill also gave an abbreviated version of literature in the nineteenth-century, treating Carlyle, "Miss Austen," Hawthorne, and Emerson. Child, who did not teach at the Annex, entrusted what was referred to as the "usual instruction in Themes and Forensics demanded in the college course" to Briggs and Wendell, and soon—given an insistent and surprising plea for more English—the pair began teaching literature there as well. Other young instructors followed, and within a decade English became, hands down, the most frequently elected subject. By 1889 there were 164 enrollments in English, 91 in history (the second most popular subject), fifty-some each in various foreign languages courses, fewer than two dozen in scientific subjects. Word spread about the new opportunities that were opening up. Young women who had studied at the likes of Vassar, Smith, and Mount Holyoke and at Midwestern state universities began enrolling, some of them in graduate level study. By 1891 English enrollments had risen to 302. This was three times more than in history, six times as many as in all other subjects combined. Meanwhile, Harvard undergraduates were complaining about the "philological gristmill" where they were made to study literature for the purpose of illustrating the history of the language. They pointed out that Shakespeare wrote his plays to be acted. And they were clamoring for opportunities to give sustained attention to the likes of *The Faerie Queene*, the better to appreciate the grounds on which classic literary works had long been admired.[13]

Briggs found in the Annex a hospitable laboratory where he could learn to teach students who were eager to be engaged and keen to meet a challenge. He designed a means of studying two seventeenth-century writers that Child's teaching only touched on, and he experimented with using class time in decidedly different ways from anything available to Harvard undergraduates. The ambitious subject matter was all Milton's works, including the prose, and all Dryden's writing apart from his plays. The class met twice a week through the whole year. The Society's annual report described what was distinctive about how Briggs conducted it: "The students themselves gave all the lectures, taking topics assigned by the instructor. Each lecture was freely criticized in the classroom, not only by the instructor but by every member of the class."[14]

As for Wendell, he set out to teach all Shakespeare's plays. He lectured on one each week. The contrast with Child's philological practices climaxed in a kaleidoscopic display of the lecturer's decided opinions. Wendell organized the first few classes by historical chronology, lecturing on *King John* and then covering the histories in the order of each monarch's reign down as far as *Richard III*. Then he took up plays from the other genres, treating early comedies and *Romeo and Juliet*. In the second term he lectured on the great tragedies and the late plays.

We can know a good deal about how Wendell taught Shakespeare through notes that he himself preserved. Unlike notes that lecturers routinely write out while preparing their lectures, his were written shortly *after* each class. He inscribed them in a bound notebook into which he eventually added for posterity the information that the course was "the first in which I have tried my hand as a teacher of literature."[15] The notes are of various kinds. Some summarize what he had talked about. Several tell about particular productions he had seen and about how well-known actors (e.g., Henry Irving, Ellen Terry) performed. Others register his affective responses to, say, a given play: *A Midsummer Night's Dream* "affected me almost as subtly as music does" (15 December 1884). Or, to his performance on a given day: My lecture was "rambling." Or, after lecturing on *As You Like It:* "I am too tired this afternoon to jot down all that I said in abuse of this popular play" (16 February 1885). Frequently, he documents exchanges that reveal an audacity on the part of the young women for which he was unprepared. On the day that he taught *Julius Caesar* he reports that "At the end of the hour, Miss Howe asked me, with touching simplicity, whether I had ever read any of the plays I talked about more than once. Eheu!" (2 March 1885).

A striking annotation in this vein was written right after the class on *Richard III* (Monday, November 24, 1884). It culminates in Wendell's enumerating "three bombshells" that startled and shook him and left him addressing in the notebook an imagined audience that was altogether discontinuous with the students in whose company he had talked about the play. Midway through the lecture, a curious and somewhat dissatisfied student, perceiving that he was not going to engage with the sorts of issues that the play raised for her, had interrupted to ask some trenchant questions. Wendell's recapitulation of what he had been saying, and not saying, reports both the student's intervention and the two phases of his reaction to it, in class and after class:

> Human beings always take more interest in a villain than in an equally complete honest man. To analyze the reason for this state of things, in the character of Richard[,] I did not attempt. And at this point in my remarks I was rather appalled by the sudden arrival of three bombshells:—viz., 1. Does the portrayal of evil character demand higher or lower literary qualities than the portrayal of good? 2. In what respect does the religious attitude of Shakspere resemble or differ from that of other dramatists of his time? 3. What, in my opinion, may be thought of the literary value of antithesis as observed in the works of Shakspere in general?
>
> In a feeble effort to rally from the shock caused by this unexpected &

> undeserved bombardment, I passed the rest of the hour. I failed, I think, to expound to my fair interlocutrix the full horror of her questions, or of the state of mind which they proved to lurk behind an engaging countenance.

Here, in the last two sentences, the implicit audience for Wendell's notes has taken a turn. His youthful writing for the *Lampoon* perhaps lies behind it. He seems almost to be rehearsing a "Can you believe this!" anecdote to be shared with male colleagues. They would recognize the impertinence of the woman's intervention. They would not tell him that his failure to make plain why such questions ought not to be asked owed anything to his assumption that "the girls" (as he referred to them) should be honored that a Harvard man would bestow upon them his impressions of Shakespeare's plays. They would recognize the real problem: his "fair interlocutrix" was unfamiliar with the manly protocols that rendered talk about anyone's religion discreetly to be avoided and that made it unthinkable that students might challenge their teacher or expose his ignorance.

We don't know what Wendell thought he had learned from his experience teaching Shakespeare at the Annex. But Child reassigned the teaching of Shakespeare there to George Lyman Kittredge (class of '82). Kittredge, Child's protégé and a scholar notably more learned than Wendell, would teach the women according to the Group One model. Nonetheless, Wendell went on to teach at Harvard new Group Two courses that had never been given before: on the drama "exclusive of Shakspere," on "English Literature of the Elizabethan Period, exclusive of Drama and Bacon," and on American literature. He took this work seriously. Exhibiting a markedly more pragmatic frame of mind, he made conventional use of the notebooks he kept while teaching these courses to write out his lectures ahead of time. They appear on the right-hand pages, with the left-hand ones free for recording revisions. The notes from his composition and Shakespeare courses provided the basis for two of the several books he went on to publish. But when, in retirement, Wendell reflected on what he had accomplished as a writer, he singled out as his most valuable publication an essay of the kind that he had taught in forensics. Titled "The Relations of Radcliffe College with Harvard," it argued in detail that having women in class would distract Harvard students from their manly work and would likely "diminish" the professors' "scholarly vigor."[16]

After Kittredge first taught a Shakespeare course at the Annex, he proceeded to teach it on both campuses for many more years. His teaching was legendary in both forums. One Radcliffe student characterized his behaviors in the classroom this way:

> Kittredge always came into class looking as if he had been up all night. Often he ran his hand through his hair, and closed his eyes. He had one deficiency I never like[d] and apparently it lasted ~~him~~ [*sic*]. He never looked his students in the eye. He used a card system. He would call a name, put a question, and then look into space just over one's head. . . . I never felt he knew me or, for that matter, any one else. There was no personal relationship. . . . Nevertheless I am glad beyond words I had the privilege and I liked even the examinations given when they came.

Of the Shakespeare course generally, she wrote: "I did not find a single minute of it boring. His comments upon the meaning and origin of ~~passages~~ [*sic*] words and phrases were so thoroughly intertwined with his striking passages of character interpretation, that it merely meant a pleasant variety."[17]

In 1894 Kittredge was appointed the Harvard's fourth professor of English, and Child gave him charge of the philologically oriented electives that for the past few years the two men had been teaching together. Kittredge also created a new course on "Metrical Romances." Meanwhile, a pair of young graduates who, like Kittredge, had been trained in the Child's methodology took over the teaching of "half-courses" on Bacon and on Milton, and Briggs invented a new Group One course on versification. Child, on the brink of retirement, inaugurated a course on his specialty, English and Scottish popular ballads. When the college reorganized the ways in which courses were categorized, the English department at last divided its course offerings into three groups: primarily for undergraduates; for undergraduates and graduates; and primarily for graduates. The Group One courses were placed almost exclusively in the third category.

As the university continued to hire recent graduates onto the faculty, the Group Two courses multiplied rapidly. Lewis Edwards Gates (class of '84) took over Hill's course on nineteenth-century prose and developed an altogether new composition course, numbered English 22. Although personally

Gates was a bit of a recluse, as a lecturer he was incomparably brilliant, and his courses proved wildly popular. At the Annex he adapted Briggs's versification course (English 16) to include the students' own original poems an integral feature of the endeavor. George Pierce Baker (class of '87) took decisive charge of the large forensics courses. He inherited Wendell's English 14 and built it into the most successful drama course in the country. Years later, when Harvard rejected the idea of building a theatre, Baker moved to Yale and took the course with him. Wendell introduced English 17 to cover Elizabethan literature "exclusive of Shakspere." He also turned the course he had created at the Annex into English 23, "The Works of Shakspere," the first course at Harvard to treat almost all the plays. (The department disallowed any student who had not already taken Child's "orthodox" course on the Bard from registering for it.) Shortly before Child died in 1896, Harvard's four professors taught together as a team that offered, "primarily for undergraduates," the college's first general survey of English literature (English 28). Each lecturer covered a different era. The ascending course numbers we have been seeing here attest to an expanding list of literature courses greater in number and influence than those offered at any other institution.

WHEN CHARLES W. ELIOT became Harvard's president, in order to raise funds to pay new faculty, he had set out to expand the size of the student body. By the early 1890s, the university had more than three thousand students, about two-thirds of them studying in the Faculty of Arts and Sciences, an incomparably larger number of students than could be found in most colleges. The English department, with twenty faculty members, was the country's largest: nearly a thousand enrollments in yearlong courses, nearly another thousand in half-courses. Optional composition courses, notably ones in which students could write on any subject they wished, proved the most popular of all the electives. Wendell, when he reported these figures in Harvard's contribution to *The Dial*'s symposium on English in American universities, insinuated that his department's success was chiefly owing to a policy whereby "when a course is given into a man's charge, . . . he is absolutely free to conduct it in any way he chooses."[18] Laissez-faire for the students as they chose their courses, absolutism for the instructor once the students entered his classroom.

But the long-standing prescription of required composition courses remained something of a hindrance. Students who had little interest in English often developed a distaste for the subject, and many teachers who read undergraduate essays lived with an uneasy recognition that they were wasting their time. (Wendell himself came to agree with Child that composition is not "University work.") While Harvard was emerging as the very epitome of the modern university, and specialized study in every discipline was growing increasingly sophisticated, the policy that required composition courses continued to rest on the naïve assumption that what English professors taught sufficiently served the purposes of all the other departments. We might wonder whether professors in other disciplines, recognizing how much work reading a student's writing entails, were content to deprive students of the opportunity to have advanced instruction in writing for their chosen field. That would have better credited the fact that writing is after all a fundamental tool for learning: it requires slowing down, reflecting, presenting complex material, and, as *The Philosophy of Style* (1852) by Herbert Spencer had emphasized, employing language that is readily accessible to readers as possible.

Another outcome of Harvard's continuing practice of locating the writing requirements in the English department proved unfortunate for English instructors who worked in other colleges. The department developed a policy whereby two instructors were exempted from teaching the prescribed composition courses to pursue their scholarship. The other eighteen were required to put in the work. This acknowledged that teaching writing is hard work and simultaneously denigrated it, conferring second-class status upon instructors who specialized in teaching writing.

It was the teaching of literature that made Harvard's English department a mecca, attracting not only a large percentage of undergraduates but an increasing number of students who had been studying elsewhere, young men who made their way to Harvard on account of its superior courses. By the 1890s the large number of literature courses available at Harvard dramatized the acuity of President McCosh's observation that English literature is too vast a subject to master. But it no longer mattered that President Eliot had forbidden "grouping" courses and that Harvard did not offer an English major. The availability of numerous electives could be confusing, and not every student exercised good judgment in choosing among them. But the department now offered a modicum of help by clarifying three desired outcomes for its courses and by dividing its offerings according to levels of difficulty. This supplemented the scuttlebutt about teachers and course content that circulated as students contemplated their choice of electives. More than the large *number* of opportunities for studying literature, the extraordinary *range* of different instructors, topics, approaches, and methods that students encountered in the department opened vistas, whetted curiosity, and begat desire. The remarkable treasure trove of materials from this period found today in the Harvard archives—circulars, printed examinations, professors' notes, syllabi, students' notebooks, dean's reports, and the like—attests to an unprecedented self-awareness, on the part of both the instructors and their students, of the historic importance of what they had been involved in.

16

The English Major at Wellesley College

A fact that strikes us as a great paradox when we look over the whole history of education is that nearly all of the reforms in pedagogy have come from radical, negative men—men who were idiosyncratic, and who departed from the beaten paths of society to such a degree as to amount to a deformity.

—W. T. HARRIS, U.S. Commissioner of Education (1898)

IN THE YEAR 1900, at the Exposition Universelle, the organizers of the largest World's Fair that had ever been held awarded the Wellesley College Department of English a gold medal. The stated purpose of the Paris Exposition, as it was known in English-speaking realms, was to celebrate the achievements of the past century and to accelerate progress into the new one. To demonstrate every sort of progress, forty countries and dozens of colonies and protectorates mounted exhibits—thousands of exhibits altogether. The conspicuous achievements on display—a Ferris wheel, escalators, diesel engines, electric vehicles, dry cell batteries, talking pictures—paid tribute to the power of technology and of industry. Education, an engine of progress, was by no means overlooked. The U.S. prepared dozens of exhibits from its secondary schools and institutions of higher learning. Some few exhibits—from Harvard, MIT, and Princeton—received gold medals. The Wellesley English department displayed materials that illustrated progress in the education of women: syllabi, course plans, and especially the books of fiction, poetry, and criticism that faculty members had authored. The exhibit made it clear that an institution for women and managed by women had, in a mere quarter-century, achieved a status comparable to that enjoyed by the most admired colleges in the United States.

In preparing for the display of vitality in America's schooling, the U.S. Commissioner of Education, W. T. Harris, composed a document to be read by those who were to be responsible for specific exhibits. Harris made the case that, among the nations of the world, the U.S. was distinctive in the ways it connected education with industry to enhance productivity. His palpable optimism about the nation's readiness for what, in retrospect, would be called "the American century" rested on his confidence that American schooling prepared students for the workplace. Colleges in particular were preparing teachers for the growing numbers of young people who would be attending them. Harris urged his readers to understand that "we" are about to "become one of a number of great powers that assume to direct the course of civilization and decide for the rest of the world its destiny. . . . Considering our wealth-producing power and the enrollment in our schools we may easily claim to be the most powerful nation in the world." The Paris Exposition would be the perfect arena in which to secure recognition: "Our claims will be recognized by the united powers of Europe and we shall be allowed our place in their councils."[1] But he warned that it would be impractical to exemplify the connection between education and industrial productivity by laying out samples of the work students were producing. Visitors to the Exposition were not going to linger over, say, term papers, even ones composed by the country's most highly accomplished students. Efficient graphics—publications, photographs, maps, charts, tables, and statistics—were to be the chief means for illustrating the great industry of American schooling. This put the focus on the teachers.

The head of Wellesley's English department, Katharine Lee Bates, was principally responsible for putting together its exhibit and for writing a visitors' guide. Five years earlier she had warmed to a similar task when *The Dial* called upon her to contribute to its fortnightly accounts of how English was being organized in American colleges and universities. She knew that there were readers likely to regard a college for women as an upstart intruder from off "the beaten paths." But in composing her piece on "English at Wellesley College,"[2] which was to be the last of the eighteen contributions to the *Dial* symposium, she saw a remarkable opportunity. Wellesley would be of greater interest to readers than the other leading women's colleges, Vassar and Smith, because it was run by women. The activities and achievements of its English faculty, in which women outnumbered men by nearly twenty to one, outstripped those described in many of the previous reports. The enthusiastic guide she wrote for the Paris Exposition five years later framed and colored everything that visitors and evaluators encountered in the exhibit: course outlines, brief descriptions of how Anglo-Saxon, Chaucer, and contemporary literature were taught; statistics (in a college with 688 students, 418 seats in literature courses had been filled by students who freely chose them); and above all publications by the faculty.[3] It turned out that European visitors were especially interested in another fact: unlike European educational institutions that were funded by the government, this college run entirely by women was funded from private wealth. Its extraordinarily abundant resources enabled it to operate independently.

LOCATED SOME FOURTEEN miles southwest of Harvard Yard, Wellesley College owed both its conception and its beautiful campus to a man: Henry Durant (1822–81), a Harvard graduate who had dreamed of becoming a renowned poet. As a young man Durant began practicing as an attorney. His flamboyant performances as a trial lawyer, and his shrewd investments in the rubber industry, made him immensely wealthy. He and his wife, Pauline, purchased some three hundred acres of uninhabited land abutting Lake Waban west of Boston, planning to develop a great family estate there. When their two offspring died in childhood, they began contemplating a utopian experiment. Aware of the country's great need for well-trained teachers and reckoning that educating young women was as important as securing women's suffrage, Durant spent eight years planning a college in which women would receive as good an education as the college he had attended furnished for young men. It would have a library as large as Harvard's, provide more up-to-date scientific laboratories than MIT, and—this would make Wellesley unique—demonstrate that a professorate comprised entirely of women could offer a caliber of teaching likely to surpass what was to be found in any other liberal arts college.

The Durants had in mind a second agenda as well. It manifested itself early on in a four-year search for the woman who would serve as president. While the institution proclaimed itself nondenominational and it was understood that teachers and students alike would be Protestant, the Durants were Christians of the evangelical sort, eager for their social experiment to induce religiously lukewarm students to undergo a conversion. They expected teachers to do double duty, serving as housemothers in the dormitories and reporting to a president who would bear responsibility for keeping both the social and the religious dimensions of the students' lives in line. The daily schedule would have the young women (sixteen was the minimum age for admission) up at six in the morning. There would be three classes each day and six additional hours assigned for study; a chapel service; two twenty-minute periods of silence for meditation; an hour for exercise and an hour for required domestic chores; and lights out at ten. In the event, Durant hired Ada Howard, a graduate of Mount Holyoke Seminary who had extensive experience overseeing the education of girls. It did not matter that she lacked the learning and credentials of the faculty that he hoped to hire, or that she would be of little use in setting up the curriculum. Academic matters, like everything else that he considered important, he meant to take charge of himself.[4]

Durant was funding the entire experiment, and he assumed the leading part in planning a realm that would be populated and operated by women who would carry out his plans. He oversaw the landscaping of the grounds. He took a daily interest in the construction of a massive structure atop a high hill that would house every facet of the institution, from classrooms and a library to kitchens and dormitories. Designed in the French Second Empire style, the building featured a beautiful central court modeled on Roman palaces of the Renaissance, with stained-glass windows and dark walnut interior paneling. Its crowning touch was to be a room devoted to the Brownings, where a bust of Elizabeth Barrett and one of her original manuscripts could be displayed. Alas, the entire structure was to be destroyed by fire in 1914. (Not a single inhabitant died.) Many alumnae and faculty had saved their papers and notes elsewhere. Today the college archives house numerous notebooks filled up by students in the 1880s, many of them providing evidence of the large place for literary study that Durant envisioned.

The college's early publications proclaimed that "literature" is "essential to woman's education." They made plain that every student was to study literature through all four years. Durant's idea was that while the affective component of literary experience might compromise the manliness that Harvard promoted, it was especially valuable for the fairer sex, whose propensity for nurture would be enhanced by becoming knowledgeable about literature. His curricular plan grouped literary study with history, composition (called "Essay-Writing"), and elocution as a single subject. Within a framework that allotted only three hours a week to these subjects, students were to master the whole history of Western literature. Freshmen (as they were denominated) were to be provided with an outline history that began in ancient Greece and Rome, moved through the early literatures of Italy, France, Spain, and Germany, and concluded with English literature from medieval times. Sophomores were to study English literature from Elizabethan times through the nineteenth century; juniors, to study three great authors—Homer, Dante, and Shakespeare; seniors, early English literature, especially Chaucer. Meanwhile, the students were assigned extracurricular reading, and they were encouraged to join reading circles overseen by faculty members.

Durant's plan for the curriculum depended on his foundational decision to curtail study of the classical languages. He had no problem hiring well-qualified women to teach both Latin and Greek, but students would not be required to study these subjects beyond their first year. Well before other colleges were offering a major, his ambitions provided for the possibility that a student might wish to specialize in a particular area. There would be several Courses to choose from, including science, classical languages, modern languages, music, and art. As things turned out, his provision for specialization was premature: few students showed interest in these options. The majority sought instruction in a broad variety of subjects and chose what was called "the General Course." The college also offered a special "Teachers Course" that did not lead to a degree. It enabled many women who simply wanted to advance their knowledge of one or two subjects—most of them already teachers, often of English—to take whatever courses they wished.

For all the preparations Durant had made, a large surprise awaited him when the college finally opened in 1875. It foreshadowed several things that would go wrong with his ambitious plans. While 314 young women enrolled, the faculty determined that only 30 were prepared to do college-level work. Instead of sending the others home, Durant improvised. He set up a preparatory department, promising it would be only temporary, and within a few years it had succeeded so well that he was able to abolish it. Meanwhile the college faculty maintained high standards by using discretion in their means for evaluating students' work, seeking to dampen students' inclination to compete for grades by informing them only whether they had passed or failed. (Wellesley students began receiving notice of their grades in the 1930s.)

The first students found Durant's elaborate plans for their educational program confusing. One month into the first year of classes, Elizabeth Stilwell wrote a letter to her mother back in Ohio about how subjects that met only once a week were overwhelming all her studies: "Wellesley is not a college," she informed her,

> The buildings are beautiful, perfect almost; the rooms and their appointments delightful, most of the professors are all that could be desired, some of them are very fine indeed in their several departments, but all these delightful things are not the things that make a college. . . . I came here to take a *college course,* and not to dabble in a little of every insignificant thing that comes up. More than half of my time is taken up in writing essays, practicing elocution, trotting to chapel, and *reading poetry* with the teacher of English literature, and it seems to make no difference to Miss Howard and Mr. Durant whether the Latin, Greek and Mathematics are well learned or not.[5]

The letter goes on to identify Mr. Durant as a powerful presence hovering over the students and teachers alike: "Every member of the freshman class has the same feeling, and not only the students but even the professors. . . . [They] have expostulated and expostulated with Mr. Durant, but all to no avail. He is as hard as a flint and his mind is made up of the most beautiful theories, but he is perfectly blind to facts. He rules the college, from the amount of Latin we shall read to the kind of meat we shall have for dinner."[6] Years later, Katharine Bates, who had been a member of the second entering class, said of her experiences with Mr. Durant, "I loved his poetic side, but his fanaticism drove me out of church and theology for all time."[7]

Durant's commitment to employing women faculty meant, practically speaking, looking westward to find candidates who had acquired academic degrees. He cultivated a relationship with James Burrill Angell, the new president of the University of Michigan, the largest full-scale university in the country.

Partial to its graduates, he hired Mary Sheldon (class of '74) to teach history and literature, two subjects closely intertwined both at Michigan and in Wellesley's curriculum. Mary had come to Ann Arbor from upstate New York, where her father was doing innovative work as a history teacher. The first inspiring teacher she found at the university was Moses Coit Tyler, who, by the ways in which he taught history and literature, reminded her of her father. Tyler got her reading literary works in their entirety, and she found, in his insistence that students learn through inquiry, a model for her own teaching. At Wellesley she introduced students to a method that began with something concrete: an object for history, an original piece of writing for literature. She got students observing the artifact and asking questions. She encouraged them to educate themselves by reading on their own. Read "the Masters," she told them—Homer, Dante, and Shakespeare (Durant's favorites)—and Goethe and Milton as well. She singled out other authors she had enjoyed: "Hawthorne most of you know, but perhaps not Thoreau. Read Thoreau[,] 'change // eyes with him and you go out of doors and see what this world is. . . .' Read everything . . . [by] George Eliot." She summed up her advice: "By the time you have read all these you will be able to judge for yourself, having standards. But don't cram; the mind as well as the body needs time to digest."[8] Although her students seem to have reciprocated her evident love for them, Sheldon left Wellesley before her third year there was over. Some members of the faculty regarded her avoidance of hearing recitations and her lecturing as a shocking omission of duty. She eventually found a better outlet for her work at Stanford, where she established an enduring reputation for innovative teaching.[9]

Durant, meanwhile, believed that he had already found a woman better suited to serve as the professor of the English language and literature. He hired Louise Manning Hodgkins, who had been teaching in Wisconsin, where Lawrence College granted her an MA degree. Inasmuch as the vast majority of Wellesley students were in the preparatory school, Durant granted Hodgkins a year's leave of absence to study in Europe. When she returned and took up her teaching duties, she was a publishing writer already in her thirties. She discovered in short order that beginning students found studying the long history of Western European literature overwhelming. She replaced the superficial study of European literatures with a course on her own specialty, nineteenth-century poetry and prose. But, in keeping with Durant's ideas for teaching literature, she introduced students to the study from a distance, preparing them to read literature in the future by giving them information about it. Her approach was bibliographically top-heavy and hardly any better than the one Durant had designed for beginning students. The course covered some twenty-six writers, eighteen English and eight American. For each author, every student was equipped with a copy of a printed pamphlet. A page or two listed significant facts about each writer's life, named his or her (Elizabeth Barrett and George Eliot were included) famous works, and provided many "Selected Books of Reference." There followed several blank pages, each headed with the single word "*NOTES*." Students were expected to write on these pages in class and in the library. As the blank pages stared up at the users, their spaciousness reinforced their teacher's daunting prediction that every graduate of Wellesley would be studying these writers for the rest of her life.

Meanwhile, Hodgkins now taught Durant's sprawling Western literature course to sophomores. Its lengthy title epitomized the ambitious expectations that Elizabeth Stilwell had been up against: "Outlines of General Literature, beginning with the corruption of the Latin Tongue; Mediaeval Epics; Early Literature of Italy, Spain, France and Germany; Outline History of English Literature." As its ultimate focus suggests, the principal purpose of the course was to provide a nationalist context for reading literature in English. Several student notebooks show that the first two classes made the rationale for building up to English explicit. Hodgkins showed students a phylogenetic tree diagram that illustrated the branching of Indo-European languages, and she had each student copy it. Then she provided an explanation of the climactic place occupied by English. Students wrote down what we would now call her bullet points. This is how they appear in one of several notebooks that attest to the underlying assumptions about the historic importance of the English as a language:

—"Political supremacy [is] always followed by linguistic / ex., Saxons [*sic*] in England"

—"a conquering nation enforces her language for the conquered

1. By making it fashionable
2. By making it the medium of all governmental and legal procedures."[10]

In conjunction with the diagram that showed that modern English derived from Anglo-Saxon, this explanation reinforced, in quasi-scientific terms, the traditional Roman idea (*translatio imperii, translatio studii*) according to which political hegemony moves westward and generates new dominant cultures. This was the opposite of a decline-and-fall theory of culture. In the English-speaking world, the idea fit neatly with current theories of evolution and progress. The British Empire found it ready to hand for justifying its territorial expansion and for voicing its ambitions for a national scholarship of the sort being created in the contemporary projects that wrought *The Dictionary of National Biography* and the *Oxford English Dictionary.* Not for nothing did Miss Hodgkins's course mix nineteenth-century English and American writers. This accustomed students to thinking of literary works written in the U.S. as an extension of English literature and integral to it. Katharine Lee Bates took the course. Years later, when she came onto the faculty herself, she began offering one of the country's earliest courses on American literature. She went on to become famous for her poem "America the Beautiful," composed in 1893 upon arriving in the Colorado Rockies via the railroads. Americans were by this time quite accustomed to crediting the idea of Manifest Destiny, and her poem celebrated the country's natural beauty "from sea to shining sea."[11] The exhibit that Bates later prepared for the Paris Exposition fulfilled the explicitly patriotic purpose articulated by the U.S. Commissioner of Education.

ON THE THIRD OF OCTOBER 1881, only six years after Wellesley College opened, Henry Fowle Durant, the patriarch who had founded it, passed from this life, and with him passed his constant surveillance of the experiment he had launched. He had been so closely involved in the college's daily operations that he had remained the principal impediment to fulfilling the unique pedagogical reform he had envisioned: a women's college operated by women. As he led women away from "the beaten paths" of higher education where men taught men, he had held the reins tightly. In the last months of his life, however, the presence of a brilliant young woman he had hired to be the college's professor of history gently began alerting him to the contradiction that he embodied. As he got to know her, he awakened to the knowledge that he had found just the person to succeed him.

Among the talented Michigan graduates that Durant hired, none contributed to the eventual eminence of Wellesley College as spectacularly as Alice Elvira Freeman (BA, University of Michigan, 1876). She and Mary Sheldon had been coleaders of a women's study group in Ann Arbor. President Angell had known Freeman personally all through her undergraduate years. When, after her graduation, he witnessed her teaching a high school class on English literature, he wrote to Durant about her incomparable industry and talent. Durant found it difficult to persuade her to accept a position, but in 1879 she took up the post as Wellesley's professor of history. Once he saw Miss Freeman's vivid personality in action for himself, Durant recognized in her an utter original. She exceeded her own reputation for learning, industriousness, and efficiency. But in no time, she was over-extending herself. As the other teachers did, she oversaw students' domestic tasks and took her turn teaching from the Bible. Soon she was everyone's favorite to hear speaking in the daily chapel gatherings, and she was the students' most sought-after counselor. She taught fifteen classes a week. Seniors often sat in on the ones in which she introduced first-year students to college studies. Everyone—students, faculty, and especially Henry and Pauline Durant—seems to have loved her radiant, joyous energy and her sympathetic demeanor. Durant, acknowledging that Ada Howard's work had become increasingly ineffectual, created a new administrative position and appointed Freeman vice president of the college. A few months later, he died from kidney disease at age fifty-nine. The time had arrived for Wellesley to be run by a woman.

Alice Freeman was only twenty-six years old when the trustees named her Wellesley's second president. Under her leadership the college moved onto the national stage and became one of the country's leading educational institutions. She traveled to high schools to tell Wellesley's story, lectured widely on women's education, and was a cofounder and president of the American Association of University Women. In an era when college presidents were among the most influential men in the country (Eliot at Harvard, White at Cornell, Angell at Michigan), she was the only woman at the head of an independent, nationally known institution. At Wellesley, she hired intellectually serious faculty, women more inclined to promote scholarship and social reform than evangelical religion, and she inspired greater professionalism.

But in 1887, after seven years of successfully hiding how harried she had been, Alice Freeman's health was deteriorating. To everyone's dismay she announced that she was resigning and that she would be getting married to Harvard philosophy professor George Herbert Palmer.[12] (At Wellesley, a faculty member's marrying and resigning were intertwined well into the twentieth century.) She and her husband continued to pursue their separate careers. She retained an active interest in the welfare of the college even as she accepted invitations for public speaking events, wrote for major magazines, and herself became the subject of magazine features and news stories. By the time Katharine Bates's piece on "English at Wellesley College" appeared in *The Dial,* Alice Freeman had accepted an offer from the recently founded University of Chicago to serve as its first dean of women, and she was spending part of every year in the bustling city where the journal was published.

As for the study of English at Wellesley, President Freeman's impact on it manifested itself slowly. But, as we will see, the benefits of her personnel decisions lasted long after she had resigned. Two innovations that she introduced during her presidency made dramatic improvements. First, to ensure that every student who entered the college would have had first-hand experience with literary works, she embedded the kind of serious English component in the admissions examination that Michigan had modeled. It required an essay on a literary masterpiece or on a historical period. The subjects to be prepared were announced in advance. The first exam was to require writing on one of the following: Shakespeare's *Julius Caesar,* Scott's *Ivanhoe,* or the age of the Spanish discoveries in America. Second, as part of a general reduction of required courses, the four years of literary study that Durant had imposed upon the entire student body were reduced to two and refocused. Second-year students now had a more manageable amount of reading on which to focus. The course still met for only a single hour each week but covered only the history of literature in English. Amidst a general expansion of electives, interested juniors and seniors had a choice among new literary electives. An ambitious lover of literature could now study authors from any and every period and could fashion for herself a specialty in English literature.

President Freeman's long-term impact on English studies resulted from the precedent she set when she persuaded two creative writers to join the faculty to teach literature. She hired them in a spirit akin to the principle enshrined in the motto of the Massachusetts Institute of Technology, *mens et manus* ("mind and hand"), which encouraged bringing on board practitioners of whatever advanced skills were to be taught. It's not that she wanted practicing writers to teach "Essay-Writing," or that she thought teaching students to write poetry and fiction should be substituted for teaching them to read literature more effectively. Rather, she trusted actual writers of literature to know best how to teach it. So, in 1885, taking the long view, she offered Katharine Bates a position as instructor in English. And two years later, she secured the services of Vida Scudder, a graduate of Smith College (BA, '84). Scudder had been one of the first women admitted to graduate studies at Oxford, where she got to know John Ruskin and became deeply interested in Fabian socialism. A born teacher and a prolific writer, as a social reformer she was destined to make a name for herself beyond the Wellesley campus.

Katharine Bates had enrolled as a student at Wellesley in 1876. She was the eldest of four children in a family struggling to make a go of it. Her widowed mother, an avid reader, was a graduate of Mount Holyoke, and she strongly supported her daughter's studies. Her sons had gone into the workplace so that their sister could attend college. By the time Katharine was a senior, she was president of her class. That year she took a course with the newly hired Miss Freeman, who became her mentor.

The offer to teach at her alma mater came to "Katie of '80" (as she was admiringly called) five years later. She was happily teaching at a nearby academy for girls, Dana Hall. When she received President Freeman's invitation to teach at the college, she knew quite well that if she accepted the offer, the pay would be slight, the work hard, and that continuing with the kinds of writing she longed to be doing—or getting married—would require her to give up the position. When she nonetheless accepted, she had no way of knowing that her mentor had made the offer in hopes that she would in time succeed Louise Manning Hodgkins. In her first two years on the faculty, however, Bates demonstrated that she had the goods. As one of her last acts as president, Alice Freeman recommended her to the trustees for promotion to associate professor.

While teaching at Dana Hall, Katharine Bates had been writing poetry and fiction for publication. Her fear that she couldn't continue writing if she took on college teaching turned out to be misplaced. In the year of her promotion, she published a successful young adult novel titled *Rose and Thorn*. Rose, its heroine, begins as a young woman unaware of how privileged she is. Gradually, she allows herself to notice the harsh realities faced by the poor people who are making their way through the same city streets where she has long walked in comfort, and she becomes increasingly empathetic towards them. The novel implicitly offered Rose as a model for its readers, and its focus on social inequalities anticipated a development that in the years to follow would become a hallmark of the Wellesley English department's approach to literature. The book won its author a $700 prize, enough money to give her hope that a year's study in Europe was possible. She boldly proceeded to take a leave of absence and spent fifteen months abroad.

In England, Katharine Bates first traveled in the north and visited sites connected with literary works she loved. Then she made her way south, stopping for a time in London, where she visited the British Museum's vast reading room. She discovered there that *Rose and Thorn* had been republished in a pirated edition and felt a wounded kind of outrage different from the outrage she had felt when she first learned about the squalor in which the urban poor were forced to live.[13] Once she settled in at Oxford, she attended coeducational "University lectures" and for the first time encountered male professors, only to be disappointed that their approach to literature was decidedly philological. But she pursued the resolve she had brought with her to learn Anglo-Saxon and made use of the Bodleian Library to study medieval drama. When she returned to Wellesley, she wrote a thesis on these subjects for which the college awarded her the MA degree. She developed her thesis into her first scholarly book. Miss Hodgkins, who had once counseled her to give up teaching and concentrate on writing children's literature, had by this time seen another kind of writing on the wall and resigned. Wellesley promoted Associate Professor Bates to full professor and named her head of the English department.

The hiring of Katharine Bates and Vida Scudder set off a rush of students electing literature courses. President Freeman's successor hired another two practicing writers, Sophie Jewett, who had been publishing volumes of poetry under a pen name, and Margaret Sherwood, a writer of fiction, poetry, and criticism. By the mid-1890s these four women had developed what they began to call a "major" in literature. As the *Dial* essay on "English at Wellesley College" announced, the college was now teaching the whole range of English literature from 1300 to the present. For the students who wanted to specialize, the faculty had arranged a panoply of possibilities. Pointedly, the literature program did not include the required composition courses, which were taught by a separate corps of instructors of "Essay-Writing."[14]

WHEN KATHARINE LEE BATES wrote about Wellesley College for *The Dial*, she recognized that she had a unique opportunity to sum up what all the previous accounts had displayed about the current state of English studies, and she was able to pinpoint "puzzles" that the many reports had left unsolved. That she had been reading these "professorial testimonies" with unusual care could be seen in the frequency and graciousness with which she cited the contributions of other reporters. She observed that the whole process of sharing information and aspirations marked a culmination of the grand "experiment" through which English had been made a legitimate college subject. She articulated questions that had been raised for her when she read about practices that differed widely among the various institutions that had contributed to the symposium. For instance: What was to be the place of Anglo-Saxon in an undergraduate curriculum? Should all students be required to study it? Should study of this language be considered as foundational and taught to first-year students, or should it crown the studies of those seniors who had taken multiple English courses? Other questions that had remained beneath the surface emerged as well: What should be the function of the lecture, and under what circumstances was lecturing likely to be effective? At what point should an undergraduate begin to encounter professional criticism? Another question acknowledged the frustration that teachers sometimes have with recalcitrant students: What should be done with—and for—a student who resists the affective and aesthetic components of the vicarious experience that literature offers?[15]

The Wellesley contribution to *The Dial* also drew on other institutions' reports to suggest a bold answer to the question about what the contents of English studies would be. Bates made the case that the distinctive place that the study of literature now occupied in the modern university warranted its being considered an independent subject, not a merely auxiliary component of composition courses. She quoted from the Yale contributor's report to the effect that a literary education necessarily involves "emotional and aesthetic faculties as well as the purely intellectual." She bolstered this view with further quotations: from Penn's having advocated for a literary study that enriches students' experience far beyond what is utilitarian; and from Chicago's insistence that "literary masterpieces should be studied chiefly for their beauty."[16] Then, urging that the "essential values" in a literary education include its provision of vicarious experience, she pointed out that the reports had "already given judgment in favor of dividing English . . . into the science of linguistics and the art of literature." She went on to observe that they showed as well that "composition and rhetoric, elocution, and comparative literature, must also be taken into account as candidates for separate departments" overseen by specialist faculty.

In proposing that English departments separate the teaching of composition from the teaching of literature Professor Bates was recommending her own institution's long-standing practice. Mr. Durant had come to respect the teaching of writing as a demanding kind of work that would benefit students for their whole lives. In recruiting faculty, he hired a group specifically to teach writing, separate from the faculty that was to teach literature. He believed that bright college graduates, working with small classes in which students received individual attention, could teach basic writing satisfactorily. To train and oversee a cadre of these instructors, whose title would be "Teachers of Essay-Writing," he had hired Margaret E. Stratton, a graduate of Oberlin. President Freeman endorsed Durant's plan and solidified Miss Stratton's position by naming her "Professor of the English Language and Rhetoric," and she empowered her to teach language and linguistics as well.

To be sure, Wellesley's teachers of literature worked closely with students as they learned to write about literary works. But the proposal for a clear separation of duties among members of an English department's faculty suggested a certain disdain for the drudgery inevitably involved in reading countless compositions. The Michigan contribution to *The Dial* had explained that the drudgery arose wherever a college administration proved unwilling to hire a sufficient number of teachers to do the work. The Stanford report gleefully proclaimed its university had eliminated the problem simply by assigning the teaching of composition to the high schools and by denying admission to applicants whose writing did not already measure up.[17] (Within a very short time, however, Stanford's administration found it necessary to install a first-year composition course.)

The Wellesley report offered an ample and generous description of how its faculty taught "Essay-Writing" courses that through all four years trained students to do increasingly more sophisticated types of writing. And as department head, Bates scored a telling point on behalf of her colleagues who specialized in teaching composition when she wryly observed that "It is unfortunate that they are themselves mortal, and have thus far been unable to accede to the desire of the other departments that all students whose technical themes and examination papers, while good in substance are bad in statement, shall be . . . turned over to the Rhetoric department for reformation."[18]

Among the answers that nineteenth-century colleges and universities gave at various times to the question "What would 'English' be?" the Wellesley practice of offering literature courses as an independent subject was neither typical nor unique. In earlier chapters we have seen that both Lafayette and Cornell anticipated Wellesley's practice of hiring faculty specially dedicated to teaching writing. We can add here that in the early 1890s Columbia University separated its English department into distinctly different divisions. For its part, Wellesley's department housed three sub-departments (English literature, English composition, and English language) long into the next century. Meanwhile, in most English departments across the country English teachers were expected, as was the case at Harvard, to teach both literature and composition.

If we take the long view, it is striking how readily nineteenth-century college administrators assigned the responsibility for teaching writing to faculty members who were pioneering the study of literature. In the traditional liberal arts colleges, the responsibility for overseeing written compositions had been considered a secondary business of the "Professor of Rhetoric," whose principal work was preparing students to do public speaking. After the Civil War, as institutions began to take in many more students and to offer new fields for study, administrators increasingly assigned the obligation to teach composition to the very faculty who were inventing the study of vernacular literature. Within a surprisingly short time, a merely convenient and contingent, not to say utterly arbitrary, melding of two separable sets of responsibilities collapsed into a routine practice that came to seem natural.

When at Wellesley Alice Freeman initiated a series of hirings that installed writers of literature as the teachers of literature, she sought to accord literary study a status that was not yet widely recognized. As it happened, these practitioners of the art richly demonstrated that it was possible to devise a major that consisted wholly of courses trained on literary works. The exhibit of their own writing at the Paris Exposition evinced both their industriousness and their productivity. It prominently included fiction (Katharine Lee Bates's *Rose and Thorn;* Margaret Sherwood's *An Experiment in Altruism* and numerous short stories she had published in magazines); volumes of poetry by Sophie Jewett (notably, *The Pilgrim*) and by Bates (*The College Beautiful* and *The Hermit*); criticism (Vida Scudder's *Introduction to the Writings of John Ruskin, The Life of the Spirit in Modern English Poets,* and *Topical Outline for the Study of Modern English Literature,* and Bates's *The English Religious Drama*); social criticism (Scudder's *Socialism and Spiritual Progress*); and a Yale PhD dissertation (Sherwood's "John Dryden's Dramatic Theory and Practice"). The array of published volumes highlighted the graphic display that the U.S. Commissioner of Education had called for. It added to the wonder that a successful college wholly run by women evoked among Europeans. And it demonstrated a progress in literary study that had quite eclipsed the old-fashioned piecemeal treatment of literary works characteristic of courses devoted to rhetoric and oratory.

Coda

A Library

Eschew the skylark and the nightingale, birds that Audubon never found.
A national literature ought to be built, as the robin builds his nest,
out of the twigs and straws of one's native meadows.

—VAN WYCK BROOKS, *The Flowering of New England*

BOXES AND CRATES, hundreds of them, thousands even, each packed with books, mostly old ones, larger ones at the bottom, forty thousand books altogether, all closed up to be moved in wagons. Heavy work for strong men and horses. In the weeks to come each book is to be liberated from its crowded coffin. After inspection, whether cursory or dawdling, its caretaker will assign it a place all its own on the chance that some patron will make it live again. Secure at last in a newly constructed library, its destiny will be to dwell in just that alcove where it is likeliest that some learned man seeking it, or seeking something like it, will make his way.

The year was 1841. Harvard College had never had a building wholly devoted to housing its books. As far as people in the Northeast knew, no other college had one either. (South Carolina College opened a freestanding college library a year earlier.) In all of greater Boston there was no structure like Harvard's first library building. Standing firm in its Quincy granite and tall with its spires reaching into the sky, it looked like a church. By design it was reminiscent of a breathtakingly beautiful college chapel built in the fifteenth century in the older Cambridge, from which the founders of Harvard College had departed to make a new home across the sea. Built for beauty and with little thought to utility, its gorgeous exterior stopped the breath—and sometimes the feet—of those whose eyes chanced to catch sight of it unawares. Five years hence a sketch of this stunning Gothic Revival building would become (and it has since remained) the principal image on the seal of the city of Cambridge, Massachusetts.

An ornate interior matches what you had been seeing as you approached. ("You," that is, if you are the right sort of person. Harvard is a privileged man's domain, and this is its inner sanctum.) The interior features twenty splendid columns rising from floor to ceiling, ten on either side of an arched nave. It stretches from north to south and invites you to look up. No altar defines either end as the intended focus for your wandering eyes. On either side between any two pillars there is an alcove, like a side chapel. The original floorplan for the ground floor shows that if you amble down to the northern end, you will see, in the last alcove on the left, books on the classical languages. Opposite, as if ready to duel with the Greek and Latin books for your attention, the easterly alcove displays poetry, drama, and fiction in your mother tongue. From the center of the building a wing juts out on each side. With nooks and crannies here and there, the first floor provides twenty-three separate lodging areas, each exhibiting a different category of books. Looking around and noticing the second floor above each alcove, you begin to wonder what further possibilities might be awaiting up the stairs. If you've come for a particular book, once the librarian looks up its shelf number and fetches it, you can take it into the reading room. It extends into the west wing. On a winter's afternoon at closing time, its windows will show you the setting sun. Several decades on, equipped at last by a new technology that harnesses electricity, the library will remain open in the evening.

Harvard's Gore Hall library was named after its principal benefactor, Christopher Gore. A former U.S. senator from and governor of Massachusetts, he had entered the college at age thirteen. No sooner had he graduated in 1776 than he joined the continental regiment. Through business dealings after the war, he amassed a fortune. He was not the first man to leave much of it to the college and its library. Harvard takes its name from a benefactor whose large bequest included, in addition to a handsome sum of money, more than four hundred books. Alas, in 1764 a massive fire destroyed most of them, and about four thousand more. Soon afterwards, thanks to many donors and above all to

Thomas Hollis, new books, growing in number, were stored in two rooms in the New Harvard Hall. Not until the building of Gore Hall, constructed entirely of stone, brick, and iron, was the lesson learned.

When the new library opened, it was expected to prove serviceable until the end of the century. Even though it looked ancient, and the architects had not thought to provide office space for the staff, a wholly modern innovation promised eventually to render its operation highly efficient. For decades, the only means that patrons had for knowing what books the library held was to own a printed catalog enumerating its holdings. Problem was, because new books were constantly added, the catalog was out of date as soon as it was printed. In the base copy kept in the library itself, every time a new book was added to the collection, someone needed to write the bibliographical data into the margin on the appropriate page. The college's librarian, Thaddeus Harris, proposed to the Harvard Corporation an unprecedented labor-saving device. By recording on a card the information about each book and then arranging the cards alphabetically, whether by author, by title, or by subject, a catalog consisting of cards could be kept up to date. The interleaving of cards made accommodating constant changes much easier. Beyond this, by adding to each card a shelf mark that noted the book's location, the librarian would find it much simpler to fetch it. (The alcoves were not freely open to patrons and certainly not to students, who had no need to consult the library's collection to prepare for their daily recitations.) Each book would have a unique three-part number indicating (1) in which alcove it was to be placed, (2) the shelf on which it belonged, and (3) where the book fit in the row of books that sat on that shelf.[1] A call number thus looked like this: 17.12.5. The transition to a card catalog would take years of work. It turned out to be women's work. It could never be finished.

Harvard's library holdings grew faster than the planners of the building could have predicted. By 1877, when a young graduate of the college took to compiling the number of volumes in some 311 U.S. college libraries, Harvard's 160,000 volumes doubled the number of the next largest collection, and a large addition to Gore Hall was already under construction.[2] The handsome appendage opened with the promise that it could hold another 250,000 books, all sitting safely on iron book stacks built right into the frame of the new "East Stacks." By the 1890s the addition proved altogether insufficient. Many volumes were being transferred to the law school and the divinity school. Yet books kept piling up along the floors. The interior of the original building was gutted to make room for another quarter-million volumes. A once beautiful dwelling place for Harvard's books descended into monstrosity and had to be torn down. Today the Widener Library, opened in 1916, stands imposingly on the site once occupied by Gore Hall.

TWO YEARS AFTER Gore Hall opened, Nathaniel Hawthorne, recently married and living at the Old Manse in nearby Concord, composed a tale that brings its protagonists right into Harvard's new library. Titled "The New Adam and Eve," it belongs to a particular moment. Greater Boston was witnessing a flirtation with utopian communes: the Alcott family began the sojourn at Fruitlands that Louisa May satirized in *Transcendental Wild Oats,* and Hawthorne himself invested in the communal experiment called Brook Farm, an episode that provided his inspiration for *The Blithedale Romance.* The suspicion of industrial technology that infused these two living experiments sometimes inflected the realm of higher learning as well.

The traditional curriculum at Harvard in the 1840s occupied but a fraction of the students' time. Teachers encouraged a preference for acquiring an easygoing knowledge of this and that. Tacitly, the students discouraged one another from digging deeply into their formal studies. Those who took to reading extracurricular materials such as novels often did so surreptitiously, lest their mates think they were "grinding." But compared to preparing for their daily recitations in Latin and Greek, the prospect of learning about modern literature seemed a breath of fresh air. The professors of romance languages, Henry Wadsworth Longfellow and later James Russell Lowell, cultivated a casual, amateur style that allowed them to ramble on about literature, as if hardly teaching. The Boylston Professor, Ned Channing, held informal discussions of classic literary works. In this atmosphere, Henry David Thoreau, class of '37, who would become Hawthorne's almost daily companion at the time he composed "The New Adam and Eve," had conceived a longing to become a poet.

Unlike a majority of students who felt or feigned indifference to their studies, Thoreau seems to have been a "digger" or a "grind." Not that he lavished all his energy on the prescribed courses. Rather he educated himself in an extracurricular realm different from the fraternal fellowship enjoyed in the literary societies by other aspiring writers. The library charging records show that he steeped himself in English literature, especially Milton, the prose as well as the poetry.[3] Four years after his graduation, his new mentor, Ralph Waldo Emerson, arranged for him to return to Harvard to make use of the splendid new library. Young Thoreau assumed that his route to becoming a poet was to look into Anglo-Saxon and pre-Chaucerian poetry and then to begin reading in earnest with Chaucer and Gower. He sought out materials kept in the alcove filled with poetry, drama, and fiction. He started reacquainting himself with the twenty-one volumes of *The Works of the English Poets from Chaucer to Cowper* that he had freely perused in his student days. While scanning their title pages, he lost heart: "looking over the dry and dusty volumes of the English poets," he wrote in his notebook, "I cannot believe that those fair and fresh creations I had imagined are contained in them. English poetry from Gower down, collected into one alcove—and so from the library window compared with the commonest nature, seems very mean. Poetry cannot breathe in the scholar's atmosphere."[4] Feeling "oppressed by an inevitable sadness," Thoreau nonetheless managed to renew his resolve. He proceeded to spend two weeks filling notebooks with striking passages gleaned from the English poets. This did not entail the sentimental Anglophilia that Channing's vaguely English accent might have encouraged. Thoreau was searching for "nuggets": a passage from Donne that strikes you with a thought you would never have conceived yourself, or one from Pope dressing up something you'd often thought yourself but had never expressed so well. A year later, in his long talks with Hawthorne, Thoreau ran into some striking ideas that gave him further reason to consider whether reading chronologically through English poetry was a natural route to becoming a poet.

"The New Adam and Eve," composed at the time when Hawthorne regarded the younger Thoreau as his best company, manifests an ambivalence about the relations between literary activity and living naturally. An explicitly didactic story, it takes Brook Farm simplicity a step further: it proposes that reading and writing are unnatural acts, hardly essential to human life. It must have reminded Thoreau of that surprising and dispiriting moment in Harvard's new library.

The narrator of Hawthorne's story urges readers to understand that he means to promote an appreciation of "how little" in "the world's artificial system . . . is natural and how much is merely the interpolation of the perverted mind and heart of man." A prophecy that "the end is nigh" was circulating widely in New England at the time. It's as if Hawthorne, setting out to write a satirical allegory, had said to himself, "Okay, I'll grant them their premise. Let me show you what happens next." The story begins once the world has ended. It has ended in the sense that, to borrow from the French, tout le monde has disappeared. The Day of Doom simply "swept away the whole race of men." It left utterly intact "the abodes of man, and all that he has accomplished, the foot-prints of his wandering, and the results of his toil, the visible symbols of his intellectual cultivation and moral progress—in short, everything physical that can give evidence" of the world in 1843.[5]

Hawthorne inserts his new Eve and Adam as belated "investigators" in the corner of that world occupied by Boston and Cambridge. His protagonists are not survivors. They have just come into being and represent the beginning of a second start for humanity, biologically discontinuous from the first. The narrative records their initial impressions as they encounter traces of a race of whose existence they know nothing. Although they are fully grown and equipped with language, they are able to name only those objects that we might call "natural." As they wander through abandoned structures to which the narrator gives generic or particular names—a dry goods store, a church, a court of law, a "Hall of Legislature," a prison, a mansion on "Beacon Street," a bank, a war memorial on "far-famed Bunker Hill," the "rich library of Harvard University," and even the "cemetery of Mount Auburn"—everything manufactured seems to them inauthentic, superfluous, and unnamable. Drawn to the bright clear sky and to such spare foliage as may be found in a city, they feel "perplexed" and remark, "Something drags us down." Through the course of the day's adventures a feeling that whatever had gone on before their arrival weighs heavily on them and increases. It will come to a head in the climactic scene in the library.[6]

The very title of Hawthorne's story recalls *Paradise Lost.* The narrator's most conspicuous allusions to the epic, including an event in Gore Hall that will reverse its tragedy, involve what we might call corrections of the ways in which Milton had retold the biblical story. When, late in the narrative, the new Adam and Eve enter "the rich library of Harvard University," Adam begins "poring over the regular columns of mystic characters" found in "a bulky folio." He feels "painfully perplexed" with a suspicion that the book bears "a mysterious relation to his mind." "I cannot help thinking," he says to Eve, "that the interpretation of the riddles amid which we have been wandering all day long might here be discovered." The narrator, in one of many apostrophes addressed to the characters, urges, "Oh, Adam, it is too soon, too soon by at least five thousand years, to . . . busy yourself in the alcoves of a library!" Then, as he reports with a sense of relief that Adam has put down the book, he intervenes to interpret his story: the "fatal apple of another Tree of Knowledge," he assures readers, remained uneaten. Adam was again capable of enjoying "a new world in our worn-out one."[7]

The narrator then proposes his own prophecy. It seeks to delay almost indefinitely the desired consummation of his tale: he predicts that, when in "the progress of centuries" Adam's descendants create a literature of their own, it "will be no interminably repeated echo of our poetry, . . . but a melody never yet heard on earth." The narrator pronounces Adam "blessed in his ignorance" and expresses a wish that "the roof of the edifice crumble down upon the whole" library. He begins to celebrate what he thinks resistance to reading "the old lore" will make possible: an utterly new literature, to be created through centuries unburdened by repeated echoes of what has already been written, a literature that offers "intellectual forms unbreathed upon by our conceptions." Was Hawthorne making a rudimentary case for an American literature that would be discontinuous with that of the mother country?[8]

MELVIL DUI. A student's name. A curious spelling. Melville Louis Kossuth Dewey began his studies at Amherst College in the early 1870s. Noah Webster, known for his dictionary, had been a founder of the college. Webster was also an advocate for a simplified system of spelling that would distinguish American from British English. Dewey, like Francis March before him, caught Webster's spirit and enlisted in the cause. He dropped his middle names and altered the spelling of the first and last names accordingly. Eventually he split the difference, and history knows him as Melvil Dewey, the inventor of the Dewey Decimal System for classifying books. His system helped to crystalize another split: an emerging one between English and American literature.

As an undergraduate Dewey had worked in the college library. After his graduation in 1874, Amherst hired him to manage it. Most libraries shelved books on the basis of their size or in the order of the dates when they were acquired. Dewey had it in mind to devise a new way to organize a library's holdings. He familiarized himself with the emerging practice of creating a card catalog. Anticipating that libraries generally would need a card catalog system, he established a business that sold index cards and file cabinets. Meanwhile he developed a classification system that, building on Francis Bacon's idea of classifying different kinds of knowledge, would gather books from similar disciplines into clusters. He would assign each book a unique number that would identify its specific class, subclass, etc. Numbers to the right of a decimal point would indicate greater specificity. In 1876 Dewey managed to copyright a forty-two-page pamphlet describing the workings of this system, and he began circulating it to elicit comments. Nine years later, an expanded second edition went to more than three hundred pages and recorded over ten thousand entries. Because the system was designed to accommodate the growth in a library's holdings and to facilitate browsing books on a particular subject, many libraries, private and public, small and large, adopted it. It became the most widely used system of classification in the world. In 1887 Dewey founded the country's first school of library science at Columbia University. He hired Annie Hutchins, who had been overseeing the work of cataloging in Harvard's Gore Hall, to teach in the program.

The Dewey Decimal System of Classification did not so much invent the distinction between "American Literature" and "English Literature" as set it in stone. In this system, three-digit numbers in the 800s to the left of a decimal identify the books of and on literature. In its earliest instantiation the numbers between 810 and 819 gathered every kind of literature written in the United States under the heading "Treatises and Collections." In the second edition Dewey changed the heading to "American Literature." Numbers 820–29 contained English literature (works written in Britain and its colonies). The 830s designated literature in German, etc., so that major language groups were covered in 800s, with the 890s designating works in languages unaccounted for between 810 and 889. Numbers to the right of the first decimal could be subdivided again and again to designate greater specificity. As libraries all across the country adopted the Dewey Decimal System and patrons found literary works written in English located in two different places, this configuration taught millions of people to take for granted the separation of American literature from English and to draw on a nationalistic framework as they read.

But the separation was not inevitable. In the same year that Dewey first circulated a description of the decimal system, Charles Amni Cutter published an account of an alpha-numeric "Expansive Classification" system. He had created it for a private library in Boston, the Athenæum, which had hired him away from Harvard's Gore Hall, where he had been assistant librarian. Cutter's system, like Dewey's, readily adapted itself to newly published materials. But it lodged together all literary works in English, whether composed in Britain, its colonies, or the United States.[9] When, early in the twentieth century, the Library of Congress created what has since become the principal alternative to the Dewey Decimal System, its system of classification (LLC) drew on Cutter's system for its subject headings and alpha-numeric methodology. But in organizing literature in English, it conformed to the precedent set by Dewey when it assigned the initial letters *PS* to American Literature and *PR* to British Literature.

IN 1877, THE YEAR AFTER Dewey and Cutter published their classification systems, Harvard opened a large addition to Gore Hall. In allocating space to literature in English it sided with Dewey. The "East Stacks," as the addition was called, had five floors, and all the literature and history books were housed there. The fifth floor lodged the library's special holdings, including an extraordinary Dante collection. On the fourth floor one could find books on language, on English history, on literary history, and all the books that constituted "English Literature," now understood as works composed by British writers. Books judged to belong to American history and literature were afforded the whole third floor to themselves, and the librarians began to create call numbers with the letters *AL* to designate American Literature. The decision to devote a distinct section of the library to "American literature" had a rich local meaning. The books there represented the fulfillment of the hope that had been famously articulated at Harvard's annual Phi Beta Kappa lecture by Edward Everett half a century earlier, when he outlined in detail the prospects for a national literature.[10]

What Harvard's library now freely designated as "American literature" made virtually no dent on the course offerings of the newly constituted English department overseen by Francis Child. This was not unusual. As professors in U.S. colleges began creating a curriculum that divided literature into historical periods, the courses that covered the eighteenth and nineteenth centuries rarely mixed American and British writers together. This may have allowed the robin to enjoy her contentment an ocean away from the skylark and the nightingale, but the sound of her voice was only faintly to be heard in the younger nation's English departments.

College administrators were slow to allow or encourage courses on American literature because it had become a standard school subject, taught by instructors who lacked serious university training.[11] Similarly, professors of English tended to regard it as a belated and relatively parochial branch of study unworthy of a place in the curriculum. Writing from the colonial period was deemed insufficiently literary. Writings from the nineteenth century were generally regarded as too modern to be considered classic. But by the 1890s several English departments began to offer courses called American literature.

There were a few notable exceptions—or rather, anticipations. In the mid-1870s at the University of Michigan, Moses Coit Tyler, while working on his book *A History of American Literature, 1607–1765*, began giving a yearlong lecture course on the subject. It met only one hour a week and was not given every year. In the mid-1880s, after Tyler had departed to teach at Cornell, his successor, Isaac Demmon, began offering an advanced undergraduate seminar on American literature.

Curiously, Princeton offered an American literature course even earlier, in 1872, as we've seen in the chapter on "Taking Notes." "Curiously," that is, in several respects. Not only did the course anticipate by two decades almost all the courses on the subject that emerged elsewhere. It met for a full year, and it was not elective: all Princeton sophomores were required to take it. The instructor was John Seely Hart, whose rhetoric textbook had long been in use in the college. Some thirty years earlier, Hart had published *The Female Prose Writers of America: With Portraits, Biographical Notices, and Specimens of their Writings.* At well over five hundred pages and with descriptions of writings by hundreds of women, the book proved especially popular among librarians, who valued its useful information. Recently, Hart had finished writing a six-hundred-page *Manual of American Literature* treating hundreds of American writers and many hundreds of publications from colonial times to the present. Literary works by Americans were now proliferating so rapidly that librarians all over the country recognized the surpassing value of Hart's volume as a help in making decisions about what to buy for their collections. Hart prompted them to think about whether literature in English belonged all in one area or whether it should be separated into distinct American and English sections on the basis of the authors' nationalities. Anticipating what the dissemination of Dewey's classification would define more sharply, he wrote in his first chapter:

> AMERICAN LITERATURE, strictly speaking is that part of English Literature which has been produced upon American soil. . . . *NOTE.*—A Literature is denominated from the language in which it is written. As Latin Literature is that written in the Latin language, and Greek Literature is that written in Greek, so English Literature is that written in the English language. It includes works written by Americans, as well as those written by Englishmen. It includes the works of foreigners even, provided those works are written in the English tongue. For convenience of treatment, however, the subject is divided into two parts. The works in English written in England have been considered in a separate volume, under the title of English Literature; those works in English written in the United States are now to be considered, under the title of American Literature.[12]

Unlike other Princeton courses from the 1870s, Hart's course on American literature has left few traces. His *Manual* gives us some clues, however, to what authors and literary works he taught and to his likely approach. In his preface he observes that "the study of literature is in fact a part of the study of history." He introduces his work as a reference book, not a textbook. He insists that it is not to be made a source of material to be memorized and recited. (Hart promoted actually reading literature, rather than reading about it.) The *Manual* provides excerpts from several recent writers, including, for poetry, Poe, Whittier, Bryant, Whitman, and Bret Harte; and James Russell Lowell for criticism. From among the writers of prose, Hart assigned his students to read Hawthorne. The *Manual* gives him pride of place among novelists and accords him a lion's share of space. "As a master of style," Hart writes, "Hawthorne is inimitable. No one ever wrote purer English." Although he "produced nothing in verse, yet he has rightfully been styled the greatest creative genius of America." Hart positions Hawthorne as the country's Shakespeare "beside the great masters, not of the age but of all time." On the page that follows, he describes Thoreau, whose *Walden* had not yet attained the esteem in which it is held today: he was "a thorough humorist in the old English sense of a man who indulges in humors." Hart endorses Thoreau's wonderfully acute power of observation, and his fine taste and skill in "word-painting," and remarks, "he might have made a first-class naturalist. His works are to the last degree original and quaint."[13] Herman Melville receives a brief notice in small typeface, *Moby-Dick* no notice at all.

Hart retired in 1874, and the required course for sophomores disappeared from the curriculum. American literature returned to Princeton at the end of the 1880s in a course on "Victorian" literature, where Irving, Hawthorne, Bryant, Longfellow, and Lowell appeared along with Tennyson, Browning, Arnold, and Carlyle. This transatlantic mingling was not a throwback to an earlier time when "English literature" referred to all literary works in English; nor did it prove to be a paradigm that would be followed in courses elsewhere. It suggests, however, that a separation of British and American literature need not have become a foundational assumption when English departments began building up a specialized faculty or when they began creating boundaries to demarcate the contents of one English course from another.

ACKNOWLEDGMENTS

I AM GRATEFUL FOR permission to reprint, in part, material that appeared in essays that I published previously. Most of what I have drawn from these essays has been redeployed for new purposes in this book.

A short passage in the introduction and much of the first half of chapter 6 distill information and ideas from "Shakespeare, Milton, and the Humanities at MIT in Its Foundational Period," *Explorations in Renaissance Culture,* 43.1 (Spring 2017): 1–29. This material is used by permission of Brill Publishers.

A few short passages that appear here and there in chapter 15 are drawn from "The Works of Wm Shakespeare as They Have Been Sundry Times Professed in Harvard College," *Shakespearean Educations: Power, Citizenship, and Performance,* ed. Coppélia Kahn et al. (Newark: University of Delaware Press, 2011), 175–200.

About two pages in chapter 15 were anticipated in an essay called "Religion and the Rise of English Studies" that appears in *The Routledge Companion to Literature and Religion,* ed. Mark Knight (London: Routledge, 2016), 27–37. This material is used by permission of the Taylor & Francis Business Group.

Some information in chapter 11 is drawn from "How John Milton Was Lodged in the Curricula of U.S. Colleges after the Civil War," Special Issue on "Milton in the Americas," *Milton Studies* 58 (2017): 223–44.; copyright © Duquesne University Press. This information is used by permission of Pennsylvania University Press.

THE SYMBIOTIC RELATIONSHIP between teachers and students may serve as a reminder of the ways in which members in the educational and scholarly communities mutually benefit one another. All of us have learned from those who have gone before us and from those who have shared our study in the classroom. In addition to the many scholars whose published work has deepened the knowledge on which this book is based, those who have invited me to present findings from my archival visits made it possible to benefit from interactions with a range of different audiences. My thanks to Raymond-Jean Frontain, Achsah Guibbory, John Guillory, Suzanne Matson, Sean McDowell, Annabel Patterson, Paul Stevens, Bob Taggart, and Dennis Taylor for bringing me into forums where knowledgeable questions challenged me and generous suggestions enriched my perspective. Conversations at conferences and in the halls at my workplace often led to fruitful collaborations. Sometimes, someone whom I'd never met, having heard about my project, wrote to encourage me to carry it out. June and Paul Schlueter sent me helpful books.

I am especially grateful to colleagues and friends who commented on drafts as the book was being written. Once I conceived a plan for writing, Rosemarie Bodenheimer offered to read my first attempts at an introduction. Now, years later, she has read virtually every page of the book, many chapters more than once. She told me when something wouldn't do, and she framed her criticisms in ways that suggested how to make things work better. I owe a great deal to conversations with her and her late husband, Andy Von Hendy.

Others commented on a chapter or on a section: Philip Alexander, Mary Thomas Crane, Mary Anne Harrington, Peter Haskin, the late Judith Herz, Coppélia Kahn, Mary Jo Kietzman, James O'Toole, Jonathan Post, Brendan Ruberry, and Margaret Thomas all offered knowledgeable advice. More people than I can mention helped me appreciate that what my research was turning up was of interest to a wider audience than the specialists for whom I had been accustomed to write. Colleagues who persuaded me of this include Bob Chibka, Paul Doherty, the late David Ferry, Carlo Rotella, Paul Schervish, Jeanne Shami, Andrew Sofer, Gary Stringer, Conevery Valencius, and Chris Wilson. But in the end, warts and all, I am responsible for what's in the book.

It was more than a stroke of good luck that I was working in a college where support for the humanities is a hallmark of the institution. I am grateful to Boston College for several small research grants and for the yearlong sabbatical during which I started writing the book. David Quigley, Provost and Dean of Faculties, waited patiently for the book and offered reassuring encouragement. The staff at the O'Neill Library, especially Anne Kenny in the Interlibrary Loan Department, was an unfailing help.

The support I have received at Boston College has extended beyond what administrators and fellow faculty members have offered. Many students have engaged in the work with me, not least a host of undergraduate research assistants that includes Denise Bracken, Sarah Goodfield, Sean Gibson, Emily Cersonsky Hayman, and Colin Ryan. Through the period of preparing the manuscript for publication, graduate students Hannah Clay and Jo Mikula proved to be astute checkers for accuracy. I appreciated their willingness to ask questions and to speak up with criticisms. Their intelligence and literary sensibility made for companionable collaborations. Former students who have read parts of the book—including Francis Adams, Laura Cressotti, Jenny Factor, and Elizabeth Fischer—also offered criticisms. Their engagement with the material confirmed my intuition that readers who majored in English, whatever they have gone on to do, are likely to feel they have a stake in how the story is told.

Writing the book would not have been possible without substantial aid from archivists and specialist librarians at virtually every institution I have visited. Dozens of archivists helped me find materials, many at institutions acknowledged in the notes: Amherst, Boston College, Bowdoin, Harvard, MIT, Michigan, Princeton, Vassar, and Wellesley. Archivists at other institutions also provided materials that broadened the base of knowledge on which I've been able to draw: Barnard, Boston University, Brown, Case Western Reserve, Columbia, Dartmouth, Johns Hopkins, King's College (London), Oberlin, Radcliffe, the Senate House Library of the University of London, Smith, Stanford, and Yale. I am especially grateful to Barbara Meloni and Robin McIlhenny. They made the Harvard Archives feel like a second home and graciously introduced dozens of my students to doing archival work. Rosalba Varallo Recchia of the Princeton Archives smoothed out tangles for me on several occasions. Roland Baumann supported me for a Frederick B. Artz grant that made it possible to spend sustained time in his archives at Oberlin College. During the winter of the pandemic, Sara Ludovissy came out into the cold to squire me into Wellesley's quarantined Clapp Library. Then she helped me sift through boxes of notes to find what the college's first students were writing in their notebooks.

As the acquisitions editor at Louisiana State University Press, James Long saw to it that I would work to develop the promise he saw in the project. Whenever I brought him a question or concern, he was always at the ready. The opportunity to work with him has been a great pleasure. Two readers for the Press made the book stronger by posing challenges that I was happy to take on. Jim Turner deserves my great appreciation for recognizing what makes the book distinctive, for spelling out what sorts of revisions would enrich it, and for providing in his own historical scholarship a model to emulate. Lee Sioles, as learned as she is smart, gracefully shepherded the manuscript through the final stages.

And, finally, I am thankful to my whole family for their love and good humor. My wife, even as she was working to finish writing her own book, set aside time and cleared space for me to write mine. I am grateful to her not least for the times I came home from visiting a distant archive and found that, in my absence, she'd undertaken and completed some large household project.

The book is dedicated to my sister and my brother.

NOTES

Introduction

1. See Geiger, *History*, chaps. 4–6.

2. Locke, *Some Thoughts*, 136.

3. Yale University, *Reports*, 3.

4. "Popular Collegiate Education," 3–4.

5. "Popular Collegiate Education," 6–7.

6. Lafayette College, *Circular 1866–67*, 7.

7. Eliot, "New Education," 203.

8. "New Education," 215.

9. [Harriet Prescott Spofford], "The Institute," 232.

10. Payne, "Introduction," 26.

1. What Was Going to College Like?

1. Bates, "Boston Books," 59.

2. The practice that we know as grading began at Yale. In the early days of the republic the faculty classified students as *optimi* (best), *secondi optimi*, *inferiores* (or *boni*, good), and *pejores* (worse). Yale seems to have originated the 4.0 marking system, where 4 was awarded to the best work. In the 1830s Harvard began using a 20-point scale for marking in rhetoric. In the 1850s Michigan went to a system of "pass/no pass." Harvard began using the 100% scale in the 1870s and in the 1880s letter grades (A through E). See Durm, "An A Is Not an A," 294–97. See also Schinske, "Teaching More." https://www.lifescied.org/doi/10.1187/cbe.cbe-14-03-0054.

3. For an in-depth account of the decades before Arlo Bates was a student, see Geiger, *History*, chaps. 4–7.

4. Mahoney, "American Catholic Colleges," 44.

5. Forward-looking exceptions could be found at Harvard and at the College of New Jersey; see Turner, "From Philology," 52–53. Cf. Winterer, *Culture of Classicism*, 52–57.

6. My proposal about the incomparable importance of achieving native fluency in one's first language finds its root in a remark made by the noted linguist Leonard Bloomfield. In a chapter on "The Use of Language" he observes, almost casually, that the acquisition within a speech-

community of "habits of speech and response in the first years of life . . . is doubtless the greatest intellectual feat any one of us is ever required to perform." See *Language*, 29.

7. The best account of how English was studied and taught under headings such as philology, belles lettrès, and rhetoric can be found in Part Two of Guillory's *Professing Criticism*. Cf. Graff, *Professing Literature*. For the most widely read account of the rise of English, see the opening chapter in Eagleton, *Literary Theory*.

8. Wells and Davis, *Sketches*, v.

9. Wells and Davis, 70.

10. Wells and Davis, 73.

11. See Syrett, *Company*, 5.

12. Wells and Davis, 55.

13. Wells and Davis, 73.

14. Wells and Davis, 79.

15. William Spalding, *History, with Appendix by Houston*, 449. See also Tilson.

16. Newman, *Practical System*, 83–84. Beth Hewett has recently sought to rehabilitate this textbook in *A Scholarly Edition*.

17. Lounsbury, "Study of English," 573.

2. Elocution and Composition

1. Noah Webster's *Grammatical Institutes* was first published in 1783 and often reprinted.

2. See Gustafson, "Eloquent Shakespeare," in Kahn et al., eds., *Shakespearean Educations: Power, Citizenship, and Performance*, 71–91.

3. Rufus Stebbins, as quoted by Katula, who offers a sustained treatment of Everett's oration. See *Eloquence*, 71–72.

4. Everett, *Orations*, 33.

5. Rush, *Human Voice;* quoted by Granqvist, 90.

6. R. W. Griswold, I.1; see also Stevens, "Milton," 789.

7. John Milton, *Paradise Lost*, I.249–55.

8. See Dittrich, "Writing Revolution," 163.

9. See the biographical notice by R. H. Dana, Jr., Channing's posthumously published *Lectures*.

10. Barber, *Practical Treatise*, 92–100.

11. For a less sympathetic account of the teaching done by Channing and Child, see Heinrichs, "Destroyed Rhetoric," *Harvard Magazine*, 37–42.

12. See Edward Channing, List of subjects for students' themes in Harvard College, 1823–1851, HUC 8823.286, Harvard University Archives.

13. John William Bacon, themes, HUC 8842.386, Curriculum Collection, Harvard University Archives.

14. Dittrich devotes an entire chapter to Henry Burroughs's writing; for the heading of this essay, 115.

15. Francis Henry Brown, Student Themes, 1855–57, HUC 8855.386, Curriculum Collection, Harvard University Archives.

16. George A. Fiske, Themes and course papers, 1859–61, HUC 8855.386, Harvard University Archives.

17. In *Rise and Fall,* where he offers a rather cavalier account of how the study of literature began at Brown and Yale, Scholes sets out a polemical genealogy of the relations between composition and literature. He subsequently renewed his prescription for a realignment of those relations in *English after the Fall.*

18. See Haverty, Natasha. "No Night There: The Life and Death of Professor Timothy Whiting Bancroft," https://repository.library.brown.edu/studio/item/bdr:115295/.

19. Genung, "Amherst College," in Payne, ed., *English in American Universities, by Professors in the English Departments of Twenty Representative Institutions,* 112, 110.

20. Scott, "English at the University of Michigan," in Payne, ed., 120–22.

3. Commencement Orations

1. Gegung, "Amherst College," in Payne, ed. 111.

2. W. S. Tyler, *History,* 636–39.

3. Amherst College, *Commencement, 1853,* 2–3.

4. See March, "Growth of Lafayette," 229.

5. See Opal, "Victorian Campus," 349; cf. *Amherst Collegiate Magazine,* 3.7 (June 1856): 223–24.

6. "Religious Condition of Colleges," Hitchcock Society of Inquiry, General. Box HS 3, Folder 5, Amherst College Archives.

7. Quoted from Syrett, *Company,* 57.

8. See W. S. Tyler, *History,* 303–4.

9. Genung, 110. "Religious Condition of Colleges."

10. Lucius Root Eastman, "Milton" [1857], Unpublished Manuscripts in Alumni Biographical Files and Class Shelves, 1821–, Amherst College Archives.

11. Henry Sabin, "Literature essential to a nation's strength" (1852), Unpublished Manuscripts in Alumni Biographical Files and Class Shelves, 1821–. Amherst College Archives.

12. Quoted by Englehardt, in "Henry Sabin," 395. This paragraph and the one that follows are based on information provided by Englehardt, 388–412.

4. Philology as a Turning Point

1. For two valuable studies that treat the early study of English literature in England, see D. J. Palmer, *The Rise of English Studies* and Buurma and Heffernan, *The Teaching Archive.*

2. Nietzsche, *Daybreak,* Preface § 5, in Hamacher, 67.

3. Turner provides an extraordinarily rich account of these phenomena in *Philology.*

4. On these developments and on the history of philology more generally, see Harpham, *Humanities and the Dream,* chap. 2.

5. See Shepherd, "Thomas Jefferson as a Philologist," 211–14.

6. Cf. Ryder, "George Ticknor," 960–72.

7. See T. Hart, Jr., "Ticknor's History," 76–88.

5. A Love for English Words

1. See Hauer, 883.

2. *Addresses at the Inauguration of the Rev. G. Wilson* McPhail, 16. Short quotations from it are excerpted passim from 3–22.

3. Quoted by Bright, cxxi–cxxii, n. 7.

4. *Biographical and Historical Record of the Class of 1835 in Yale College,* 112. Although March may have been the first Professor of English in the U.S., some three decades earlier, before the incorporation of London University, University College in London named the Rev. Thomas Dale Professor of English. For the extensive influence of Scottish universities on the rise of English studies, see the essays in Crawford, ed., *Scottish Invention.*

5. "Within the last fifty years a complete revolution has taken place in the ideals and purposes of the scholarly class. The highest words of the old scholars were 'culture' and 'beauty.' . . . The highest words of the new scholars are 'progress' and 'power.'" March, "Spelling and Progress," 131.

6. Comparative Grammar of the Anglo-Saxon Language; see *Athenaeum,* January 7, 1871; quoted following the title page in Selected Writings.

7. March, "Growth of Lafayette," 224.

8. March, "Study of Anglo-Saxon," 233.

9. See March, "Method of Philological Study," 252.

10. March, *Method of Philological Study,* iii–iv.

11. See "Method," 254–55.

12. Owens, 34.

13. MacKenzie, 95, 98, 92.

14. See Campbell, 65–66.

15. March, *Introduction to Anglo-Saxon.*

6. Professors of English in the Scientific Schools

1. See the introduction, 14.

2. Angulo, *William Barton Rogers,* 124–52.

3. Atkinson, *Classical and Scientific Studies,* 31; 70 n.; 30.

4. Atkinson, "Liberal Education," 20.

5. MIT Department of General Studies, Curriculum Materials, AC 485:1, Archives of the Massachusetts Institute of Technology. At this time the Institute enrolled about 175 students, the majority of whom, because they were not seeking a degree, were not required to follow the nonprofessional studies curriculum. The registrar's summary of enrollment figures since the inception of the Institute is arrayed in tables in *The President's Report* for 1907–8, 54–65.

6. E.g., "Atkinson's Classical and Scientific Studies," 578–84.

7. Atkinson, "Liberal Education," 15.

8. Atkinson, *Books and Reading*, 42–43.

9. Her name was Augusta R. Curtis; see Alexander, *Widening Sphere*, 33–34. Cf. MIT Committee on Instruction Records, 1 (Dec. 14, 1870).

10. Emerson's essay "Shakespeare; or, the Poet" appeared as Lecture V in *Representative Men*.

11. Atkinson, "Study of Literature," 106.

12. See Atkinson's report to the Committee on Instruction, 1870, 3. See also Atkinson's May 1872 report to the President on Instruction in English, in the *President's Report* for 1871–72, 79–84.

13. See Atkinson's report on the Department of English and History, in the *President's Report* for 1873–74, 75–76. See also the account of Atkinson's address in the Folders on First Faculty, MC 431, Series 2:8, Julius Stratton Papers, Archives of the Massachusetts Institute of Technology.

14. From a letter of August 27, 1871, transcribed by Stratton during the preparation for his book, *Mind and Hand* and found in Julius Stratton Papers, MC 431, Series 2:8.

15. A transcription of parts of Atkinson's letter of 1878 to Rogers is in MC 431, Series 2:8; see F17-F18, Julius Stratton Papers.

16. See Schiff, "'Select Course,'" 22–23.

17. See Chittenden, *History*, 1: 140. Cf. also Schiff.

18. Lounsbury, "Study of Literature," 584, 600–601, 582, 584.

19. Lounsbury, 595.

20. Lounsbury, 592–93, 582.

21. Lounsbury, 585.

22. Lounsbury, 585–87.

23. Lounsbury, 587, 589.

7. An Ardent Desire to Learn

1. Douglass, *Narrative of the Life*, 78, 84, 120.

2. Du Bois, "Training of Black Men," 292.

3. Cf. Talty, *Mulatto America*, 96–97.

4. Over half a century later, Walter Dyson reprinted a reconstruction of Emerson's talk; see *Howard University*, 366.

5. See Henneman, "English in the South," 180–97.

6. See the requirements for seniors listed in the college catalogs beginning in the mid-1870s.

7. Tuckerman, "Sketch of American Literature," 511.

8. Quoted in Majors, *Noted Negro Women*, 105; Frederick Douglass, Letter dated 21 December 1877, General Correspondence, 1877 July–December, Frederick Douglass Papers, Library of Congress; see also Douglass, "The Color Line," 568.

9. See McCallister, "Shakespeare Visits the Hilltop," in Kahn et al., eds., 219–46.

8. Competing with the Boys

1. Thwing, "College Women," 546–53.

2. Juliet Amelia Adams, Letter of September 1869, Vassar Student Letters, Vassar College Digital Library. https://digitallibrary.vassar.edu/collections/other-collections/vassar-college-student-letters/1651de21-92bc-4397-bf67-bc755c62c7ff.

3. Henry Barmby Buckham, "Report of the Professor of Rhetoric and Letters for 1st College Year ending June 27, 1866," Vassar College Biographical Files, Archives and Special Collections Library, Vassar College Libraries.

4. Mary M. Badgley, Letter of 15 October 1866, Vassar Student Letters, Vassar College Digital Library. https://digitallibrary.vassar.edu/collections/other-collections/vassar-college-student-letters/f29f04f8-4f94-4761-90c1-ace9d73681fc.

5. Quoted by Edelman, "History" (2011), 6.

6. William Smith, ed., *History*, 7–22, passim.

7. Backus, *Shaw's New History*, 6–13, passim.

9. Acting English Plays

1. Justin Gest, "What the 'Majority Minority' Shift Really Means for America." *New York Times*, 24 August 2021.

2. The quotation from Edmund Spenser's *View of the Present State of Ireland* is crucial in Canny's article on "English Colonization."

3. "Fr. John Bapst Survives."

4. See Donovan, *Boston College*, 153, 151.

5. West, "Democracy of Studies."

6. Connolly, ed., *English Reader*, 19.

7. The plays acted at Vassar were precisely extracurricular, staged by the students themselves.

8. Boston College student theater collection, BC 1991.081, John J. Burns Library, Boston College.

9. Cf. Wilder, *Ebony and Ivy*.

10. Entrance Examinations

1. Allen, letter to the *Pall Mall Gazette*, 272–73.

2. See Lawrie, *Beginnings of University English*. For Scotland, see Crawford, *Devolving*.

3. Eliot, "Liberal Education," 29–30.

4. National Center for Education Statistics. "Historical summary."

5. *Cornell University Register*, 3rd ed., (1874–75), 103.

6. Some questions come from the 1872–74 *Register* as well; see 96, 122–23.

7. Harvard University Catalogue, 1873–74, 53.

8. See Hill, "An Answer," 236.

9. These were gathered into a volume titled *Twenty Years of School and College English.*

10. *Twenty Years,* 26.

11. *Twenty Years,* 27–28.

12. Calendar of the University of Michigan for 1880–81, 29.

13. Calendar of the University of Michigan for 1894–95, 38–39.

14. In this and the following paragraph, I quote passages as Denise Albanese has made them available in an essay to which I am indebted here: "Canons before Canons," 156–74.

15. Cf. The Stanford Eugenics History Project. https://www.stanfordeugenics.com/.

11. Taking Notes

1. Quoted by Kraig, *Woodrow Wilson,* 14.

2. Hunt, "Rhetorical Science," 675.

3. Hart, *Composition and Rhetoric.*

4. The administration assigned Hart to teach a full-year required literature course to sophomores. This was an unusual development, both in that the college had not been offering courses on literature in English, much less requiring them, and because the subject of the course was American literature, which other colleges would not be offering, even as an elective, until two or three decades later. See "Coda: A Library," 219–21.

5. Quoted in Kraig, 16.

6. Kraig, 14, 23–24.

7. Duffield, "Rhetoric/Life of Christ," Hunt, Theodore /McCosh, James; AC052, Box 31, Folder 3, Lecture Notes Collection, Princeton University Archives, Department of Special Collections, Princeton University Library. (The pages in Duffield's notebook are unnumbered.)

8. Theodore Hunt, Rhetoric 1873–74, AC052, Box 31, Folder 2, Lecture Notes Collection, Princeton University Archives, Department of Special Collections, Princeton University Library.

9. Cf. Van Lennep, William Bird; AC104-02, Box 149, Undergraduate Alumni Records, 19th Century, 1800–1899, Princeton University Archives, Department of Special Collections, Princeton University Library.

10. Van Lennep, 32; Theodore Hunt, Rhetoric 1873–74.

11. Van Lennep, 27; Theodore Hunt, Rhetoric 1873–74.

12. See *Athletics at Princeton,* 57.

13. "English Electives," 6. Cf. Hunt, "Place of English."

14. Murray, *The Study of English,* 22. Cf. James Ormsbee Murray, Notes on English Literature / from lectures, PR 481 M877 1882, Lecture Notes Collection, Princeton University Archives, Department of Special Collections, Princeton University Library.

15. William Reed Barricklo, Notes, James Murray, English Literature, 1877–78, AC052, Box 41, Lecture Notes Collection, Princeton University Archives, Department of Special Collections, Princeton University Library.

16. William R. Wilder, Notes, James Murray, AC052, Box 44, Folder 7, English Literature,

1877–78, 1, Lecture Notes Collection, Princeton University Archives, Department of Special Collections, Princeton University Library. For Wilder's notes on the Milton lectures, see 26–77.

17. Wilder, in Murray, 65, 68.

18. On twentieth-century criticism, cf. John Guillory, *Professing Criticism.*

19. Wilder, in Murray, 1.

20. Hunt, PhD, "English in the College Curriculum."

21. Report to the Board of Trustees of the College of New Jersey, 13 November 1885, Office of the President Records: Jonathan Dickinson to Harold W. Dodds Subgroup, AC117, Box 39, Series II, James McCosh Records. Princeton University Archives, Department of Special Collections, Princeton University Library.

22. Report to the Board of Trustees, 10 November 1887, Box 39.

12. The Study of Masterpieces

1. See Thwing, *American Colleges.*

2. Thwing, 10–11.

3. Information to which no endnotes are attached comes from the University of Michigan Calendar for the relevant year.

4. See VanOverbeke, chaps. 2–3.

5. See Kammen, "Moses Coit Tyler, 63.

6. Tyler, Letter to Messrs. G. P. Putnam's Sons, 97–99.

7. Cf. Tyler, Preface to *A Manual of English Literature*, viii–x.

8. Isaac N. Demmon, AM, "Course in English Masterpieces (1884)," JA 1868.D382 C8, Bentley Historical Library, JA 1868.D382 C8. The quotation from Thomas Carlyle comes from *On the Choice of Books*, 2nd. ed., 1866.

9. Demmon, "Course in English Masterpieces (1884)."

10. Edwin C. Goddard Papers, 851364 Aa2, Box 2 (of 2), Lectures I and II, 12 and 19 October 1888, unpaginated, "Notes on Isaac Demmon's Study of Masterpieces" (1888), University of Michigan Archives. University Records refer to Goddard as "Edwin C." He regularly signed himself "C. E. Goddard."

11. For information about Mary Elizabeth Clark, I am grateful to Mary Jo Kietzman and Paul Gifford. See Census for 1850, Michigan, Lapeer County, 778, and *History of Lapeer County*, 52, 106–7.

12. Mary Elizabeth Clark, Student notebooks, 88171 Aa 2 Ac, University of Michigan Archives.

13. Clark, Student notebooks.

14. Henry Sherring Pratt, "*Paradise Lost,*" 34 (35 pages), 89194 AA, Notes on History and Literature Courses, University of Michigan Archives.

15. Pratt, essay on Shakespeare's *I Henry IV*, 6 (41 pages).

16. Pratt, Notes on History and Literature Courses.

17. Goddard, "An Essay on Shakespeare's Sonnets," 19 (43 pages), Masterpiece Course, U. of M. Nov. 1888, Box 1, Folder 19, Goddard Papers.

18. Goddard, untitled address to teachers on teaching literature in school, 4 (12 pages), 851364 Aa2, Box 1, Folder 4, Goddard Papers.

19. Shirley Wheeler Smith, "Milton's *Areopagitica*," 2 (25 pages), 86711 Aa 2 UAm, Box 14, Shirley Wheeler Smith Papers, 1881–1959, University of Michigan Archives.

20. Smith, 20–21.

21. Smith, 23.

13. The Idea of a Major

1. Johns Hopkins University, *Register for the Second Year, 1877–78*, 18. In the two paragraphs that follow, the words *course*, *department*, *major*, and *minor* appear in quotation marks whenever, as in this paragraph, I am employing them in the specific senses that they were being used at Hopkins.

2. See Rudolph, *American College*, 269.

3. Johns Hopkins University, *Circular* No. 4 (April 1880), 39–40.

4. See Gilman, "Group System," 565–76; cf. Payton, "Origin of Terms," 57–63.

5. Anderson, "Instruction in English," 167, 168.

6. See Sampson, "English at Indiana," 92–98. Sampson, who had received an MA degree in 1890, had taught at Stanford for a year, before coming to Indiana. He seems to have been under the mistaken impression that the opportunity for Indiana's undergraduates to specialize in English had begun only when he arrived in 1893.

7. William Morton Payne, "Introduction," 7–28.

8. Hodell, "Standpoint of the Student," 176.

14. English as a Special Subject at Cornell

1. The phrase, apparently first spoken in 1868, was incorporated into the university's seal.

2. See Nash, "Entangled Pasts," 451–2.

3. Cornell University Register for 1868–69, 28.

4. On the uneven development of White's thinking on this matter, see "The President's Report," in the *Register* for 1871–72, 43.

5. See the PhD dissertation by Welden, *Hiram Corson*, 15.

6. Welden, 87.

7. Welden, 113.

8. Hiram Corson, *Aims of Literary Study*, 21, 99.

9. Corson, "English at Cornell," 62.

10. *Register* for 1872–73, 108.

11. Gilman, "Growth of American Colleges," *Register* for 1871–72, 62.

12. *Register* for 1872–73, 110–11.

13. *Register* for 1872–73, 132.

14. *Register* for 1873–74, 141–42.

15. Corson, "Aims of Literary Study," 67–68.

16. *Register* for 1874–75, 119.

17. *Register* for 1873–74, 119–21.

18. *Register* for 1874–75, 146–47.

19. Corson, "English at Cornell," 63.

15. A Concentration in English Studies at Harvard and the "Harvard Annex"

1. *Annual Report of the President and Treasurer of Harvard University,* 1884–85, 45. Unless otherwise indicated, statistical data and assertions about course offerings, their dates, and their enrollments in this chapter are based on the *Annual Reports,* available online, https://guides.library.harvard.edu/harvard-radcliffe-online-historical-reference-shelf.

2. See Hill, "An Answer," 236.

3. See an anonymous commentary, *Harvard Advocate* (October 1886): 98–99.

4. "[Harvard] "Department of English: containing an announcement for 1887–88," 3, Harvard University Archives, HUC 8523.5.

5. *Annual Report,* 1886–87, 14.

6. McCosh, *New Departure,* 15.

7. Palmer, *Possible Limitations,* Part I, 575.

8. Eliot, "What Is a Liberal Education?" in *Early Reform,* 29.

9. Palmer, Part II, 15.

10. "Announcement for 1887–88," 3–4.

11. Santayana, *The Middle Span,* 2:172.

12. See Newkirk, "Politics of Intimacy," 115–31; cf. M. Connolly, "Wendell," 322.

13. See, for instance, an unsigned editorial in *Harvard Monthly,* 9 (April 1889): 76–8.

14. See Society for Collegiate Instruction, 13.

15. Wendell, "Shakespeare Course at Radcliffe, 1886–88," HUG 1876.54.14, Harvard University Archives. Wendell began keeping the notebook when he first taught Shakespeare at the Annex, in 1884–85. It formerly bore this title, pasted on its spine. That title, with its anachronistic naming of the place, seems to have been based on a note that Wendell wrote into the book on 23 May 1893. He misremembered the dates during which he actually taught the course.

16. Wendell, "Relations of Radcliffe," 8.

17. Ethel Winward Howland, Autobiography typescript, 36–37, undated, SC113, Box 1, Folder 5, Radcliffe College Archives.

18. Wendell, "English at Harvard" In Payne, ed., 48.

16. The English Major at Wellesley College

1. Harris, "Educational Exhibit," *Education,* 1–11.

2. Bates, "English at Wellesley College," 141–48.

3. See Onderdonk, "Curriculum," 140.

4. On the extensive reach of Henry Durant's influence over what went on in the college, see Palmieri, "*Incipit Vita,*" 59–78.

5. Quoted by Converse, *Wellesley,* 43–44.

6. Quoted by Converse, 44.

7. Quoted in Glassock et al., ed. *Wellesley College,* 17.

8. This advice was recorded by Mary Ella Whipple, Notebook, 1873, Box #1, Records of the Class of 1879, 6C-1879, Wellesley College Archives, Library and Technology Services, Wellesley College.

9. See Bohan et al., "Mary Sheldon Barnes."

10. Maud Hadley, Sophomore Literature notebook [1885], Records of the Class of 1888, C6-1888, Wellesley College Archives, Library and Technology Services, Wellesley College.

11. Various musical settings of "America the Beautiful" made in the twentieth century have served to broaden the appeal of the lyrics.

12. In *Alice Freeman Palmer,* Bordin draws on and critiques George Herbert Palmer's account of the courtship; see chap. 7, "Dilemma."

13. This account of Katharine Bates's time in England is indebted to Ponder, *Katharine Lee Bates,* chap. 5.

14. The courses are described in detail in a document headed "Courses for -'95–'96," English Department Records, 3L-English, Wellesley College Archives, Library and Technology Services, Wellesley College.

15. Bates, "English at Wellesley College," 147–48. As they appear here, the questions are a mix of quotation and paraphrase.

16. Ibid., 141.

17. Scott, "English at the University of Michigan," 121–22 (116–23); Anderson, "English at Stanford University," 51.

18. "English at Wellesley College," 146.

Coda

1. See *An Index Guide to the Shelf Classification.* My thanks to James Capobianco of the Houghton Library for information about the history of call numbers in the successive Harvard libraries.

2. See the appendix in Thwing, *American Colleges.*

3. Library charging records, UA III.50.15.60, vols. for 1834 through 1837, Harvard University Archives.

4. Thoreau's entry for November 30, 1841, in *Journal*, i, 337–39.

5. Hawthorne, "New Adam," 146.

6. "New Adam," 147–56.

7. "New Adam," 153–54.

8. "New Adam," 154.

9. See, in addition to Cutter's *Expansive Classification,* the volume he created for users of the Boston Athenaeum, Cutter, *Boston Athenæum*.

10. See above, chapter 2, "Elocution and Composition," 32–34.

11. See Renker, *Origins,* 110–13.

12. John S. Hart, Manual of American Literature, 25.

13. Hart, 475–77.

BIBLIOGRAPHY

THE ARCHIVAL COLLECTIONS that house many items referred to in the notes are listed below. References that identify the locations of discrete archival holdings (private letters, students' notebooks, professors' unpublished lecture notes, and the like) do not appear here, however. The specific locations of these materials are provided in the notes appended to the chapters where they are relevant. References for information derived from college catalogs, registers, and circulars are also to be found in the notes.

Manuscript Collections

Curriculum Collection. Harvard University Archives. Pusey Library. Harvard University.

Division of Rare and Manuscript Collections, Cornell University Library.

Edwin C. Goddard Papers, c. 1884–1940. Bentley Historical Library. University of Michigan.

English Department Records. Wellesley College Archives. Library and Technology Services. Wellesley College.

Julius Stratton Papers. Massachusetts Institute of Technology Archives. Department of Distinctive Collections. Building 14N. Massachusetts Institute of Technology.

Lecture Notes Collection. Princeton University Archives. Department of Special Collections. Seeley G. Mudd Manuscript Library. Princeton University.

National Center for Education Statistics. "Historical summary of faculty, students, degrees," etc. https://nces.ed.gov/programs/digest/d07/tables/dt07_178.asp

Radcliffe College Archives. Schlesinger Library. Harvard University.

Shirley Wheeler Smith Papers, 1881–1959. Bentley Historical Library. University of Michigan.

Unpublished Manuscripts in Alumni Biographical Files and Class Shelves, 1821. Amherst College Archives. Amherst College.

Vassar College Digital Archives. Vassar College.

Printed and Online Materials

Addresses at the Inauguration of the Rev. G. Wilson McPhail as President of Lafayette College. Philadelphia: William S. & Alfred Martian, 1858.

Albanese, Denise. "Canons before Canons: College Entrance Requirements and the Making of a National Educational Shakespeare." In Kahn et al., eds., 156–74.

Alexander, Philp N. *A Widening Sphere: Evolving Cultures at MIT.* MIT Press, 2011.

Allen, Grant. Letter to the *Pall Mall Gazette*. In *The Nineteenth-Century History of English Studies,* edited by Alan Bacon, 272–74. Ashgate, 1998.

Amherst College. *Commencement, on the Thirty-Second Anniversary of Amherst College, Thursday, August 11, 1853*. Amherst: Adams, Printers, 1853.

Amherst Collegiate Magazine 3.7 (1856): 223–24.

Anderson, Melville B. "English at Stanford University." In Payne, ed., 49–59.

Anderson, Melville B. "The Instruction in English at Stanford University." *The Dial* 16 (January–June 1894): 167–70.

Angulo, A. J. *William Barton Rogers and the Idea of MIT.* Johns Hopkins University Press, 2009.

Athletics at Princeton: A History, ed. Frank Presbrey and James Hughes Moffatt. FB&C Limited, 2018. Originally published under the advisory and supervision of the Graduate Committee, 1901.

Atkinson, William P. *Books and Reading: A Lecture*. Boston: Crosby, Nichols, 1860.

Atkinson, William P. *Classical and Scientific Studies, and the Great Schools of England: a lecture before the Society of the arts of the Massachusetts Institute of technology, April 6, 1865*. Cambridge, MA: Sever and Francis, 1865.

Atkinson, William P. "Liberal Education of the Nineteenth Century." *Popular Science Monthly* 4 (1873): 1–26.

Atkinson, William P. "The Study of Literature." *Technology Quarterly* 1.2 (1887): 96–106.

"Atkinson's Classical and Scientific Studies." Review of *Classical and Scientific Studies,* by William P. Atkinson, *The North American Review* 101 no. 209 (1865): 578–84.

Backus, Truman J., ed. *Shaw's New History of English Literature, prepared on the basis of "Shaw's Manual."* New York: Sheldon, 1874.

Bacon, Alan, ed. *The Nineteenth-Century History of English Studies.* Ashgate, 1998.

Baird, Theodore. *English at Amherst: A History.* Amherst College Press, 2005.

Barber, Jonathan. *A Practical Treatise on Gesture.* Cambridge, MA: Hilliard and Brown, 1831.

Bates, Arlo. "Boston Books and Bookmen." *The Book Buyer.* New York: C. Scribner and Co., 5, no. 2 (1888): 59.

Bates, Katharine. "English at Wellesley College." In Payne, ed., 141–48.

Berlin, James A. *Writing Instruction in Nineteenth-Century American Colleges.* Southern Illinois University Press, 1984.

Biographical and Historical Record of the Class of 1835 in Yale College. Reprinted, Wentworth Press, 2019.

Bledstein, Burton J. *The Culture of Professionalism: The Middle Class and the Development of Higher Education in America.* Norton, 1976.

Bloomfield, Leonard. *Language.* New York: Henry Holt, 1933.

Bohan, Chara Haeussler, et al., "Mary Sheldon Barnes: An Educator's Life in Historical Context." *Social Studies Research and Practice* 6.2 (2011): 85–94.

Bordin, Ruth. *Alice Freeman Palmer: The Evolution of a New Woman.* University of Michigan Press, 1993.

Bright, James W. "An Address in Commemoration of Francis Andrew March, 1825–1911." *PMLA* 28 (1913): cxvii–cxxxvii.

Buurma, Rachel Sagner, and Laura Heffernan. *The Teaching Archive: A New History for Literary Study.* University of Chicago Press, 2021.

Campbell, James Oscar. "II: The Department of English and Comparative Literature." In *A History of the Faculty of Philosophy, Columbia University.* Columbia University Press, 1957.

Canny, Nicholas P. "The Ideology of English Colonization: From Ireland to America." *William and Mary Quarterly* 30.4 (1973): 575–98.

Channing, Edward T. *Lectures Read to Seniors in Harvard College.* Boston: Ticknor and Fields, 1856.

Chittenden, Russell H. *History of the Sheffield Scientific School of Yale University, 1846–1922,* 2 vols. Yale University Press, 1928.

Connolly, Edward, S.J., ed. *The English Reader.* New York: Benziger Brothers, 1887.

Connolly, Michael. "Barrett Wendell: New England Orderly Idealist." *The Modern Age* 48.4 (2006): 320–29.

Converse, Florence. *The Story of Wellesley.* Little, Brown, 1915.

Corson, Hiram. *The Aims of Literary Study.* 1894; New York: Macmillan, 1896.

Corson, Hiram. "English at Cornell University." In Payne, ed., 60–64.

Crawford, Robert. *Devolving English Literature.* 2nd ed. Edinburgh University Press, 2000.

Crawford, Robert, ed. *The Scottish Invention of English Literature*. Cambridge University Press, 1998.

Cutter, C. A. *Boston Athenæum: How to Get Books, with an Explanation of the New Way of Marking Books*. Boston: Press of Rockwell and Churchill, 1882.

Cutter, C. A. *Expansive Classification: Part I: The First Six Classifications*. Boston: C.A. Cutter, 1891–93.

DeVane, William Clyde. "The English Major." *College English* 3 (1941): 47–52.

Dittrich, Bradfield Edward. "Edward Channing's Writing Revolution: Composition Prehistory at Harvard, 1819–1851." PhD diss., University of New Hampshire, 2017. https://scholars.unh.edu/dissertation/163.

Donavan, Charles F., S.J. *Boston College: Glimpses of the Past*. University Press of Boston College, 1994.

Douglass, Frederick. "The Color Line." *North American Review* 132: 295 (1881): 568.

Douglass, Frederick. *Narrative of the Life of Frederick Douglass, an American Slave* [1845]. Edited by Houston A. Baker. Penguin Books, 1982.

Du Bois, W. E. B. "Of the Training of Black Men." *Atlantic Monthly* 90.539 (1902): 289–97.

Durm, Mark W. "An A Is Not an A Is Not an A: A History of Grading." *The Educational Forum* 57.3 (1993): 294–97.

Dyson, Walter. *Howard University, the Capstone of Negro Education; 1867–1940*. The Graduate School of Howard University, 1941.

Eagleton. Terry. *Literary Theory: An Introduction* (1983). Anniversary edition., 2nd ed. Blackwell Publishers, 2008.

Edelman, Violet. "The History of the Vassar College English Department," 2011, https://150.vassar.edu/histories/english/.

Eliot, Charles W. "The New Education." *Atlantic Monthly* 23 (February 1869): 203–20; (March 1869): 358–67.

Eliot, Charles W. "What Is a Liberal Education?" *Century Magazine* 28, no. 2 (June 1884): 203–12. Reprinted, in *Early Reform in American Higher Education*, edited by David N. Portman, 17–46. Nelson-Hall, 1972.

Emerson, Ralph Waldo. *Representative Men*. Boston: Phillips, Samson, 1850.

"Endgame: Can Literary Studies Survive?" Chronicle Review, *Chronicle of Higher Education*, (January 2022).

Englehardt, Carroll. "Henry Sabin (1829–1918)." *The Annals of Iowa* 48.7–8 (1987): 388–412.

"English Electives." *Princetonian*, 2.2 (10 May 1877): 6.

Everett, Edward. *Orations and Speeches on Various Occasions*. Boston: C. C. Little and J. Brown, 1850.

"Fr. John Bapst Survives Tar & Feathers, Becomes 1st Boston College President," New England Historical Society, https://newenglandhistoricalsociety.com/fr-john-bapst-survives-tar-fathers-becomes-1st-boston-college-president/.

Franklin, Phyllis. "English Studies: The World of Scholarship in 1883." *PMLA* 99.3 (1984): 356–70.

Geiger, Roger, ed. *The American College in the Nineteenth Century.* Vanderbilt University Press, 2000.

Geiger, Roger. *A History of American Higher Education: Learning and Culture from the Founding to World War II.* Princeton University Press, 2015.

Genung, John F. "English at Amherst College." In Payne, ed., 110–15.

Gest, Justin. "What the 'Majority Minority' Shift Really Means for America." *New York Times,* 24 August 2021.

Gilman, Daniel Coit. "On the Growth of American Colleges and the Present Tendency to the Study of Science." *Cornell Register* (1871–72), 56–65.

Gilman, Daniel Coit. "The Group System of College Studies in the Johns Hopkins University." *The Andover Review* 5.30 (1886): 565–76.

Glasscock, Jean, et al., eds. *Wellesley College 1875–1975: A Century of Women.* Wellesley College, 1975.

Graff, Gerald. *Professing Literature: An Institutional History* (1987); Twentieth Anniversary edition with a new Preface. University of Chicago Press, 2007.

Graff, Gerald, and Michael Warner, eds. *The Origins of Literary Studies in America: A Documentary Anthology.* Routledge, 1989.

Granqvist, Raoul. *Imitation as Resistance: Appropriations of English Literature in Nineteenth-Century America.* Fairleigh Dickinson University Press, 1995.

Griswold, R. W. *The Prose Works of John Milton, with a Biographical Introduction.* 2 vols. Philadelphia: Herman Hooker, 1845.

Guillory, John. *Cultural Capital: The Problem of Literary Canon Formation.* University of Chicago Press, 1993.

Guillory, John. *Professing Criticism: Essays on the Organization of Literary Study.* University of Chicago Press, 2022.

Gustafson, Sandra M. "Eloquent Shakespeare." In Kahn et al., eds., 71–91.

Hamacher, Werner. *95 Theses on Philology.* Translated by Catharine Diehl. Fordham University Press, 2015.

Harpham, Geoffrey Galt. *The Humanities and the Dream of America.* University of Chicago Press, 2011.

Harris, W. T., "Our Educational Exhibit at the International Exposition in Paris in 1900." *Education* 19, no. 3 (1898): 1–11.

Hart, John S. *Manual of American Literature: A Text-Book for Schools and Colleges.* Philadelphia: Eldredge & Brother, 1872.

Hart, John Seely. *A Manual of Composition and Rhetoric: A Text-book for Schools and Colleges.* Philadelphia: Eldred, 1873.

Hart, Thomas R., Jr. "George Ticknor's History of Spanish Literature: The New England Background." *PMLA* 69.1 (1954): 76–88.

The Harvard Advocate 42.3 (1886): 98–99.

The Harvard Monthly. Unsigned editorial, 9 (April 1889): 76–78.

Harvard University. *Annual Reports of the President and Treasurer of Harvard University.* Various Years. https://guides.library.harvard.edu/harvard-radcliffe-online-historical-reference-shelf.

Harvard University. *Twenty Years of School and College English.* Cambridge, MA: Harvard University, 1896.

Haskin, Dayton. "Religion and the Rise of English Studies." In *The Routledge Companion to Literature and Religion,* ed. Mark Knight, 27–37. Routledge, 2016.

Haskin, Dayton. "The Works of Wm Shakespeare as They Have Been Sundry Times Professed in Harvard College." In Kahn et al., eds., 175–200.

Hauer, Stanley R. "Thomas Jefferson and the Anglo-Saxon Language." *PMLA* 96.5 (1983): 879–98.

Hawthorne, Nathaniel. "The New Adam and Eve." *United States Magazine and Democratic Review* 12 (February 1843): 146–55.

Heinrichs, Jay. "How Harvard Destroyed Rhetoric." *Harvard Magazine* (July–August 1995), 37–42.

Heller, Nathan. "The End of the English Major." *New Yorker* (27 February 2023).

Henneman, J. B. "The Study of English in the South." *Sewanee Review* 2.2 (1894): 180–97.

Hewett, Beth L., ed. *A Scholarly Edition of Samuel P. Newman's A Practical System of Rhetoric.* Brill, 2020.

Hill, Adams Sherman. "An Answer to the Cry for More English." *Good Company* 4 (1879–80): 236.

History of Lapeer County, Michigan. Chicago: H. R. Page, 1884.

Hodell, Charles W. "The Study of English Literature from the Standpoint of the Student." In Payne, ed., 175–78.

Hunt, Th. W., PhD. "The Place of English in the College Curriculum." *PMLA* 1 (1884–5): 118–31.

Hunt, Rev. Theodore. "Rhetorical Science," *Presbyterian Quarterly* 3.12 (1874): 660–78.

An Index Guide to the Shelf Classification of the Harvard College Library. Printed for the Library, 1905.

Johns, Adrian. *The Science of Reading: Information, Media, and Mind in Modern America.* University of Chicago Press, 2023.

Johns Hopkins University. *Circular* no. 4 (April 1880), 39–40.

Johns Hopkins University. *Register for the Second Year, 1877–78*, 18.

Kahn, Coppélia, Heather S. Nathans, and Mimi Godfrey, eds. *Shakespearean Educations: Power, Citizenship, and Performance*. University of Delaware Press, 2011.

Kammen, Michael. "Moses Coit Tyler: The First Professor of American History in the United States." *The History Teacher* 17.1 (November 1983): 61–87.

Katula, Richard A. *The Eloquence of Edward Everett: America's Greatest Orator*. Peter Lang, 2010.

Kimball, Bruce. *The Inception of Modern Professional Education: C. C. Langdell, 1826–1906*. University of North Carolina Press, 2009.

Kraig, Robert Alexander. *Woodrow Wilson and the Lost World of the Oratorical Statesman*. Texas A & M University Press, 2004.

Lafayette College. *Circular. Pardee Scientific Course in Lafayette College. 1866–67.*

Lawrie, Alexandra. *The Beginnings of University English: Extramural Study, 1885–1910*. Palgrave Macmillan, 2014.

Locke, John. *Some Thoughts Concerning Education*, § 164 [1693], in *The Harvard Classics*, ed. Charles Eliot. Vol. 37. Collier and Son, 1909.

Lounsbury, T. R. "The Study of English." *The New Englander* (1870): 572–601.

Lynch, Deidre. *Loving Literature: A Cultural History*. University of Chicago Press, 2015.

MacKenzie, James C. "Dr. March as a Teacher." In *Addresses Delivered at a Celebration in Honor of Prof. Francis A. March, LL.D., L.H.D., at Lafayette College, October 24, 1895*. Easton, PA: Lafayette Press, 1895.

Mahoney, Kathleen A. "American Catholic Colleges for Women: Historical Origins." In *Catholic Women's Colleges in America*, ed. Tracy Schier and Cynthia Russett, 25–54. Johns Hopkins University Press, 2002.

Majors, M. A. *Noted Negro Women: Their Triumphs and Activities*. Chicago: Donohue & Henneberry, 1893.

March, Francis A. *A Comparative Grammar of the Anglo-Saxon Language*. New York: Harper & Brothers, 1871.

March, Francis A. "The Growth of Lafayette: A Post-Prandial Address." In *Selected Writings*, 222–30.

March, Francis A. *Introduction to Anglo-Saxon: An Anglo-Saxon reader, with philological notes*. New York: Harper & Brothers, 1870.

March, Francis A. "Method of Philological Study of English in Lafayette College, Easton, Penn." In *Selected Writings*, 252–55.

March, Francis A. *Method of Philological Study of the English Language*. Reprinted, New York: Harper and Brothers, 1886.

March, Francis A. *Francis A. March: Selected Writings of the First Professor of English*. Edited by Paul Schlueter and June Schlueter. Friends of Skillman Library, 2005.

March, Francis A. "Spelling and Progress." In *Selected Writings,* 130–32.

March, Francis A. "The Study of Anglo-Saxon." In *Selected Writings,* 231–39.

Massachusetts Institute of Technology. Committee on Instruction Records, 1 (December 14, 1870).

Massachusetts Institute of Technology. *The President's Report,* various years.

McCallister, Marvin. "Shakespeare Visits the Hilltop: Classical Drama and the Howard College Dramatic Club." In Kahn et al., eds., 219–46.

McCosh, James. *The New Departure in College Education. Being a Reply to President Eliot's Defense of It in New York.* New York: Charles Scribner's Sons, 1885.

Milton, John. *The Complete Poetry and Essential Prose.* Edited by William Kerrigan et al. Modern Library, 2007.

Murray, James O. *The Study of English Literature: Its Scope and Method.* Providence: Brown University, 1886.

Nash, Margaret A., "Entangled Pasts: Land-Grant Colleges and American Indian Dispossession." *History of Education Quarterly* 59.4 (2019): 437–67.

Newkirk, Thomas. "The Politics of Intimacy: The Defeat of Barrett Wendell at Harvard." In *Taking Stock: The Writing Process Movement in the '90s,* edited by Lad Tobin and Thomas Newkirk, 115–31. Boynton/Cook, 1994.

Newman, Samuel P. *A Practical System of Rhetoric, or, the Principal Rules of Style Inferred from Examples of Writing.* Portland, ME: William Hyde, 1827.

Nietzsche, Friedrich. *Daybreak,* Preface § 5. In Hamacher, *95 Theses.*

O'Toole, James. *Ever to Excel: A History of Boston College.* Institute of Jesuit Sources, 2021.

Onderdonk, Virginia. "The Curriculum." In Glasscock et al., eds., 122–63.

Opal, J. M. "The Making of the Victorian Campus: Teacher and Student at Amherst College, 1850–1880." *History of Education Quarterly* 42.3 (2002): 342–67.

Owens, W. B. "Dr. March and His Work for Lafayette." In *Addresses Delivered at a Celebration in Honor of Prof. Francis A. March, LL.D., L.H.D., at Lafayette College, October 24, 1895.* Easton, PA: Lafayette Press, 1895.

Palmer, D. J. *The Rise of English Studies.* Published for the University of Hull by Oxford University Press, 1965.

Palmer, George Herbert. *Possible Limitations of the Elective System,* Part 1 in the *Andover Review* 6, no. 36 (1886), 569–75; Part 2 (January 1887), 1–18. Reprinted, Boston: Houghton, Mifflin, 1887.

Palmieri, Patricia. "*Incipit Vita Nuova:* Founding Ideals of the Wellesley College Community." *History of Higher Education* 3 (1983): 59–78.

Payne, William Morton, ed. *English in American Universities, by Professors in the English Departments of Twenty Representative Institutions.* Boston: D. C. Heath, 1895.

Payne, William Morton. "Introduction," In Payne, ed., 7–28.

Payton, Phillip W. "Origin of the Terms 'Major' and 'Minor' in American Higher Education." *History of Education Quarterly* 1.2 (1961): 57–63.

Peckham, Howard H. *The Making of the University of Michigan 1817–1992*. Edited by Margaret and Nicholas Steneck. Bentley Historical Library, 1994.

Phelps, William Lyon. *Autobiography with Letters*. Oxford University Press, 1939.

"A Plea for Shakespeare and Spenser—Student Opinion." *The Harvard Monthly* 9 (1889): 76–77.

Ponder, Melinda. *Katharine Lee Bates: From Sea to Shining Sea*. Windy City Publishers, 2017.

"Popular Collegiate Education." *Nassau Monthly* 4 (1844): 1–9.

Renker, Elizabeth. *The Origins of American Literature Studies: An Institutional History*. Cambridge University Press, 2007.

Reports of the President of the Massachusetts Institute of Technology. Boston: various years.

Rudolph, Frederick. *The American College and University: A History*. Introductory Essay and Supplementary Bibliography by John R. Thelin. University of Georgia Press, 1990.

Rudolph, Frederick. *Curriculum: A History of the American Undergraduate Course of Studies Since 1636*. Jossey-Bass, 1978.

Rush, James. *The Philosophy of the Human Voice; Embracing its Physiological History; together with a System of Principles*. 2nd ed. Philadelphia: Grigg & Elliott, 1833.

Russell, David R. "Romantics on Writing: Liberal Culture and the Abolition of Composition Courses." *Rhetoric Review* 6.2 (1988): 132–48.

Russell, Robert. "The Question of Composition—A Record of Struggle." *College English* 21 (1969): 171–77.

Ryder, Frank G. "George Ticknor and Goethe—Boston and Göttingen." *PMLA* 67.7 (1952): 960–72.

Sampson Martin W. "English at the University of Indiana." In Payne, ed., 92–98.

Santayana, George. *The Middle Span*, vol. 2: *Persons and Places*. Charles Scribner's Sons, 1945.

Schiff, Judith Ann. "A 'Select Course' that helped reshape Yale." *Yale Alumni Magazine* 82.6 (2019): 22–23.

Schinske, Jeffrey, and Kimberly Tanner. "Teaching More by Grading Less (or Differently)," 2017. https://www.lifescied.org/doi/10.1187/cbe.cbe-14-03-0054.

Scholes, Robert. *English After the Fall: From Literature to Textuality*. Iowa University Press, 2011.

Scholes, Robert. *The Rise and Fall of English: Reconstructing English as a Discipline*. Yale University Press, 1998.

Scott, Fred N. "English at the University of Michigan." In Payne, ed., 116–23.

Shaw, Thomas B. *A History of English Literature. By Thomas B Shaw, M.A.* A New Edition. Enlarged and Re-written. Edited, with Notes and Illustrations, by William Smith, LL.D. London: John Murray, 1864.

Shepherd, H. E. "Thomas Jefferson as a Philologist." *American Journal of Philology* 3.10 (1882): 211–14.

Smith, William, ed. *A History of English Literature. By Thomas B Shaw, M.A.* A New Edition. Enlarged and Re-written. Edited with Notes and Illustrations, by William Smith, LL.D. London: John Murray, 1864.

The Society for the Collegiate Instruction of Women. *Report of the Treasurer and Secretary, 1889–90*. Cambridge, MA, 1890.

Spalding, William. *The History of English Literature, with an outline of the origin and growth of the English language, illustrated by extracts.* New York: D. Appleton, 1862.

Spalding, William. *The History of English Literature with an Outline of the Origin and Growth of the English Language Illustrated by Extracts,* with Appendix by W. Houston. Toronto, Ontario: Adam Miller, 1876.

[Spofford, Harriet Prescott]. "The Institute of Technology." *Frank Leslie's Illustrated Newspaper* 29, no. 742 (December 18, 1869): 232, Supplement.

Stevens, Paul. "Milton in America." *University of Toronto Quarterly* 77.3 (2008): 789–800.

Stratton, Julius A., Loretta H. Mannix, and Catherine Stratton. *Mind and Hand: The Birth of MIT.* MIT Press, 2005.

Syrett, Nicholas L. *The Company He Keeps: A History of White College Fraternities.* University of North Carolina Press, 2009.

Talty, Stephan. *Mulatto America: At the Crossroads of Black and White Culture: A Social History.* Harper Collins, 2003.

Thayer, Vivian Trow. *The Passing of the Recitation.* D. C. Heath, 1928.

Thoreau, Henry David. *Journal 1: 1837–1844*. In *Journal,* edited by John C. Broderick et al. Princeton University Press, 1981.

Thwing, Charles F. *American Colleges: Their Students and Work.* New York: G. P. Putnam's Sons, 1879.

Thwing, Charles F. "What Becomes of College Women." *North American Review* 161, no. 468 (1895): 546–53.

Tilson, Alistair. "Who Now Reads *Spalding?*" *English Studies in Canada* 17.4 (1991): 469-78.

Tuckerman, Henry. "A Sketch of American Literature." In *A Complete Manual of English Literature,* by Thomas Budd Shaw. New York: Sheldon and Co., 1867.

Turner, James. "From Philology to the Humanities: Fragmentation and Discipline Formation in the United Kingdom and the United States." In *Writing the History of the Humanities: Questions, Themes, and Approaches*, edited by Herman Paul, 47–64. Bloomsbury Academic, 2022.

Turner, James. *Language, Religion, Knowledge: Past and Present*. University of Notre Dame Press, 2003.

Turner, James. *Philology: The Forgotten Origins of the Modern Humanities*. Princeton University Press, 2014.

Turner, James. *Religion Enters the Academy: The Origins of the Scholarly Study of Religion in America*. University of Georgia Press, 2011.

Tyler, Moses Coit. Letter to Messrs. G. P. Putnam's Sons. 28 March 1876. In *Moses Coit Tyler 1835–1900: Selections from His Letters and Diaries*, edited by Jessica Tyler Austen, 97–99. Doubleday, Page, and Co., 1911.

Tyler, Moses Coit. Preface to *A Manual of English Literature by Henry Morley, thoroughly revised, with an entire re-arrangement of matter, and with numerous retrenchments and additions, by Moses Coit Tyler*. New York: Sheldon and Co., 1879.

Tyler, W. S. *History of Amherst College during its First Half Century, 1821–1871*. Springfield, MA: Clark and W. Bryan, 1873.

VanOverbeke, Marc A. *The Standardization of American Schooling: Linking Secondary and Higher Education, 1870–1910*. Palgrave Macmillan, 2008.

Welden, Linda Frances. *Hiram Corson: Interpretative Reader, English Teacher, Literary Scholar. LSU Historical Dissertations and Theses*. 3141. Louisiana State University, 1977. https://repository.lsu.edu/gradschool_disstheses/3141/doi/10.31390/gradschool_disstheses.3141.

Wells, D. A., and S. H. Davis. *Sketches of Williams College*. Williamstown, MA: H. S. Taylor, 1847.

Wendell, Barrett. "English at Harvard University." In Payne, ed., 44–48.

Wendell, Barrett. "The Relations of Radcliffe College with Harvard." *Harvard Monthly* (October 1899): 1–10.

West, Arthur F. "Is There a Democracy of Studies?" *The Atlantic Monthly* 84 (1899): 821–27.

Whately, Richard. *Elements of Rhetoric*, last enlarged and revised edition. Nashville, TN: Southern Methodist Publishing, 1861.

Wilder, Craig Steven. *Ebony and Ivy: Race, Slavery, and the Troubled History of America's Universities*. Bloomsbury Press, 2013.

Winterer, Caroline. *The Culture of Classicism: Ancient Greece and Rome in American Intellectual Life, 1780–1910*. Johns Hopkins University Press, 2002.

Yale University. *Reports on the Course of Instruction in Yale College; By a Committee of the Corporation, and the Academical Faculty.* New Haven, CT: Hezekiah Howe, 1828.

Zimmerman, Jonathan. *The Amateur Hour: A History of College Teaching in America.* Johns Hopkins University Press, 2020.

INDEX

Abbott, Edwin, 177
Adams, John, 62
Addison, Joseph, 25, 99
admissions examinations. *See* entrance examinations
Agassiz, Louis, 101, 114
AI (artificial intelligence), 2
Alcott, Louisa May, 213
American Association of University Women, 202
"America the Beautiful" (Bates), 201
Amherst College, 10, 21, 42, 43–49, 64, 69, 122, 216–17; and Commencement Day, 44
Andover Theological School, 136
Allen, Grant, 105
Allen, William Grant, 85
Angell, James Burrill, 112, 135, 198–99, 202
Anglo-Saxon, 8, 29, 49, 55, 62–70, 80, 91, 93–95, 101, 108, 126–27, 130, 139, 143, 157, 159, 162, 164–66, 170, 173, 177, 179, 184, 195, 205, 206; and racial pride, 94–95
Ann Arbor, Michigan, 15, 136, 138, 143, 145, 199, 202
archives, 3–6, 20, 38–42, 45, 74, 120–30, 140–48, 184, 192, 196, 198, 200–201
Arnold, Matthew, 105, 221
Arnold, Thomas, 137
Athenæum (library), 218
Athenaeum (publication), 66
Atkinson, William P., 72–77, 81–82
Atlanta University, 84
Atlantic Monthly, 12, 99
Audubon, John James, 210
Austen, Jane, 185; *Pride and Prejudice*, 8, 111
Backus, Truman, 91–95
Bacon, Francis, 22, 68, 79, 144, 179, 189, 217; *New Atlantis*, 139
Bacon, John, 39
Badgley, Mary Mills, 92
Baker, George Pierce, 190
Bancroft, George, 57, 67
Bancroft, Timothy, 41
Bapst, Johannes, 96, 98
Barber, Jonathan, 37–38
Barnard College, 101
Barricklo, William Reed, 129–30
Bates, Arlo, 19–22, 28–30
Bates, Katharine Lee, 194, 198, 201, 203–9; "America the Beautiful," 201; *Rose and Thorn*, 204–5
Beadle's Dime Novels, 136
Beecher, Henry Ward, 44
Bentley Historical Library (Michigan), 142
Blood of the Nation, The (Jordon), 114–15
Bloomfield, Leonard, 227n6
Bodleian Library, 205
Book Buyer, 19, 21
Boston, 13–14, 19, 57, 58, 72, 97, 98, 136, 210, 213, 215–16
Boston College, 83, 96–101; acting plays, 99–101
Boston Tech, 72, 77. *See also* Massachusetts Institute of Technology
Bowdoin College, 21–22, 28, 46, 65, 86, 107
Briggs, LeBaron, 110–12, 116, 179, 183–86, 189–90
Bright, James Wilson, 70
British Museum, 205

Brontë, Charlotte: *Jane Eyre,* 93, 144; *Shirley,* 144
Brook Farm, 213–14
Brooks, Van Wyck, 210
Brosnahan, Timothy, 99
Brown, Francis Henry, 40–41
Brown University, 41, 162
Browning, Elizabeth Barrett, 165, 196, 200; *Aurora Leigh,* 93
Browning, Robert, 69, 75, 159, 165; Browning Society, 166, 173, 221
Bryant, William Cullen, 166, 220–21
Buckham, Henry, 91–92
Bunyan, John, 69
Burke, Edmund, 25, 36, 119, 125, 139–40, 144
Burns, Robert, 128
Buurma, Rachel Sagner, 6, 229n1
Byron, George Gordon, Lord, 128

Calvino, Italo, 8
Cambridge, Massachusetts, 185, 210–11, 215
Cambridge University, 1, 56, 66, 72–73, 210
Carlyle, Thomas, 134, 139, 144; *Sartor Resartus,* 140, 144, 185, 221
Carr, William Otis, 46
Central College (New York), 85
Channing, Edward Tyrrel, 27, 35–39, 40, 42, 43, 213–14, 228n12
Chaucer, Geoffrey, 8, 29, 37, 69, 79, 128, 132, 143, 157, 159, 165–67, 171–73, 179, 195, 197, 214; *The Canterbury Tales,* 80–81, 172
Chicago, Illinois, 15, 156, 203
Child, Francis, 39–42, 43, 70, 125, 176–91, 219
Chironomia, 37
Christian Union, 136
Clark, Mary Elizabeth, 142–45
Classical Course, 6, 10–11, 66–68, 77, 87, 154
Cogswell, Joseph Green, 57
Coleridge, Samuel Taylor, 165
Colgate University, 91
College of New Jersey. *See* Princeton University
Columbia University, 1, 70, 122, 208, 217
comparative philology, 55, 65–67, 126–27, 155, 169
composition, 31–42, 45–48, 68, 79–80, 93, 99, 110–11, 118–19, 126–27, 133, 157–58, 168–69, 176–78, 181, 183–85, 191; and "Essay-Writing," 197, 204, 206, 208; in entrance examinations, 110–16; and specialized writing faculty, 41, 66, 79, 158, 164, 191, 204, 206
Cooke, Increase, 32
Cooper, James Fenimore, 36
Cornell, Ezra, 161–66
Cornell University, 70, 107–10, 114, 134, 136, 138, 156, 158, 160, 161–75, 202, 208, 219; choice of "Special Subject," 161, 173. *See also* Gilman, Daniel Coit
Corson, Hiram, 70, 161, 164–74; *The Aims of Literary Study,* 165, 168; and examinations, 168, 71–74
Cowper, William, 25, 129, 132, 214
Cromwell, Oliver, 144
Cutter, Charles Amni, 218

Dana Hall, 204
Dante, 197, 218; *The Divine Comedy,* 27
Darwin, Charles, 73
Davidson College, 117
Davis, Henrietta Vinton, 88
deliberative rhetoric and style, 32–33, 35
Demmon, Isaac Newton, 138–43, 146, 219
DePauw University, 159–60
De Quincey, Thomas: *Confessions of an English Opium Eater,* 138
Dewey, John, 77
Dewey, Melvil, 216–18, 220
Dewey Decimal System, 216–18, 220
Dial, The (Chicago), 15, 156–57, 159–60, 174, 190, 194, 203, 205–7
Dickens, Charles, 23, 36; *A Christmas Carol,* 112; *Little Dorrit,* 93
Dickinson, Emily, 44
Dictionary of National Biography, The, 201
Donne, John, 4–5, 184, 214
Douglass, Frederick, 83–88, 89, 90; and importance of reading, 83
Dowden, Edward, 178
Dryden, John, 79, 125, 129–30, 143, 179, 186, 209; *Absalom and Achitophel,* 140
Du Bois, W. E. B., 84–85
Duffield, John Fletcher, 120–28
Durant, Henry Fowle, 195–203, 207

Eagleton, Terry, 228n7
Edinburgh Review, 28, 144
elective system, 158, 175–76, 180–82
Elements of Rhetoric. *See* Whately, Richard
Eliot, Charles W., 12–14, 21, 71, 95, 99, 106, 132, 175–85, 190–91, 202; "The New Education" 12, 71
Eliot, George, 54, 174, 199, 200; *Silas Marner*, 140
Eliot, T. S., 4, 184
elocution, 23, 31–37, 65, 93, 119, 132–33, 162, 165, 169, 197–98, 207
Emerson, Ralph Waldo, 15, 44, 58, 86, 185, 214; "The American Scholar" (speech), 24; essay on Shakespeare, 75; lecture at Howard University, 86
Englehardt, Carroll, 229n12
English Course, 6
English in American Universities (Payne), 15, 158
entrance examinations, 91, 95, 105–16; English exam decisive, 106–7; published specimens, 107–9; and set literary texts, 110–12
epideictic rhetoric and style, 32–33
"Essay-Writing," 197, 204, 206–7. *See also* composition
Everett, Edward, 24, 32–33, 38, 47, 57–58, 67, 119, 218

Female Prose Writers of America (Hart), 219
Fielding, Henry, 36
Fiske, George A., 40
forensics, 36, 176–77, 183, 184, 185, 188, 190
Fowle, William B., 32
Fowler, William Chauncey, 46–47, 65, 67–68
Frank Leslie's Illustrated Newspaper, 13–14, 72
fraternities, 25, 64
Freeman, A. E., 1
Freeman, Alice Elvira, 202–5, 207–9
Friedrich Wilhelm University (Berlin), 39
Fuller, Margaret, 15

Garfield, James A., 41
Gates, Lewis Edwards, 189–90
Genung, John Franklin, 42, 43, 45, 47
Gibbon, Edward, 100
Gilman, Daniel Coit, 154–56, 169
Goethe, Johann Wolfgang von, 57–58
Goddard, Edwin C., 141–42, 145–47, 149
Goldsmith, Oliver, 25, 36, 125; *The Vicar of Wakefield*, 110
Gore, Christopher, 211
Gore Hall, 211–13, 215, 217–18
Göttingen, 39, 57–58
Gower, John, 214
grading, 20–21, 92, 123, 167, 198, 227n2
Graff, Gerald, 228n7
Great Awakening (Second), 10
Grimm brothers, 39, 125; law of phonetic change, 169
Guillory, John, 228n7

Hadley, James, 125
Hahnemann Medical College, 123
half-courses, 7, 179
Harris, Thaddeus, 212
Harris, W. T., 193–94, 201
Hart, John Seely, 119; *Female Prose Writers of America*, 219–20
Harte, Bret, 165, 220
Harvard University, 7, 12–14, 20–21, 25, 27, 32, 36–43, 46, 56–60, 72–73, 78, 101, 106–7, 110–11, 125, 127–28, 134, 145, 157, 160, 164, 166, 193, 195–97, 210; "Annex" (*see* Society for Collegiate Instruction of Women); and concentration in English, 175–92; and debates about the elective system, 132, 175–76, 180–82; English 14 (drama course), 19–20, 179, 190; and evolution of its entrance examinations, 110–12; and Lawrence Scientific School, 11–12, 77; and *Lampoon*, 183, 188; libraries, 210–16, 218–19. *See also* archives
Haverford College, 145
Hawthorne, Nathaniel, 3, 28, 131, 165, 185, 213–16, 220–21; *The Blithedale Romance*, 213; "The New Adam and Eve," 213–16
Heffernan, Laura, 6, 229n1
Hellenism, 57
Herbert, George, 181
high schools, 9, 21, 70, 96, 111–12, 114, 135, 146, 185, 202, 207
Hill, Adams Sherman, 41, 176, 178–81, 183, 185, 189

History of American Literature During the Colonial Period, The (Tyler), 137–38
Hodell, Charles W., 153, 158–59
Hodgkins, Louise Manning, 199–201, 204–5
Hollis, Thomas, 211–12
Homer, 11, 29, 60, 70, 107, 197, 199
Hopkins, Mark, 41
Howard, Ada, 196, 198, 202
Howard, Oliver Otis, 86
Howard University, 85–88, 89, 93, 95, 96, 101; dramatic club, 88
Howe, Julia Ward, 89
Howison, George, 76–77
Hume, David, 129
Hunt, Rev. Theodore Whitfield (T. W.), 118, 120–28, 131–33
Hutchins, Annie, 217

Idea of the University, The (Newman), 100
immigrants, 11, 23, 83, 85, 95, 96–98, 101
India civil service examination, 93, 106
Ireland, 97
Irish immigrants, 97–98, 101
Irving, Henry, 187
Irving, Washington, 221
Istanbul, 122

Jefferson, Thomas, 10, 58, 62–63, 131
Jesuits, 96–100
Jewett, Sophie, 205, 209
Johns Hopkins University, 3, 118, 153–54, 156, 176
Johnson, Samuel, 69, 100, 129
Jordan, David Starr, 114–16, 156, 159; *The Blood of the Nation,* 114–15

Kimball, Bruce, 5
Kittredge, George Lyman, 188–89
Know-Nothing Party, 98

Ladies Course, 6–7
Lafayette College, 49, 54, 62–70, 81, 125, 158, 177; Pardee Scientific School, 11
Langdell, C. C., 5
Latin, as a living language, 98–99
Lawrence College (Wisconsin), 199
Lawrence Scientific School. *See* Harvard University
Lehrfreiheit ("freedom to teach"), 55
Library of Congress, 218
linguistics, 81, 158, 207
Literary Course, 87
literary societies, 24–25, 64, 93, 119, 128
Locke, John, 10
Longfellow, Henry Wadsworth, 27, 28, 164–65, 213, 221; *Hyperion,* 164; *The Song of Hiawatha,* 165
Lounsbury, Thomas, 28, 77–80, 132, 174; "The Study of English," 78–80
Lowell, James Russell, 27, 164, 213, 220–21

major (origins of the term), 153–54
Mann, Horace, 48
Manual of American Literature, A (Hart), 219–20
March, Francis, 49, 54, 60–61, 63–70, 81, 91, 125–26, 132, 164, 177, 216; *Comparative Grammar of the Anglo-Saxon Language,* 66; *Method of Philological Study of the English Language,* 60
Martineau, Harriet, 89
Massachusetts Institute of Technology (MIT), 12–14, 71–77, 81 174, 193, 195, 204; curriculum of, 73–77
McCallister, Marvin, 231n9
McCosh, James, 122, 132, 180, 191
McPhail, G. Wilson, 63–64, 66
Melville, Herman, 221
Messina, Sicily, 100
Milton, John, 25, 28, 34–36, 45, 47, 68, 73, 79, 99, 125, 130, 148, 157, 179, 186, 189, 199, 214–15; *Areopagitica,* 139, 147–48; "Il Penseroso," 34; "Lycidas," 172–73; *Of Education,* 144; paired with Shakespeare, 11, 19, 27, 28, 31, 45, 47, 70, 75, 129–30, 173; *Paradise Lost,* 108–9, 140, 145; and portrayal of Eve, 144
minor, 154. *See also* major
Mitchell, Maria, 90
Modern Language Association, 131
More, Thomas: *Utopia,* 139
Morley, Henry, 137
Morrill Land-Grant Act, 11, 161

Mount Holyoke Seminary, 10, 186, 196, 204
Müller, Max, 105
Murray, James Ormsbee, 128–32

Nassau Herald (Princeton), 122
Nassau Monthly (Princeton), 10–11, 19, 28
National Center of Education, 1–2
National Education Association, 95, 113–14
National Teachers Association, 74
Nativist party, 97
"New Adam and Eve, The" (Hawthorne), 213–16
"New Education, The" (Eliot), 12, 71
Newman, Samuel: *A Practical System of Rhetoric*, 28, 65
New York, 9, 19, 85, 89, 98, 122, 136, 161, 162, 199
Nietzsche, Friedrich, 54, 56

Obama, Barack, 1
Oberlin College, 10, 207
Old English, 62, 94, 155, 179. *See also* Anglo-Saxon
oratory, 44, 93, 112, 162–63, 209. *See also* professors of rhetoric and oratory
Oxford English Dictionary, The, 154, 201
Oxford University, 1, 56, 66, 72–73, 105–6, 114, 156, 204, 205

Pall Mall Gazette, 105, 109–10
Palmer, George Herbert, 175, 177, 181–82, 203
Palmieri, Patricia, 237n4
Paris Exposition (1900), 193–95
Pater, Walter, 105
Payne, William Morton: *English in American Universities*, 157–58
Penobscot language, 98
Perry, Bliss, 132–33
Phelps, William Lyon, 184
philology, 53–61, 65, 80–81, 94, 118, 123, 125–26, 132, 157, 169–70
Plato: *Republic*, 139
PMLA (*Publications of the Modern Language Association*), 131
Poe, Edgar Allan, 69, 220
polygenesis, 101
Ponder, Melinda, 237n13
Pope, Alexander, 25, 79, 100, 130–31, 132, 214; *An Essay on Man*, 140; *The Rape of the Lock*, 138, 140
Poughkeepsie, NY, 89
Pratt, Henry, 145
Princeton, New Jersey, 10, 28
Princeton University, 66, 117–33, 193, 219–20; archives of, 120–21; and baseball team, 120, 122, 127–28
Princetonian, 119, 128–29
professors of rhetoric and oratory, 3–4, 24, 27, 31, 35, 38, 45–47, 65, 86, 117–19, 132–33, 169, 176–77
Proto-Indo-European, 56

Queen Elizabeth I, 97
Quickenings, 46, 49

Radcliffe College. *See* Society for the Collegiate Instruction of Women
Raymond, John H., 91–92
Ratio Studiorum ("Plan of Studies"), 98–100; dramatic performances prescribed, 100
recitation periods, 22–23
Renker, Elizabeth, 238n11
Rensselaer Polytechnic, 9–10
rhetoric, 24, 26–47, 36, 65–67, 75–76, 86–87, 91–93, 113, 138–39, 158, 162–64, 169, 176–77, 207–9, 219, 228n11. *See also* professors of rhetoric and oratory
rhetorical science, 118, 124
Richardson, Samuel, 36
"Rise of English," 2, 53–54
Rogers, William Barton, 71–72, 76–77
Rollin, Caroline, 164
Rush, James, 35
Ruskin, John, 105, 204, 209

Sabin, Henry, 47–49
Saginaw, Michigan, 146–47
Santayana, George, 183–84
Schiff, Judith, 231n16
Scholes, Robert, 229n17
Scientific Course, 6, 11, 66, 154
Scott, Fred, 42

Scott, Walter, 9, 36, 80, 113, 203; *Ivanhoe*, 110
Scudder, Vida, 204, 206, 209
Seneca Falls Convention of 1848, 89
Shackford, Charles Chauncey, 164, 167–71, 173–74; examinations, 167–71
Shakespeare, 8, 23, 29, 36, 60, 75, 79–81, 86, 88, 93, 99–101, 124–25, 132, 157, 177, 186, 197, 221; Harvard rotation of plays, 178–79; courses and public readings at Cornell, 165, 167, 170–73; enrichment courses at Hopkins, 155; G. L. Kittredge's course, 189; paired with Milton, 11, 19, 27, 28, 31, 45, 47, 68, 69, 70, 75, 129–30, 173; and rhetoric and oratory study, 24, 27, 32, 34–35, 38, 40–41; seminar course at Michigan, 138, 140, 145–46, 149; set texts of, 110, 112–13, 203; "Shakspere" as the Harvard spelling, 178; and Barrett Wendell's course for women, 186–88
—plays: *All's Well That Ends Well*, 178; *Antony & Cleopatra*, 178; *As You Like It*, 40, 130, 187; *Coriolanus*, 100; *Hamlet*, 32, 34, 40–41, 159, 170, 178; *Henry V*, 178; *I Henry IV*, 100, 145, 178; *Julius Caesar*, 27, 32, 35, 37, 60, 67, 100, 110, 112, 143, 159, 178, 187, 203; *King Lear*, 100, 130, 178; *Macbeth*, 132, 170, 178; *The Merchant of Venice*, 34, 66, 100, 110, 114–15, 130, 132, 159; *A Midsummer's Night Dream*, 187; *Much Ado About Nothing*, 132; *Othello*, 5, 28, 101, 132, 178; *Richard III*, 100, 187; *Romeo & Juliet*, 88, 178; *The Tempest*, 110, 130, 178; *Twelfth Night*, 27, 111; *The Winter's Tale*, 132, 178
Shakespeareana, 139
Shaw, Thomas Budd: *A Complete Manual of English Literature*, 93, 125, 137; *Outlines of English Literature*, 26, 29, 87, 93, 109
Sheffield Scientific School. *See* Yale University
Sheldon, Mary, 199, 202
Shelley, Percy Bysshe, 1
Sherwood, Margaret, 205, 209
Smith College, 101, 186, 195, 204
Smith, Shirley Wheeler, 147–48
Smith, William, 93
Society for the Collegiate Instruction of Women ("Harvard Annex"), 185–89
South Carolina College, 210
Spalding, William: *A History of English Literature*, 26
"Special Study" at Cornell, 163
Spencer, Herbert, 73; *The Philosophy of Style*, 191
Spenser, Edmund, 36, 69, 125, 128, 140, 157, 166–67, 179; as bureaucrat in Ireland, 97; *The Fairie Queene*, 128–29, 140, 172, 186; and Spenserian stanza, 172
Sprague, Homer, 163–64
Stanford, Leland, 156
Stanford University, 114–15, 156–57, 199, 207
STEM subjects, 1–2
Stilwell, Elizabeth, 198, 200
St. John's College, Annapolis, 165
Stratton, Margaret E., 207
"Study of Masterpieces" seminar, 135, 138–49
Swarthmore College, 2
Swift, Johnathan, 25, 100, 125, 129
Syrett, Nicholas L., 228n11

Talty, Stephan, 231n3
Teachers Course (Wellesley), 197
Tennyson, Alfred, Lord, 75, 132, 173, 221; *The Princess*, 140
Terry, Ellen, 187
Thoreau, Henry David, 37, 213–14; *Walden*, 221
Ticknor, George, 27–28, 39, 57–60; *History of Spanish Literature*, 59; *Syllabus for Spanish Literature*, 58–59
translatio imperii, translatio studii, 33, 201
Turner, James, 5, 53, 229n3
Tyler, Moses Coit, 135–39, 141, 143, 148–49, 166, 174, 199, 219; *The History of American Literature During the Colonial Period*, 137–38

University of California, 77
University of Chicago, 203, 207
University of London, 106
University of Michigan, 11, 42, 112–13, 139–49, 162, 166, 174, 175, 198–99, 202–3, 207, 219, 225, 227n2; entrance requirements and examinations, 112–14
University of North Carolina, 10, 25
University of Pennsylvania, 207
University of Vermont, 91
University of Virginia, 10, 62

Van Lennep, William, 122–28
Vassar College, 83, 89–95, 96, 101, 107, 109, 186, 195, 225; chaos in the English department, 90–92; English course offerings, 94; English entrance examination, 91
Vassar, Matthew, 89–90
Virgil, 23, 29, 60, 107, 173

Washington, DC, 85
Webster, Daniel, 24, 31, 32, 34, 119, 164
Webster, Noah, 32, 64–65, 216
Welden, Linda Frances, 235n5
Wellesley College, 90, 101, 160, 193–209
Wendell, Barrett, 20–21, 179, 183–88, 190–91; "The Relations of Radcliffe College with Harvard," 188
West Point, 9–10, 86
Whately, Richard: *Elements of Rhetoric*, 27, 65
White, Andrew Dickson, 136, 138, 156, 161–64, 166–67, 169, 174, 202
Whitman, Walt, 220
Whitney, William Dwight, 125
Whittier, John Greenleaf, 165, 220
Whittlesey, Eliphalet, 86
Widener Library, 213. *See also* Harvard University: libraries
Wilberforce University, 84
Wilder, Craig Steven, 232n9
Wilder, William, 130–31
Williams College, 24–26, 41, 132
Wilson, Rev. Joseph Ruggles, 117
Wilson, Thomas Woodrow, 117, 119, 122, 127–30, 133
Winterer, Caroline, 5, 117
Wordsworth, William, 99, 105, 167; *The Excursion*, 140

Yale University, 7, 10, 21–22, 38, 73, 77, 81, 86, 127–28, 136, 156, 166, 184, 190; belated appearance of English in college curriculum, 77–78; granting the PhD degree, 154, 209; and report of 1828, 10; and Select Course, 77–78; and Sheffield Scientific School, 12, 14, 22, 28, 71, 73, 77–82, 174
Young, Edward, 25

www.ingramcontent.com/pod-product-compliance
Lightning Source LLC
LaVergne TN
LVHW102044161026
850310LV00030B/151

* 9 7 8 0 8 0 7 1 8 7 2 4 1 *